# Researching Hospitality
# and Tourism

First published 2008
Reprinted 2011

SAGE Publications Ltd
1 Oliver's Yard
55 City Road
London EC1Y 1SP

SAGE Publications Inc.
2455 Teller Road
Thousand Oaks, California 91320

SAGE Publications India Pvt Ltd
B 1/I 1 Mohan Cooperative Industrial Area
Mathura Road
New Delhi 110 044

SAGE Publications Asia-Pacific Pte Ltd
33 Pekin Street #02-01
Far East Square
Singapore 048763

**Library of Congress Control Number: 2007930765**

**British Library Cataloguing in Publication data**

A catalogue record for this book is available from the British Library

ISBN 978-1-4129-0391-2
ISBN 978-1-4129-0392-9 (pbk)

Typeset by C&M Digitals (P) Ltd, Chennai, India
Printed in Great Britain by the MPG Books Group
Printed on paper from sustainable resources

MIX
Paper from
responsible sources
FSC® C018575

For Penny – my one and only love and soul mate.

# Contents

Preface      x

1    **The Nature and Relevance of Research**      1
Key Concepts and Issues      1
1.1   Introduction      1
1.2   The Nature of Research      2
1.3   The Characteristics of Scientific Research      6
1.4   Types of Research      12
1.5   The Main Research Approaches      16
1.6   Research Issues, Questions and Problems      19
Summary      22
Further Reading      22

2    **Research Philosophies and Schools of Thought**      24
Key Concepts and Issues      24
2.1   Introduction      24
2.2   The Nature of Knowledge and Reality      25
2.3   Positivism and Phenomenology      30
Summary      40
Further Reading      40

3    **Developing the Research Proposal and Plan**      42
Key Concepts and Issues      42
3.1   Introduction      42
3.2   Finding and Refining A Topic      43
3.3   Refining the Research Question(s)      50
3.4   Developing Aims and Objectives      51
3.5   Putting the Research Proposal Together      54
3.6   Ethical Considerations      55
Summary      57
Further Reading      57

4    **Sourcing and Reviewing the Literature**      59
Key Concepts and Issues      59
4.1   Introduction      59
4.2   Why is a Literature Review Necessary?      60
4.3   What is Literature?      63

4.4  What is a Literature Review?                                65
4.5  Sourcing, Searching and Accessing the Literature           67
4.6  Evaluating and Reviewing the Literature                    70
4.7  Writing the Literature Review                              72
Summary                                                         75
Further Reading                                                 75

5  **Developing the Conceptual Framework**                        77
Key Concepts and Issues                                         77
5.1  Introduction                                               77
5.2  The Conceptual Framework                                   78
5.3  Constructs and Concepts                                    81
5.4  Variables                                                  82
5.5  Theories and Models                                        89
5.6  Hypotheses                                                 90
5.7  Operationalisation                                         92
5.8  Measurement and Scales                                     95
5.9 Establishing Good Measures                                 100
Summary                                                        103
Further Reading                                                103

6  **Choosing the Empirical Research Design**                    105
Key Concepts and Issues                                        105
6.1  Introduction                                              105
6.2  Experimental Research                                     108
6.3  Survey Research                                           112
6.4  Comparative Research                                      119
6.5  Case Study Research                                       122
6.6  Observational Research                                    126
6.7  Action Research                                           127
Summary                                                        129
Further Reading                                                129

7  **Collecting the Empirical Data**                             131
Key Concepts and Issues                                        131
7.1  Introduction                                              131
7.2  Questionnaires and Questions                              132
7.3  Interviewing                                              151
7.4  Observation                                               154
7.5  Projective Techniques                                     157
Summary                                                        161
Further Reading                                                161

8   **Sampling**                                                            163
    Key Concepts and Issues                                                 163
    8.1  Introduction                                                       163
    8.2  What is Sampling and Why is It Important?                          164
    8.3  Quantitative Data Sampling                                         168
    8.4  Qualitative Data Sampling                                          171
    Summary                                                                 173
    Further Reading                                                         174

9   **Analysing Quantitative Data**                                         175
    Key Concepts and Issues                                                 175
    9.1  Introduction                                                       175
    9.2  General Issues                                                     176
    9.3  Descriptive Statistics                                             182
    9.4  Bivariate Analysis                                                 188
    9.5  Inferential Statistics                                             195
    9.6  Data Reduction Techniques                                          202
    Summary                                                                 205
    Further Reading                                                         205

10  **Analysing Qualitative Data**                                          207
    Key Concepts and Issues                                                 207
    10.1  Introduction                                                      207
    10.2  What Kind of Qualitative Data do You Have?                        208
    10.3  Basic Principles and Stages in Qualitative Data Analysis          210
    10.4  Qualitative Data Analysis Techniques                              211
    10.5  Justifying Qualitative Data Analysis Choices                      213
    Summary                                                                 214
    Further Reading                                                         214

11  **Writing Up the Research Project**                                     216
    Key Concepts and Issues                                                 216
    11.1  Introduction                                                      216
    11.2  Style, Presentation and the Reader                                217
    11.3  The Contents                                                      220
    11.4  References in the Text and Bibliography                           222
    Summary                                                                 229
    Further Reading                                                         230

*References*                                                               231
*Index*                                                                    235

# Preface

This text has been designed specifically for undergraduate students undertaking degree programmes in hospitality and/or tourism, though postgraduate students on these types of programmes may also find this material useful. It has been written to assist students undertaking the type of research project frequently required in the final year of such programmes that is associated with the production of a dissertation or research project report. In terms of its structure and contents, essentially it takes you through the issues and decisions that need to be considered and made to conceive, plan, conduct and write up the type of research project you are likely to be required to complete for such a course, unit or module. In this sense it seeks to take you through each decision and action stage of the research process, from identifying a topic and formulating the research question or aim and objectives to writing up the final document.

In putting this text together, I have been acutely aware, as a result of my long experience of teaching undergraduate hospitality and tourism students the type of 'research methods' module frequently included within a programme, to provide students with the methodological issues, tools and techniques necessary for conducting a research project, because students often find it a somewhat alien area compared to much of the other content within these types of programmes. On many occasions I have encountered the view from students that all this 'methodology stuff' and research is not as important as other vocational and/or business management material, which they can see the relevance and potential usefulness of studying. Often, research and its associated methodological considerations are seen by students as just a task that has to be done to fulfil the requirements of the degree and 'all this research stuff' is just an academic exercise that really has no value in the real world after graduation because it's what academics do while practitioners get on with the important business of managing companies.

Of course, this is true to a certain extent, but it is a fallacy to believe that the knowledge and skills developed in studying and undertaking research will not be of practical use in the real world. The intellectual development this engenders is invaluable in its own right but also, beyond this, the business world is rapidly becoming a more complex and dynamic environment within which conventional knowledge and accepted practices become outdated much more frequently. Indeed, in your future as a hospitality or tourism manager, it is reasonably certain that the fundamental basis of existing business models will be challenged and changed because of new ideas, concepts, products, processes and so on much more rapidly than has been the case in the past. In turn, the rationale for change is likely to be derived from research activity, be it conducted by academic, commercial or company researchers – that is seeking to challenge the status quo and develop new knowledge and techniques. Similarly, you may well be a manager who receives research reports and has to evaluate their results to make sound business decisions based on this information or, equally, you may have to commission research from professional research organisations and will need to provide them with a brief and evaluate their proposed methodology before agreeing a contract with them. Whatever the reason, a sound, critical knowledge and understanding of research and its associated methodological considerations will be an increasingly invaluable part of the future hospitality or tourism manager's toolkit.

I hope you enjoy reading this book and find it helpful. In writing it I have tried to take you from your real world of experience to the research methodology jargon by providing vignettes and examples to illustrate that perhaps the language of research and research methodology is not as alien as you may feel when first encountering it. I have also tried to indicate and explain why, when designing and undertaking a research project, various aspects of the research process have to be thought through, why decisions have to made in selecting alternative perspectives, research designs, data collection instruments and analysis techniques and, just as importantly, why these have to be logically supportive of and explained/justified to convince the, perhaps sceptical, recipient of the research that it should be regarded as credible.

Finally, I must record my thanks to my wife Penny, who has endured my preoccupied mind and absence from her life while at the computer keyboard for long periods writing with her usual cheerful stoicism. I would also like to extend my thanks to Chris Rojek at Sage who was not only a significant influence in commissioning the text in the first place but has also been extremely understanding and supportive during the writing process when difficulties arose to slow down the delivery of the final manuscript beyond the original date envisaged.

Bob Brotherton (November 2006)

# Chapter 1

## The Nature and Relevance of Research

---

### KEY CONCEPTS AND ISSUES

» *The nature of research.*
» *Experience, common sense and theory.*
» *The characteristics of scientific research.*
» *Good and bad research.*
» *Theoretical and applied research.*
» *Exploratory, descriptive and explanatory research.*
» *Inductive and deductive approaches to research.*
» *Issues that require research solutions.*
» *Some problems that may be encountered.*

---

## 1.1 Introduction

The purpose of this chapter is to provide you with a clear understanding of what research is and what it is designed to do. To achieve this, we will explore the nature of research in terms of its main purposes, functions and characteristics. We will also examine different types of research and focus on how these might be used to address or solve theoretical or practical problems, as well as the two basic approaches used to design and conduct research. We will also consider the features that characterise research regarded as good or bad and highlight some of the problems and issues that can arise in any research project, regardless of its scope and size. At the end of this process, you should not only have a clearer understanding of these issues but should also feel more confident that undertaking research is perhaps not quite as daunting as you may have believed and developing research skills is not just something you have to do because it is required on your course but that these will actually be useful to you when you become a practising manager.

## 1.2 The Nature of Research

Research is often seen by students on hospitality or tourism courses as a necessary evil to be confronted. This is especially the case when tutors inform students that they will have to undertake an undergraduate research project or dissertation. This type of activity may be viewed as something different, larger and much more challenging than the normal pattern of learning on a programe and, because it is outside the normal experience of attending lectures and seminars, writing relatively short pieces of coursework and/or sitting the examinations that tend to characterise most modules or units on a programme, there may naturally be some apprehension about having to undertake such a venture.

In many respects, hospitality and tourism courses, and the people engaged in them, have strong practical and applied emphases. Indeed, it is perhaps unlikely that you see yourself as a traditional high-flying academic who naturally wishes to engage in theoretical or applied 'research' within a chosen academic field or discipline. That sort of thing may be seen as okay for the physicists, chemists, computer scientists, economists and historians of this world, but, you might be asking what relevance does it have to the more practical and pragmatic world of hospitality and tourism? Well, before we go on to consider this question read Exhibit 1.1, as this may help to demystify some of the misgivings you may have about doing research.

---

### Exhibit 1.1    Research – Do I Need to be Einstein to Do It?

Sarah has just started her final year as an undergraduate student on a BA (Hons) International Tourism Management course and she also works as a part-time waitress at the Mexican Sunrise restaurant. She is usually very bubbly and enthusiastic in her work and well liked by regular diners at the restaurant. However, Carlos Ramirez, the restaurant manager, has noticed that Sarah has looked worried and preoccupied during her recent shifts and this is beginning to affect how she deals with the customers. So, he asks her if she can come to see him in his office after her current shift finishes.

Carlos said, 'Hi Sarah, come in and have a seat and don't look so worried – I'm not about to sack you! It's just that I've noticed lately that you don't appear to be quite your effervescent self with the customers and I wondered if there was a problem I could help with.' Relieved, Sarah said, 'Well, you're right, I am a bit worried about something. When I started the final year of my course, the tutors told me that a major part of this year was going to be taken up with the individual research project and this will account for 30 per cent of my final marks and have a major impact on the degree I get. As if that wasn't bad enough, they then scared us out of our wits by saying it would be the real test of how good we are and, because we have never done anything like this before, we had better get on it with it quickly because we will have to deal with things like research philosophy, deduction and induction, hypothesis testing, collecting empirical data and probably use inferential statistics to analyse this. My God, it's like another language and I don't think I can cope.'

Carlos smiled, 'Ah, so that's it. I knew there was something up. Okay Sarah, let's see if we can't put your mind at rest a little over some of these things. When I was in your position I felt the same. I felt like I needed to be Einstein to be able to do it, but I learned that, really, all this research stuff is not as daunting as you think. A lot of it is new jargon that you haven't encountered before and, once you learn the research language a little, it will not be so frightening. Let me give you an example. Remember when you first came to work here, you were a little lost because of the jargon we use in the restaurant until I explained it for you in terms you were already familiar with?'. Sarah nodded. 'Well, it's pretty much the same with research', Carlos said and continued, 'You know more than you think you do. Do you remember when I asked you to come up with some ideas on how we could improve the service in the restaurant?' Sarah nodded again. 'Well, you did, and some very good ones as well. So how did you do it?'

Sarah replied, 'I'd already had some ideas from what I'd read and studied on the course, from my experience of working here and I went to suss out how a couple of other restaurants operated. Then I thought, well, if we could do X then that might improve Y because I could see the connection between the two. So, if you remember, we set this up as a trial for a couple of weeks to see if it was true.'

'And how did we decide whether it was or not?' Carlos asked.

'We compared the restaurant's performance before the trial with its performance during the trial and then I wrote this up in a report for you, which proved my original thoughts were right', said Sarah.

'Exactly,' said Carlos, 'So, let me put this into research jargon for you, because this is what you did, you conducted a piece of research! You began by examining existing evidence on how to organise restaurant service, then you used this to formulate some educated guesses, or hypotheses, on likely causes and effects. What we then did, through our trial, was to set up a type of experiment to test your hypotheses to see if they were correct or not. How did we find these out? By analysing the restaurant's performance figures, or data, and then we came to the conclusion that this information indicated the original hypotheses were correct. So, when you wrote up these findings in the report, this gave us the rationale for changing the service system.'

'Wow, when you put it like that, I guess I do know more than I thought I did and maybe it's not going to be such a worry after all. Thanks, Carlos – you've put my mind at rest and I think I'll be okay now. It's really very good of you to take the time and trouble to help me in this way.'

'No problem, Sarah', Carlos said, 'After all, I do have an ulterior motive. If you're happier and more relaxed, you'll be back to your old self at work and the customers will be happier again.'

'Ah', said Sarah, 'What was it you said about Einstein earlier? I think you are smarter than you let on!'

Hopefully Exhibit 1.1 will have helped to convince you that research is less highbrow and complicated than you may have thought! As an aspiring hospitality or tourism manager, you will know that most of your time as a manager will be spent managing, dealing with real-time, practical issues and problems. Decisions will have to be made within tight timescales, often on the spot, and this implies a more pragmatic approach to solving problems and answering questions. Experience, common sense and quick thinking will be important in this type of environment. There may not be time for an extended investigation, reflective theorising and procedures designed to ensure that the answer arrived at is based on sound and comprehensive facts or data and, therefore, the most valid and reliable one available.

That said, however, and notwithstanding the value of timely managerial decision making, not all managerial decisions can be successfully made on the basis of experience, common sense or quick thinking. One of the problems with these as a basis for determining answers, finding solutions and making decisions is that they are likely to have, at best, a fairly shaky evidence base and tend to be idiosyncratic and inconsistent over time.

Let us just consider this issue for a moment. An individual's experience is unique to that individual and is comprised of all the experiences he or she has encountered and how that person has thought about, reacted to and learnt from those experiences. Therefore, one person's experience can never be the same as another's. Even if the people concerned share similar past experiences, the ways in which they perceive them and learn from them will differ. Thus, answers, solutions and decisions based on experience will tend to be idiosyncratic because the underlying evidence base – the individuals' experiences and cognitive abilities – used to generate them varies from one person to another.

Similarly, what is common sense? Common sense is a generally accepted view or belief of what is seen to be a sensible way to act or understand certain questions, issues or events. Such a view or belief may indeed be accurate, but, equally, it may not. The problem is that there is rarely, if ever, an opportunity to prove or validate views based on common sense because it is invariably unclear where the origins of the commonsense view in question lie and any evidence base underlying the view is likely to be fragmented, diffuse and indistinct at best. Hence, when challenged, the person using common sense as the rationale or justification for an answer, solution or decision only has recourse to the, rather mythical, strength of the commonsense belief as evidence to support it. Typically the question 'How do you know that is correct or the right way to do things?' is answered with the statement 'Because it's common sense' – an answer that invites the questioner to agree with the commonsense belief of the proponent. What happens, though, if the questioner does not accept this? Can there be a logical discussion, with reference to data that could support or refute the claim, to establish which view is correct? No, of course not. The very nature of a belief is just that – it is something people believe for some reason, but is not something that necessarily can be proved one way or the other. I may believe in God, you may not, but there is no way that we could find irrefutable or incontestable evidence to support either view.

So, although not without value, answers and solutions based on experience or common sense alone may have inherent flaws and lead to inconsistent, if not conflicting, policies and practices if they are the sole basis for managerial decision making. In addition, where questions arise that cannot be answered by reference to prevailing common sense or accumulated experience, perhaps because they are entirely new or much more complex, we have to resort to other techniques and methods. Among these is research.

As a practising hospitality or tourism manager, you will have to engage in various aspects of research then – because the questions and problems facing the contemporary manager are increasingly becoming ones that are new and complex and cannot be answered or solved by using experience or common sense alone – but you do actually undertake research in your daily life now. Consider the following issues for a moment: you want to go on holiday, you want to buy a car, you want to find a suitable venue for your twenty-first party, you want to get the best return you can on your savings. How do you decide where to go on holiday, which car to buy, where to hold your party and which form of investment will give you the best return? In a word, research. All of these issues have alternative answers or solutions and you need to find and select the one that fits your needs or criteria the best. How would you do that? Simply by collecting information to identify the options associated with each, then by analysing the information and selecting the best option. In short, you would research the issue in order to identify the most suitable solution.

Many textbooks refer to, or define, research in terms of it being an activity that creates or generates new knowledge or as something that produces a contribution to the existing body of knowledge. The types of words that are commonly used in definitions of what research is include 'discovery', 'investigation', 'new facts', 'advancement of knowledge', 'original insights' – all of which seem to suggest that undertaking research is likely to be a rather daunting task and create the impression that all research is something very difficult, complicated and requires a high level of intellectual ability on the part of the researcher. However, as we have seen above, in the example of undertaking some research to choose a holiday, a car, a party venue and so on, even these simple 'research projects' will involve investigation, discovery and, at least for you as the researcher, the generation of new insights and knowledge. Therefore, it is perhaps preferable to think about research in contextual terms such as these. Indeed, the type of research you will be expected to undertake for an undergraduate project or dissertation, or even a Masters thesis, will be relatively limited in scope and expectations.

By now I hope you are convinced that research is not as difficult as you may have imagined. Of course it has its challenges, but, as indicated earlier, you already do research in your everyday life and the type of research you will be required to do as an undergraduate, or even as a Masters, student is not of the kind necessary to win a Nobel prize. Just in case you are still in doubt, let us consider a couple of views from the literature. Sekaran (2000: 4) suggests that research is, 'an organised, systematic, data-based scientific enquiry or investigation into a specific problem which is undertaken with the objective of finding solutions or answers to it'. By contrast, Wilson (1997: vi) takes the view that, 'research is a process of "principled compromise", informed by professional knowledge of the techniques and limitations of research methods, driven by personal energy, and presented with whatever honesty and objectivity that can be mustered'.

Sekaran's view of the nature of research is one that we might refer to as conventional. Although it would be difficult to argue against the value of having a process that had a clear focus and purpose, that was organised and systematic and based on data capable of being verified or challenged, Sekaran's definition implies that this process is linear in nature and one that can be conducted objectively by using the 'scientific method' to eliminate the influence of subjective values and bias. Wilson's view challenges much of this. His more alternative or, arguably, realistic stance contends that research is inherently subject to personal influence and bias and the idea that a 'method', scientific or otherwise, can somehow create an objective, bias-free process is an illusion. Put simply, because the tools and techniques used to implement the method are chosen by the researcher and it is the researcher who decides how the results are to be presented, it is inevitable that personal preferences and biases will influence the whole process.

So, who is correct? Is research always objective and value-free or is it subjective and value-ridden? The answer is that, in reality, it tends to lie somewhere on a continuum between these two extremes. Perhaps one way to think about the significance of this is to consider, as some, but not all, researchers do, the objective, value-free view as 'ideal'. Unfortunately, as is the case with most ideals, it is unlikely to be achieved. In that case, you might ask, why bother? The answer to this is that, although you may not be able to achieve what is regarded as the ideal by some, the closer you can get to this the better it will be. This leads us to consider the notions of what constitutes 'good' and 'bad' research.

## 1.3 The Characteristics of Scientific Research

Logically, good research should reflect the characteristics of the 'ideal', bad research the opposite. The 'ideal' is variously called scientific enquiry, scientific research or the scientific method and is regarded as having nine general characteristics to distinguish it from other forms of research. As we will see, each of these, both individually and collectively, is quite sensible and, if embodied in a piece of research, tends to make it more believable or credible. Whether or not they can all be achieved, however, is another matter, as we have discussed above!

## 1.3.1 *Purposeful*

Any research project should have a clear focus that is achievable as the research process itself is a means to an end. For example, it is a way to obtain answers to a question or solutions to a problem. To make this clear, an overall aim and associated objectives should be specified before the research begins. The aim defines what the overall purpose and output of the proposed research are and the objectives indicate what has to be completed if the aim is to be successfully achieved. For example, the aim of the research might be 'To determine the critical success factors (CSFs) for UK budget hotel operations'. To achieve this overall result, a number of tasks or stages will have to be completed. These will be the research objectives and, in this case, might be expressed as follows.

1 To conduct a literature review to identify the nature of CSFs, both in general and in relation to the budget hotel operations context of the project.
2 To develop a theoretical framework/conceptual model of the CSFs from the literature review and produce associated hypotheses.
3 To collect empirical data from budget hotel companies and other appropriate organisations and/or individuals associated with the project's context.
4 To analyse the empirical data and test the study's hypotheses.
5 To produce conclusions and recommendations for further research.

If these objectives are achieved successfully, then, collectively, they should enable the overall aim to be achieved.

## 1.3.2 *Rigorous*

This characteristic is concerned with the quality of the design and how the research is conducted. Essentially, if a piece of research has been conducted in a rigorous manner, it is more likely that it will be seen as credible and the results believed and accepted than would otherwise be the case. To produce a piece of research that is regarded as rigorous requires sound and logically consistent thinking to produce an appropriate overall design (methodology) and the adoption/use of appropriate tools and techniques (methods). A rigorous piece of research will have a sound underlying conceptual basis and will have been conducted in a manner that is both transparent and defensible.

## 1.3.3 *Testable*

Testability is concerned with the nature of the question being researched. For the research to be able to answer the question it is designed to address, the question must be answerable. This means that the question, or a hypothesis derived from it, must be written or phrased in a form that will enable it to be tested or proved. Essentially, this means phrasing the issue clearly in either positive or negative terms so that it can be determined whether the proposition can be supported by the evidence or not. Using our example from above, we might produce a series of such propositions or hypotheses relating to the factors that could be critical for a budget hotel's operations to be successful. Having reviewed the literature on this topic, we are likely to have identified a range of factors that it is suggested may be very important or critical for such success. What we would then need to do is test the assertions by collecting evidence to see if it supports them or not. However, to be able to conduct such tests, we need statements that are testable. For example, one factor that could be regarded as critical for this type of hospitality operation is the cleanliness of the guest bedrooms. So, we might speculate, or hypothesise, that the higher the levels of cleanliness, the more successful the budget hotel would be. Alternatively, we might state that our survey respondents – budget hotel general managers – would indicate guest bedroom cleanliness to be extremely important for the success of the hotel. As we will see in Chapter 5, there are varying forms of hypothesis statements that are capable of being tested and so we may not always want to express them in the form we have used here.

## 1.3.4 *Replicable*

If the design and procedures used to undertake a piece of research are transparent and available in the public domain for others to see, then other researchers will be able to replicate or repeat that research to test the rigour of its processes and the accuracy of its findings. This is the same idea as one researcher repeating the same experiment a number of times to see if the same results are obtained. If the results from this process are the same, or at least sufficiently similar, then people are likely to have confidence that they are accurate. I am not suggesting here that you will have the time or resources to repeatedly test your research findings, but you may wish to test previous research findings within a different context as the basis for your project. For example, in previous studies on your topic/research question, other researchers may have designed and used particular data collection/analysis instruments, procedures and techniques, but in a different context. Their studies may have been conducted in other countries to the one you are using in your project and so you may be interested in whether or not these could also be applicable to your country or they may have been undertaken a long time ago and need updating because conditions have changed. Alternatively, these might have been conducted within the context of an industry other than hospitality or tourism and you will then want to test if these would also be applicable to your industry.

Whatever the context, the key issues here are those of comprehensiveness and transparency. For you to be able to replicate someone else's study or for someone else to repeat yours, the process used must be recorded in detail. So, the assumptions made, the hypotheses tested and the data collection and analysis procedures and techniques used must be reported comprehensively and transparently to enable others to test the validity of the findings by repeating the work.

## 1.3.5 *Precision*

Because of the scale, scope and complexity of most real-world situations, we are often forced to restrict our research to a subset or sample of the full population. Where this is the case, we face an issue concerning the extent to which the findings we obtain from our sample are a true reflection of the population as a whole. If the two are the same, then we can say that they are very precise or accurate. As we may want to generalise the findings from our sample to apply to the larger population, the more precise the findings are, the more we will be able to do this successfully.

There are many issues associated with this, particularly those concerned with sample design/selection, that will be dealt with later in this book (see Chapter 8), but just consider the following example, which is likely to be familiar to you, as an illustration of why precision is important.

In all countries there are commercial companies that conduct 'polls' or surveys on behalf of clients. For example, Gallup and Mori are well-known names in the UK. These companies conduct, among others, political polls designed to estimate such things as voting intentions, the popularity of political parties or even specific politicians. So, for example, when an election is due, polls will be conducted to try and predict which political party is going to win. As the UK probably has a voting population of around 40 million people, it would clearly be impossible to ask every voter which party he or she intended to vote for. Therefore, the poll has to be conducted on a much smaller number than this. This may be as low as 2000 or 3000 people, which is clearly a very small percentage of the whole voting population. The results from this sample will then be used to predict the overall election results based on millions of voters' behaviour. As you can see, if the results obtained from the sample polled are not precise, then the prediction of the election result is likely to be wildly inaccurate.

## 1.3.6 *Confidence*

This is related to precision and is concerned with the likelihood, or probability, that the findings from the sample are correct or, put another way, how confident we can be about the accuracy of the research findings. If we can be 100 per cent confident, then, effectively, we can say that we are certain the same result will be obtained all the time. However, we can never be certain because there is always some potential for error in research work. So, what level of confidence is acceptable?

The general convention is that a 95 per cent level of confidence is the minimum acceptable. This means that the probability of the findings being incorrect is only 5 per cent and, conversely, 9½ times out of every 10 they will be correct. If we can demonstrate that our findings have such a high level of probability of being correct, they are going to appear to be robust and other people will have confidence in them. The importance of this is that we cannot simply expect other people to believe, or have confidence in, our results without presenting some proof to justify our claims in this respect.

## 1.3.7 *Objective*

As we have seen earlier, this characteristic is one that has received criticism in terms of whether or not it is really possible for any individual to be truly objective and value-free when designing and conducting research. Whichever stance you accept, the principle here is that the greater the objectivity in the research, the less subjective bias it will have. So, there is an inverse relationship between objectivity and subjectivity – that is, as one increases, the other declines. If the 'ideal' is total objectivity, then the closer you can get to that the better it is.

We probably cannot be perfect, but we can try to get as close to being so as possible. Given that we would probably accept it is not possible to eliminate all our subjective impulses, we should be aware that we are likely to bring these into play and constantly challenge ourselves to either not do this or limit it as much as we can. In addition to this, we should be aware of where our subjectivity has influenced the research and be prepared to recognise this and the impact it may have had.

## 1.3.8 *Generalisable*

It is self-evident that all research is undertaken within a particular context or situation, but this does not mean that the findings from this research will be applicable to other contexts or situations that are related or unrelated to the original context in which the research was conducted. However, it would increase the value of the research if it were to be generally applicable rather than relevant only to that one context. Therefore, the ability to generalise from the results of a research project to other contexts is clearly desirable. Thus, the ability to generalise research results widely increases their value.

The problem with this is that, to maximise the generalisability of the research results, considerable thought, time, effort and, often, money, would have to be devoted to the research design and procedures. In the type of research that you are likely to be conducting, this may not be possible for obvious reasons, in which case you may have to accept that the ability to generalise from your findings may be limited at best.

The most important issue here is not to over-claim the generalisability of your findings. If the results from your study are clearly limited to a particular company, industry sector, country, culture or time period, then it is important to state this when you write up the findings. Of course you may speculate that the findings could be applicable to a wider context, but you should make it clear that it is precisely this, a speculation, and not a strong or definitive claim to generalisability.

You may encounter this generalisability issue from two possible directions. First, the one described above, where you examine the extent to which your research findings may be capable of generalising to other contexts. Second, your research may be designed to test the extent to which previous research findings can be generalised to the context in which you are conducting your research. For example, you may take an existing theory or set of research findings that have been derived from other contexts and seek to test the extent to which they are applicable to the hospitality or tourism context you have chosen for your study. This is generally known as a 'replication' study, where you repeat or replicate the original, but in a different context. In principle, this procedure is analogous to repeating an experiment under different conditions to test how robust the original findings are when the original conditions are altered. In short, how generalisable the results may be.

## 1.3.9 *Parsimonious*

This characteristic is essentially concerned with simplicity. Any issue being researched is likely to be one that could be influenced by a wide range of factors, but not all of these possible influences will be equally strong or important to the overall answer. For example, you may ask the question 'What determines the level of customer satisfaction in this type of hotel, restaurant, destination, theme park?' When you think about this, it is clear there will be quite a number of factors that could have some influence on the level of customer satisfaction. These might be related to the nature of the product, the abilities and attitudes of staff, accessibility of the premises, price charged, quality of the experience and so on, but they are unlikely to have an equal influence. The question is, which have the largest influence on satisfaction?

Research designed to look for a parsimonious answer would seek to answer this question as well, not just the wider one. Not only would a parsimonious approach to designing the research help to make it more economical and manageable but it would also mean that the results would be likely to have greater practical value.

To illustrate this, think of yourself as a manager who has commissioned some research to answer the broader customer satisfaction question above. If the researchers came back to you and said, there are 15 factors that our research indicates have an influence, how useful would this be? On the other hand, if they came back to you and said 'Our findings show that, of the 15 factors we have identified as ones influencing satisfaction, the results clearly show that, of these, there are two that have a much greater influence than all the others', then it would be much more useful for you to concentrate your resources and efforts on improving those, knowing that, if you did, the chances of achieving an improvement in customer satisfaction and a return on this investment would be pretty good.

## 1.4 Types of Research

Research is research, isn't it? Well, yes and no! Research may be regarded as sound and good or flawed and bad. It may be viewed as scientific or unscientific. It may be theoretical or more practical in nature. It can be conducted in laboratories or in real-life situations. It may take place at one point in time or over a period of time. It might be limited to one country or could possibly embrace a number of different countries. It may be designed to test existing knowledge to establish how valid it is or to establish entirely new knowledge. It may be concerned with collecting and analysing quantitative or qualitative data. It could be designed to explore, describe or explain the phenomena in question.

So, where do we start? In the first instance, it may be useful to distinguish between what may be referred to as different types of research purpose compared to judgements regarding the quality of research. Descriptors such as 'good' or 'bad' clearly refer to the quality of a piece of research and are, at least in some respects, subjective, although criteria may be employed to distinguish between research that is regarded as good or bad. For example, research regarded as scientific is more likely to be seen as good research than that which is unscientific. The reason for this is that scientific research will embody the characteristics of scientific research discussed in the previous section of this chapter that, as we saw, are desirable features of any piece of research for a number of reasons.

### 1.4.1 Exploratory, descriptive and explanatory

In terms of differing purposes, exploratory research is really self-evident. Where, perhaps, the situation is very new, has been previously inaccessible for some reason or the research problem is too large and complex to address without some initial, exploratory work, an attempt to generate some initial insights and understanding would be of value. In this sense, a piece of exploratory research designed to surface the key issues and questions may be appropriate as it would help to make the situation clearer and, possibly, set the research agenda.

Descriptive research will be designed to establish a factual picture of the issue under investigation, whereas explanatory research will be concerned with explaining the why and how of the situation (see Table 1.1 for a comparison of the goals of these three types of research).

Explanatory research frequently includes descriptive elements but goes beyond this to identify and explore the causes lying behind the effects and the nature of the relationships between the two. Taking our earlier example of the

**Table 1.1**   The goals of exploratory, descriptive and explanatory research

| Exploratory research | Descriptive research | Explanatory research |
|---|---|---|
| Become familiar with the basic facts, people and concerns involved. | Provide an accurate profile of a group. | Determine the accuracy of a principle or theory. |
| Develop a well-grounded mental picture of what is happening. | Describe a process, mechanism or relationship. | Find out which competing explanation is better. |
| Generate many ideas and develop tentative theories and conjectures. | Give a verbal or numerical picture. | Advance knowledge about an underlying process. |
| Determine the feasibility of doing additional research. | Find information to stimulate new explanations. | Link different issues or topics under a common general statement. |
| Formulate questions and refine issues for more systematic enquiry. | Present basic background information or a context. | Build and elaborate a theory so it becomes complete. |
| Develop techniques and a sense of direction for future research. | Create a set of categories or classify types. | Extend a theory or principle into new areas or issues. |
| | Clarify a sequence, set of stages or steps. | Provide evidence to support or refute an explanation. |
| | Document information that contradicts prior beliefs about a subject. | |

*Source*: Adapted from Neuman, *Social Research Methods,* pp. 19–20. Published by Allyn and Bacon, Boston MA. © 1984 by Pearson Education. Reprinted by permission of the publisher.

factors that might influence customer satisfaction, a descriptive study would only identify these factors and perhaps speculate about their relationship to satisfaction. In contrast, an explanatory study would seek to differentiate between, and measure, the relative influence of the factors and explain the cause and effect relationship between them. In this sense, the explanatory study clearly has more applied value than the descriptive one.

However, you should not necessarily be led by this to conclude that you should aim to produce an explanatory study rather than a descriptive one. Other things being equal, it would be preferable, but, depending on the existing state of knowledge on the subject, it may be that a good descriptive study is what is required at a particular point in time. For example, although today scientists and doctors are able to prove and explain the relationships and mechanisms between such things as smoking (cause) and lung cancers (effects), it was not the case many years ago. Without earlier, more descriptive, studies that found correlations (non cause and effect relationships) between these two things, it is possible that the more detailed, explanatory work would not have taken place.

## 1.4.2 *Pure and applied*

You will also find that the research methods literature will almost universally distinguish between pure, or basic, and applied research as two types of research with very different purposes (see Table 1.2). Pure research, sometimes called 'blue sky thinking', is an activity that has no immediate utility or application to real-life problems. It is designed to contribute new thinking or knowledge to an existing field of enquiry in its own right, without having any other specific purpose. Its role is to expand and/or improve the body of knowledge, in its broadest sense, within the field concerned. Therefore, it is not utilitarian in nature, although it is quite possible that such intellectual advancements may be translated into more practical circumstances in the future. Pure research is invariably conceptual or theoretical in nature and concerned with intellectual reflection, discovery and invention. It is driven by intellectual interest and curiosity rather than a need to address a particular real-world problem.

Applied research, on the other hand, as the name suggests, is a more practical and focused type of research. It is generally concerned with practical problem-solving and finding solutions to real-world problems. In this sense, it is much more focused and goal-directed than pure research and, therefore, more utilitarian. It has a clear use value and concentrates on the explanation, action and implementation of solutions. This is likely to be the type of research you will be more interested in as it has more immediate relevance to the type of applied course you are engaged on and the challenges you will face as a hospitality or tourism manager.

## 1.4.3 *Theoretical/empirical and primary/secondary*

Similar, but not quite the same, to the distinction between pure and applied research is that between theoretical and empirical and primary and secondary research. The distinction between the latter pairing is one based on the type of data or information to be used in the research project. Secondary research relies on data that already exist – in short, those contained in the literature relating to the issue in question – whereas primary research involves the collection of new data. Another way to think about this distinction is to consider something that is obtained first hand (new) as compared to that which is obtained second hand (old). Although virtually all the research that collects and analyses primary data will also use the same basic procedures for secondary data, secondary research is limited to the use of secondary data alone. Though there is a close connection between these two types and theoretical and empirical research, the two pairings are not necessarily synonymous.

**Table 1.2** Pure and applied research compared

| Pure research | Applied research |
|---|---|
| Research is intrinsically satisfying and judgements are made by other academics. | Research is part of a job and is judged by sponsors from outside the academic discipline. |
| Research problems and subjects are selected with a great deal of freedom. | Research problems are 'narrowly constrained' in line with the demands of employers or sponsors. |
| Research is judged by the absolute norms of scientific rigour and the highest standards of scholarship are sought. | The rigour and standards of scholarship depend on the uses of the results. Research can be 'quick and dirty' or may match high scientific standards. |
| The primary concern is with the internal logic and rigour of research design. | The primary concern is with the ability to generalise from findings to areas of interest to sponsors. |
| The driving goal is to contribute to basic, theoretical knowledge. | The driving goal is to have practical pay-offs or uses for results. |
| Success comes when results appear in a scholarly journal and have a broad impact on others in the scientific community. | Success comes when results are used by sponsors in decision making. |

*Source*: Adapted from Neuman, *Social Research Methods,* p. 22. Published by Allyn and Bacon, Boston MA. © 1984 by Pearson Education. Reprinted by permission of the publisher.

Often, theoretical research is viewed as secondary research in nature and practice and, in the main, this is probably a reasonable view as it tends to take an abstract, conceptual and reflective stance in relation to the existing body of knowledge. Its role is to improve and extend the conceptual and, ultimately, concrete understanding of the issue. This invariably means that existing, secondary knowledge is questioned, tested, re-evaluated and revised. Nevertheless, theoretical research can be conducted by means of the collection and use of primary data and, hence, will be empirical in nature. Let us return to the smoking and lung cancer example we used above to illustrate this.

By collecting empirical data on the connection between people who smoked and the incidence of lung cancer, researchers began to analyse this data and develop theories to explain the relationship between the cause and the effect, so these theoretical developments were stimulated by the collection of new primary data, at least in the first instance.

Therefore, theoretical research may be conducted by using secondary or primary data. It is not the type of data that is critical here but the purpose of the research – whether it is conceptual or theoretical understanding. On the other hand, empirical and primary research are synonymous in the sense that the former always involves the collection of the latter kind of data, though, as we have seen, such data may be used for theoretical or applied research purposes.

One thing that should be clear from the above discussion is that it is not always easy to decisively separate these so-called different types of research into totally discrete categories. Indeed, most research is likely to involve secondary and primary data, both theoretical and empirical considerations, and to contain descriptive and explanatory elements. The question is not if a piece of research is definitively one or the other, but what its main emphasis and purpose is. This leads us to consider what are often termed the two main approaches to research – induction and deduction.

## 1.5 The Main Research Approaches

### 1.5.1 Induction

This is an approach that essentially works by going from the unknown to the known. As Figure 1.1 illustrates, the starting point for an inductive approach to conducting research is the identification of the problem or question to be addressed. In this respect it is synonymous with the deductive approach, but that is where the similarities end, as will become evident as we proceed to examine the two approaches. As the main purpose of induction is to build new theory, rather than test existing theory, its main empirical focus is on collecting data from the real world as a resource to be used in developing explanations or theory. Thus, the collection of empirical data occurs much earlier in the inductive approach than in the deductive approach and its role is different from that found in deduction. The inductive approach is generally regarded as one that favours the use of 'ideographic' methodologies, which we will explore further in Chapters 6 and 7, such as case studies or 'in the field' enquiries – that is, participant or non-participant observation (Gill and Johnson, 1991; Robson, 1993) – because it is rooted in a philosophical view of the world that emphasises social construction, perceptions, meanings and subjectivity as important in understanding and the development of knowledge. As we shall see, this is known as phenomenology or, sometimes, interpretivism and, in Chapter 2, this is discussed in more detail.

Having collected the empirical data, the inductive researcher then has to make sense of it by analysing it for patterns, connections, relationships and so on in order to interpret its significance and produce meaningful explanations or theories. Ultimately, although these may be tested by other researchers using a deductive process, that is not the purpose of inductive research. As the philosophical beliefs and types of methods used by the inductive researcher are likely to value rich, narrative, descriptive information far more highly than statistical data, inductive research invariably involves the collection of qualitative rather than quantitative data. In this sense, inductive research is frequently seen as synonymous with qualitative research and, as we shall see below, the reverse is true of the deductive approach.

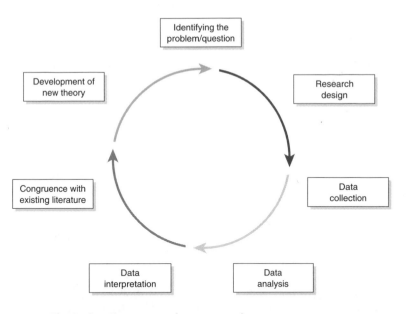

**Figure 1.1**   The inductive approach to research

However, some caution should be adopted in uncritically accepting this deceptively simple distinction. Inductive research could be conducted by means of the collection of quantitative data and deductive research by collecting qualitative data. Indeed, many research projects, adopting one or the other approach, are designed to collect both types of data. Inductive research may collect basic numerical data to facilitate the description or indicate the scope and boundaries of the situation being studied. For example, in a case study of a company, the research findings may well include data relating to its size (turnover, capital employed, number of employees or operating units and so on) and perhaps the volume of its operations (output, sales and so on). Similarly, a deductive study designed to discover the volume of a market and understand the preferences of different types of consumers in that market would probably collect quantitative data relating to the size of the market – that is, the number of consumers and qualitative data to explain why they buy certain items and not others.

One question we have not addressed yet is when would it be more appropriate to use an inductive rather than deductive approach to conduct research? Apart from the influence of the researcher's fundamental beliefs regarding the nature of the real world and knowledge, the use of induction would generally be more appropriate when the topic is so new or unique that the existing body of knowledge on it is non-existent or very limited or when it has not previously been possible to gain access to the real-world contexts in question to collect the

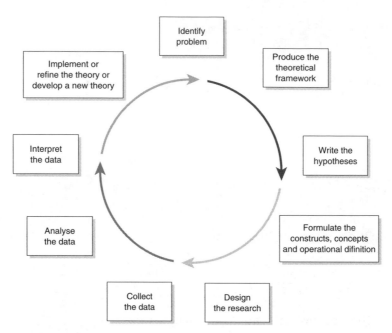

**Figure 1.2**   The deductive approach to research

data. In short, when, for a variety of possible reasons, there is not a sufficient body of knowledge in the literature to sensibly adopt a deductive approach.

## 1.5.2 *Deduction*

This is the approach to research adopted by archetypal scientists who believe that the world and knowledge are factual and objective. This is based on a set of beliefs known as positivism and we shall explore these beliefs and their implications further in Chapter 2.

As Figure 1.2 shows, this approach takes the existing body of theoretical and empirical knowledge as its primary starting point. It is embodied in the literature existing on the issues being researched and is accessed by conducting a review of this literature (see Chapter 4) to determine the theory, or theories, that will be tested in the research. So, deduction is concerned with testing existing theory, whereas, as we have seen, induction seeks to create new theory.

Once the literature has been reviewed, the deductive researcher will be in a position to develop the theoretical framework that informs and helps to structure and guide the remainder of the research process. We shall consider this in more detail in Chapter 5, but it should indicate to you that the deductive approach is generally more highly structured, focused and constrained, in terms of how the data collection and analysis procedures are designed and implemented, than is the inductive approach. This is highlighted even more when you consider that what the deductive research process will test are the logical consequences of the theory, the hypotheses. As these will be highly specific and relatively limited in number, they focus the design of the data collection procedures and instruments to ensure that only the data required to test them are collected. At the end of the process, once the data have been analysed, the theory tested during this process will either be supported, or confirmed, by the evidence or it may require modification in the light of the evidence or, in extreme cases, it may need to be replaced by an entirely new theory.

## 1.6 Research Issues, Questions and Problems

We shall consider, in more detail, many of the considerations relating to choosing a research topic and formulating the question(s) or problem(s) to be addressed in the research project in Chapter 3, but here it is worthwhile to briefly reflect on the types of issues and questions that practising hospitality or tourism managers may wish to grapple with or answer and speculate on how they might use research principles and methods to achieve this. Consider the following questions, which are probably the fairly typical issues such managers would be interested in.

- How can we increase the level of satisfaction among the guests who stay in our hotel?
- What would be the best types of location for our new, branded restaurant outlets?
- How can we reduce the level of staff turnover?
- Which advertising media and methods would give us the greatest return for our expenditure?
- What do we have to do in order to attract more visitors to this part of the country?
- Why have fewer people visited our theme park this year than in previous years?

These all represent common practical issues and problems faced by hospitality or tourism businesses. At the same time, however, they all suggest a relationship between at least two things – a cause and an effect. Often, but not always, we know what the effect is, but the cause of it may be far more uncertain. In the questions above, we know that the levels of customer satisfaction are not as high as we would like them to be, the level of staff turnover is too high, some locations are likely to be preferable to others for our restaurant operations, visitor numbers are not as high as we would like or have declined for some reason and certain types of advertising media/methods are likely to be more efficient for our purposes than others, but which ones?

So, we know what the problem is, but not how to solve it. We know what we would like to achieve, but not how to get there. This is the case because our knowledge and understanding are not sufficient to enable us to close the gap. To remedy this, we need to increase our knowledge and understanding to help find the solution. The question then is, how do we do that? We could attempt to simply guess why the effects have occurred. We could commission or employ others – consultants and so on – to investigate the problem for us or undertake some type of more systematic investigation or analysis of the problem ourselves.

Of course, which route is chosen is likely to be influenced by the amount of time, expertise and resources at our disposal. If we had little time and lacked the necessary expertise, but had the resources, we might consider commissioning an outside agency, such as a consultancy company or specialist research organisation, to do the research for us. Although this undoubtedly would produce some answers and solutions, it may be very expensive and not as timely as we might wish for. Of course, buying in external expertise has its value, but, often, we need answers more quickly than they can provide them and may want to develop our own, in-house, knowledge base and expertise for the future. To do this, we need to develop our own research skills. In addition, even if we were to commission an external agency to undertake the research for us, we would want to have an understanding of the principles, techniques and procedures likely to be adopted by such people because we would have to give them a brief in the first instance and to then be capable of critically interpreting their methods and findings (Shoemaker, 1994). So, either way, this type of knowledge is useful to a practising manager.

To give you some indication of the areas of hospitality and tourism businesses where research is being undertaken by managers in such companies, consultancy organisations and public-sector bodies, I conducted a piece of small-scale, exploratory research when preparing this text. This essentially constituted the design and implementation of a survey, using a mailed questionnaire to a sample of 845 members of a UK professional body, The Tourism Society. The questionnaire listed a range of possible areas where research might have been taking place and asked the respondents to indicate if they were involved in any of these.

The overall response to this was a little disappointing, with only 45 questionnaires returned, a response rate of 5.4 per cent, but it illustrates one of the issues discussed earlier. Being dependent on the goodwill of the potential respondents, when they are very busy people and there is nothing of obvious benefit to them in filling such a questionnaire in, can often produce low response rates, over which we have little or no control. The obvious problem this raises here is the validity of the results. Put simply, how can we be sure that the 95 per cent who didn't respond would have made similar choices to those of the 5 per cent who did? The answer is, of course, that we cannot, so the results need to be viewed with some degree of caution in terms of whether or not they are representative of the types of research activity being undertaken across the hospitality and tourism industries as a whole. In addition to this, the composition of the 45 respondents included very few managers from private hospitality or tourism companies. Most of the people who responded were from public-sector bodies, consultancy companies and trade associations. Therefore, there is a potential problem of bias in the pattern of the results.

These issues demonstrate that even a small-scale, simple piece of research can have similar problems to those endeavours that are much larger in scale. The point here is not the existence of the problems per se, but how they

**Table 1.3**    What types of research activity do managers engage in?

| Area of research activity | Percentage involved |
|---|---|
| New product/service development | 44 |
| Market research | 55 |
| Competitor intelligence | 26 |
| Site/location feasibility | 35 |
| New equipment evaluation | 4 |
| Recipe/dish development | 2 |
| Menu development | 4 |
| Pilot/test studies | 17 |
| Employee surveys | 26 |
| Customer surveys | 42 |
| Raw material/supply sourcing | 4 |
| Advertising effectiveness | 37 |
| Service quality measurement | 33 |
| Benchmarking | 44 |
| Environmental scanning | 4 |
| Energy management | 4 |
| Investment analysis/appraisal | 17 |
| IT systems/applications | 20 |
| Ecommerce | 13 |
| Business process re-engineering | 9 |
| Facilities design | 9 |
| | |
| Other areas: | |
| economic impacts of tourism | 4 |
| sales force management | 2 |
| revenue planning and management | 2 |
| distribution and channel management | 2 |
| training assessment | 2 |
| tourism master planning | 2 |
| tourism sector reviews | 2 |
| destination branding | 2 |
| visitor management plans | 2 |
| customer/marketing studies | 2 |
| cultural and heritage tourism | 2 |
| consumer choice criteria | 2 |
| accommodation quality standards | 2 |
| brand research | 2 |
| skills audits | 2 |

are recognised and dealt with. Any research you undertake may suffer from similar problems, but this is not necessarily disastrous. As we shall see in Chapter 11, it is what you claim and don't claim in relation to your results that is important. If you produce conclusions and make claims that are not supported by the evidence within your research, then you will be heavily criticised.

Table 1.3 shows that the areas or topics of greatest research activity for the respondents are market research, new product/service development, benchmarking and customer surveys, followed by advertising effectiveness, site location/feasibility and service quality measurement. Bearing in mind the reservations expressed above, and perhaps not unsurprisingly, it would seem that there is a general emphasis on those aspects of hospitality and tourism business directly concerned with markets, customers, competitors and the product/service. These are all areas that tend to be complex, difficult to control and can be problematic to understand and predict, while, at the same time, being critical to success or failure. They are also areas where change can be rapid and innovation may be crucial to succeed. Indeed, if the 'other' areas indicated by the respondents were added to these, this view would be further reinforced as many of them are also concerned with markets, customers and competitors. These are also areas where it is often difficult to be as sure as possible of the relationships between causes and effects. Given that these environments are complex and dynamic, it is invariably problematic to isolate one or even a few factors that are the main causes of the effect/s and, hence, knowledge and understanding of them tends to be less than perfect.

## SUMMARY

» Research is a purposeful activity designed, planned and undertaken to investigate and discover answers to questions and solutions to problems.

» It can be exploratory, descriptive or explanatory in purpose and theoretical or applied in emphasis.

» It can help to develop our conceptual and practical knowledge and make us better practitioners.

» There are two basic approaches that can be adopted to inform the design of research and how it is conducted – induction and deduction.

» To design and undertake research that will produce credible results, there are a number of issues to be considered – the characteristics of scientific research.

» Although research can be carefully designed, planned and executed, there are invariably elements that we cannot predict or control and, therefore, despite our best intentions, successful outcomes do have an element of luck.

## Further Reading

Blaxter, L., Hughes, C. and Tight, M. (1996) *How to Research*. Buckingham: Open University Press. Chapter 1.

Gill, J. and Johnson, P. (1991) *Research Methods for Managers*. London: Paul Chapman. Chapters 1 and 3.

Finn, M., Elliot-White, M. and Walton, M. (2000) *Tourism and Leisure Research Methods: Data collection, analysis and interpretation*. Harlow: Pearson Education. Chapter 1.

Hussey, J. and Hussey, R. (1997) *Business Research: A practical guide for undergraduate and postgraduate students*. Basingstoke: Macmillan. Chapter 1.

Jankowicz, A.D. (1991) *Business Research Projects for Students*. London: Chapman & Hall. Chapter 6.

Johns, N. and Lee-Ross, D. (1998) *Research Methods in Service Industry Management*. London: Cassell. Chapter 1.

Orna, E. and Stevens, G. (1995) *Managing Information for Research*. Buckingham: Open University Press. Chapter 1.

Preece, R. (1994) *Starting Research: An introduction to academic research and dissertation writing*. London: Pinter. Chapter 1.

Saunders, M., Lewis, P. and Thornhill, A. (2003) *Research Methods for Business Students*, 3rd edition. Harlow: Pearson Education. Chapter 1.

Sekaran, U. (2000) *Research Methods for Business: A skill-building approach*, 3rd edition. New York: John Wiley. Chapters 1 and 2.

Sharp, J.A. and Howard, K. (1996) *The Management of a Student Research Project*, 2nd edition. Aldershot: Gower. Chapter 1.

Veal, A.J. (1997) *Research Methods for Leisure and Tourism: A practical guide*, 2nd edition. Harlow: Pearson Education. Chapter 1.

# Chapter

## Research Philosophies and Schools of Thought

---

### KEY CONCEPTS AND ISSUES

- » *What is knowledge and how is it created?*
- » *The influence of different philosophies and perspectives.*
- » *Ontology, epistemology and methodology.*
- » *Objectivity and subjectivity.*
- » *Independent factual and socially constructed reality.*
- » *Positivism.*
- » *Phenomenology.*

---

## 2.1 Introduction

The purpose of this chapter is to introduce you to issues, debates and controversies relating to the philosophical strands of thought that are the most appropriate for informing and guiding your approach to designing and conducting research.

In common with everyday life, there are differences of opinion in the academic world regarding what constitutes knowledge, how this should be established and the most appropriate ways to achieve this end. In the same way that you might decide to follow a particular political or religious philosophy in your everyday life rather than others that are available, academics have to make similar choices in terms of what they believe is the right or correct set of perspectives to adopt. So, by the time you have read this chapter, you will be familiar with these issues and more confident about deciding on the philosophical basis of the approach you will take in your research.

## 2.2 The Nature of Knowledge and Reality

In Chapter 1, we touched on some of the issues associated with common sense and more scientific approaches to research and the enhancement of knowledge. However, it was a rather limited exploration of these areas and we do need to take things further in this chapter. It might be tempting to think that 'knowledge is knowledge' and that 'reality is reality' or, in other words, that a fact is a fact and what is real is real. Life would be that much simpler if these were true but, unfortunately, these are not. Of course there are shared and agreed, or non-contested, facts and views of what is real between people. Indeed, life would be even more difficult if this were not the case. On the other hand, not all 'knowledge' is agreed unconditionally and people do have different views and perceptions regarding the nature of reality and what should properly be regarded as fact or truth. Before we consider some of the academic thinking and jargon related to these issues, let us consider them in a more easily understandable context.

Read Exhibit 2.1, which contains a short, perhaps fairly typical, conversation between a hypothetical general manager and the members of his departmental management team, discussing a problem that has arisen at their hotel, and think about how the different characters react to the so-called problem in terms of their acceptance of it, their perceptions of what could be done to address it and what they accept as factual and real.

---

### *Exhibit 2.1    Knowledge and Reality*

Bill Soames, the General Manager of the hotel, opens a meeting with the words, 'Welcome to this week's management meeting. One of the main problems we need to discuss this week is the fact that our room occupancy levels have declined quite significantly over the past two weeks. We need to try and do something about this. Who has some ideas?'

'Well, common sense suggests that we could look to discount our rates more to try and attract extra bookings and guests', ventured Janet Faulkner, the Restaurant Manager.

'Perhaps we should set up a guest satisfaction feedback system to find out what our guests particularly like or dislike and then we could use this to improve things and get more repeat bookings', offered John Thames, the Human Resources Manager.

'How about setting up a reward scheme – like air miles – so that the more guests stay with us, the more reward points they get to redeem for another stay?' added the Marketing Manager, Justin Bones. 'I think that we should invest in better vacuum cleaners and other equipment so that we can improve the cleanliness and hygiene in the guest bedrooms and make them more attractive', Carmen Hoyes, the Housekeeping Manager, chipped in.

*(Cont'd)*

'Hang on, hang on', Paul Gestalt, the Rooms Division Manager, cried. 'Are we in danger of seeing a problem here when there isn't one?'

'What do you mean Paul?', said Bill Soames. 'We obviously have a problem when occupancy levels are going down.'

'Yes, perhaps, but we need to look at this in a wider context', replied Paul, who went on to explain what he meant by this. 'This is our low period during the year and, if we were to look at the occupancy levels for this period over the last five years, we would see that this always happens at this time. It is a natural consequence of the seasonal highs and lows. All our experience indicates that we will have periods of higher and lower occupancy during the year and we just have to accept it.'

'Well, I'm not sure I agree with you Paul', said Caroline Oast, the newly appointed Conventions and Meetings Manager. 'Yes, we all know that high and low periods can and do occur, but, just because they have in the past does not mean that they have to in the future or that we should accept this as inevitable. I think such a proposition can be challenged. For example, not all hotels have this problem at this time of year, so it is not universal, and we could try to boost our meetings and special events business at this time, when other sources of demand for accommodation are lower'.

'Good idea', Bill replied, 'we'll explore that after the meeting. Now for the next item …'

Paul remained unconvinced and muttered, 'There's a lot to be said for experience and common sense in these matters, everyone knows that for a fact.'

Clearly different views are expressed in this piece regarding whether there is a problem or not and, if there is, whether it is something that just has to be accepted or can be addressed. Some of the people involved make what may appear to be reasonable suggestions to try and address it, but there are assumptions about both the possible causes of the low occupancy problem – that is, room prices are too high, the rooms are not clean enough, insufficient incentives are being offered to encourage repeat business and so on – and, therefore, what may be appropriate solutions.

These suggestions could have a positive effect on occupancy levels, of course, as could the suggestion of looking to increase meeting and special events business, but on what basis is this problem–solution connection being addressed? Is it being addressed in a subjective or objective manner? Are the managers presenting any evidence to support their solutions or just using guesswork to advocate these? To what extent are experience and common sense driving their thinking? Are they assuming that this is a universal problem or one specific to the hotel concerned – that is, is it seen as a general rule or only one applying to that hotel at that point in time? To what extent are they simply accepting things as being known and factual?

What the conversation reveals is that what is known, or knowledge, and what is regarded as factual, and therefore non-contestable, are not always universally agreed. Similarly, when people suggest, implicitly or explicitly, that there is a relationship or connection between two or more things, they will often be making and using assumptions about the nature of this relationship, but where do they get these assumptions from? They might be based on experience, as Paul states, or on Janet's commonsense view of the influence of price on the demand for accommodation, or on John's speculation that guests might be interested in, and motivated by, some kind of reward scheme, or on Caroline's transference view that what works well in other hotels could work in this one.

Paul's assumption is that the factors and conditions that have influenced demand in the past remain the same. Janet's is that demand is sensitive to price. John's is that guests are interested in something more than the basic product and Caroline's is that the factors and conditions influencing demand in other contexts will apply equally in this one.

The problem here would appear to be that none of these proposed relationships, and consequent solutions, have been supported by any kind of objective evidence or logical argument. Therefore all, or none, of these could be correct. So, how do we decide which is and which is not? This is clearly a problem in itself. If we were to use experience as the sole basis for making this decision, it would be problematic because people accumulate widely divergent experiences that will have influenced how they perceive and interpret such situations and, thus, what they believe to be correct or incorrect. Using common sense may generate a consensus, but it may be largely subjective and not amenable to proof one way or the other. Accepting uncritically what appear to be logical propositions, such as Caroline's, may also be problematic, but evidence could be collected to test the view based on this.

What the example highlights is the fact that anyone grappling with questions concerning connections between different factors or events or the causes of observed effects uses, explicitly or implicitly, assumptions about them that are invariably derived from a type of personal viewpoint or philosophy of what is required to know something and the processes that support or justify statements of what should be generally regarded as known or factual.

In the academic jargon, these three things are known as ontology, epistemology and methodology (the 'ologies') and, collectively, they have quite a fundamental influence on how people design and conduct research. Ontology, for example, is concerned with views on the nature of reality. For example, some researchers – particularly those in the physical and natural sciences – believe that there are universal truths waiting to be discovered, while others suggest that reality is more complex and dynamic as it is shaped and interpreted by human action and intellect and, therefore, because of the multitude of differing situations and interactions that this gives rise to, it is more contextually determined rather than universal or contextually independent.

These differing ontologies suggest different beliefs concerning the appropriate way to develop a knowledge of the world and what the researcher's relationship to this process should be. For example, those adopting an ontological position based on a belief in universal truths are likely to advocate and adopt an epistemology that regards neutral, independent and objective inquiry as preferable as this is seen to be an approach best suited to minimising potential contamination and bias. On the other hand, those preferring the ontological position of multiple, contextually determined truths or realities would advocate a very different epistemological stance. For such researchers, the belief that research can be conducted in a neutral, independent and objective manner would be seen as a type of 'fool's paradise'. Therefore, their epistemological position would be that the most appropriate approach to developing knowledge would be one in which the researcher interacted with the subjects of the enquiry in order to understand their perspectives and feelings.

Similarly, differing ontological and epistemological positions suggest different views of what the most appropriate means, or methodologies, are to develop knowledge. Experimentation – particularly experiments conducted in a laboratory – is a very different methodology to participant observation. Those researchers advocating experimentation as the most appropriate methodology to uncover truth would have very different ontological and epitemological beliefs from those advocating participant observation.

Taylor and Edgar (1999: 27) succinctly summarise the relationship between ontology, epistemology and methodology: 'the belief about the nature of the world (ontology) adopted by an enquirer will influence their belief as to the nature of knowledge in that world (epistemology) which in turn will influence the enquirer's belief as to how that knowledge can be uncovered (methodology)'.

To illustrate this further, think about the following example. In every democratic country, there will be political parties with different philosophies, policies and assumptions about the type of society that is regarded as preferable. As a result, these parties are likely to take very different stances over the same issues. Excluding the extremes of fascist and communist parties, broadly speaking, it is possible to distinguish between political parties on the right of the political spectrum – conservative or republican – and those on the left – socialist or democrat. So, if we take the issue of a society's economy, we are likely to find that politicians from the right tend to employ the assumption that the free market is the natural and preferable way to organise economic activity because it is a logical consequence of a philosophy that emphasises the desirability of individualism and freedom with minimal state intervention. By contrast, politicians from the left tend to assume that a totally free market is not the most preferable form of economic structure for a society because the underlying philosophy of this type of political stance emphasises more collective and egalitarian values and, to achieve this, more state intervention is required to regulate and modify the dysfunctional aspects of unfettered freedom and individualism in order to ensure greater social justice.

In the political sphere, in common with many others, what is seen to be a problem by one side may not be for the other, what are regarded as the facts by one are likely to be disputed by the other, views of how society (reality) works and should work differ, the policies seen to be desirable and positive to one side may be seen as undesirable and damaging by the other. In short, the point here is that there are a great many situations and issues where disagreements arise over what are regarded as the appropriate basic assumptions, philosophy and approaches to developing knowledge. The importance of this is that if the underlying philosophy, assumptions or processes used to obtain what is being presented as knowledge can be seriously questioned or discredited, the knowledge derived from them also becomes less credible. Thus, although these considerations may appear to be rather abstract, esoterical and to have little immediate, practical value, if the foundations on which the knowledge has been built are weak or inappropriate, then the knowledge will be also. Let us think about this using the analogy of a building. If the foundations of the building are not constructed properly, you may well expect the walls, floors and roof constructed on them to be suspect and unsafe.

As it is self-evident that there are groups of people in society sharing different views of the world based on different philosophical, political, religious or cultural beliefs, it should not surprise you to know that such divisions also exist in the world of academic enquiry. Within most academic disciplines there are groups of people who subscribe to different views regarding what is most important in their field and the most appropriate ways to approach and explain these things. They tend to align themselves according to different views of what constitutes knowledge, the shared sets of assumptions derived from this and the approaches to developing knowledge these imply. In short, each different group will tend to have a different view of the most appropriate philosophical stance, or epistemology, ontology and methodology that should be used to develop knowledge.

Such groups are often referred to as 'schools of thought'. For example, in economics there are, among others, monetarist and Keynesian schools of thought. To illustrate in a simple way the implications of the differences between these two schools of thought, we might consider their views on how to manage an economy. Unsurprisingly, the monetarist school believes that it is money and, more specifically, the supply of money, that are the prime determinants of economic activity and outcomes. Consequently, and logically, if it is possible to control and manipulate the supply of money in an economy, usually via interest rates, then the economy itself can be controlled and manipulated. Alternatively, while not denying that money has importance, the Keynesian school believes that other factors are more important than the supply of money in determining the state of an economy and would suggest that the use of fiscal measures (taxation and government expenditure) to manipulate the economy are likely to be more effective than changing interest rates. Therefore, the epistemology, ontology and methodology adopted and advocated by the two schools of thought are different.

Why is this important? It is important for obvious reasons and perhaps some that are not quite so obvious. In terms of the former, a political party adopting

As you might expect, given their respective backgrounds, Justin and Randolph have very different views about the most appropriate approach to take and methods to use to address the issue they face. There are, of course, advantages and disadvantages to each of their preferred options, but what this situation highlights is the difference between the stance a positivist (Justin) and a phenomenologist (Randolph) would take in response to the same issue or question.

Although they agree that the issue is important and requires some investigation to explore it further, their respective epistemological, ontological and methodological preferences and beliefs push them in very different directions in terms of how they advocate the investigation should be designed and conducted and the reasons they give to justify these preferences. In short, they subscribe to different paradigms.

This leads us into a consideration of what are generally regarded as the two main philosophies or paradigms – positivism and phenomenology – that influence the way research is conducted. We shall examine the basis of each of these in turn and then summarise their differences.

## 2.3.1 *Positivism*

Positivism is a belief based on, and derived from, the view that a 'real' world of tangible social and physical phenomena exists independently – that is, objectively – of how such phenomena are perceived and conceptualised by people and what is required to understand and explain these is impartial, value-free, logical, empirical, scientific research. In short, the truth is out there and it can be revealed by applying an appropriate methodology.

As you might expect, positivism is the mindset of the archetypal white-coated laboratory scientist, but it is also a significant, if not the most dominant, philosophy in management research, including that into hospitality and tourism. The positivist assumes that people and/or organisations behave in a self-interested, logical and rational manner. Phenomena and events can be explained by general, or universal, cause–effect laws because knowledge and cause–effect relationships, while probabilistic and conditional, are not contextual. In other words, because there is always room for error and doubt, it is difficult to be absolutely certain that a cause–effect relationship is correct, but we can say there is a very high probability something will be the cause and, if the necessary conditions are present, it will not be influenced by other contextual features.

Positivism, therefore, contends that the theories and laws established via research must be logically consistent and explain empirical reality. In addition to this, proponents would also take the view that this theoretical empirical consistency should be replicable. This is logical because, if a general law is to be accepted, it must be applicable across a range of different contextual circumstances, so, if the research is repeated or replicated, it should deliver the same results whatever the context. To be capable of achieving this, positivists would take the view that scientific research is the only way to discover the truth and it must be conducted in an objective manner, deterministic in purpose (to determine cause–effect relationships), mechanistic in process and use well-established and validated methods.

Positivists take the view that the 'best', or most valid, way to learn the truth is to conduct experiments. Experimentation – or, more specifically, laboratory experimentation – is the preferred method of the positivist because it enables the research to be designed and conducted with the maximum degree of control. Although it may be unlikely that you will be conducting experimental research in laboratory conditions, this issue of control is important in a more general sense and something you would need to give consideration to if you were undertaking research from a positivistic perspective using other methods, such as a survey. The significance of being able to control the inputs to the research, the processes used and the conditions all this occurs under is that it enables the researcher to eliminate or, at the very least minimise, the possible effects that other influences may have on the results. In addition, because control is complete, it will also allow the researcher to measure the relative effect of different influences that have been designed into the research.

Because most phenomena and events are not caused by one factor acting in isolation from others, especially in the real world, this complexity makes it difficult to distinguish between the most and least important influences and be certain, or as near as is possible, of what the nature and mechanism of the cause–effect relationship is. For example, we might identify that the numbers of tourists coming to the UK from other countries have been declining in recent years and there is a range of possible influences that could be contributing to this. Our problem is discovering which of these is, or are, the most important or significant. All of them may have some degree of influence, but some are likely to have had a stronger influence than others. If this was something we could investigate using a laboratory experiment, we could take each influence in turn, control the process and conditions and test to measure the strength of its effect. Unfortunately, this is not possible, but there are other ways of doing so, although they are not as ideal in terms of control as experiments. Often, such techniques are statistical in nature (as we shall see in Chapter 9), but there are techniques designed to achieve similar aims with qualitative data (Chapter 10).

The key issue here is the degree of control that can be exerted over the design, process and conditions of the research. The closer we can get to the 'ideal' conditions for control — that is, the laboratory experiment – the more likely it is that we will be able to justify the accuracy of the findings. If you think about this from the reverse direction, it may become even clearer. If there is a range of factors that could be influencing or causing the effect we are investigating, but we cannot isolate or control for the influence of one from the others, it would be difficult to state with any degree of confidence what the relative influence of each is and what the nature of the mechanism (the cause–effect relationship) between each of these and the effect actually is. In these circumstances we may be able to say that there would appear to be a connection, or correlation, between the possible causes and the effect, but we would not be able to state and explain the mechanism that connects the causes and the effect.

Another problem we would have in this situation would be trying to meet the positivist's condition that research must deal with what we can see and measure – that is, real, concrete things. This is not a problem in the context of a laboratory, where we can control everything and observe and measure the outcomes from the experiment, but, in the real world, it usually is. In our example above of the reductions in the numbers of tourist, there are certain things that are concrete and measurable. The numbers of people arriving at border points – that is, airports, seaports and so on – from other countries can be seen and measured fairly easily. The exchange rate(s) between the two countries' currencies will also be known, as perhaps will the travel costs, such as air fares. We could also identify things associated with the ease of travel, such as the number and frequency of flights from the other countries to ours. All of these things would be factual and easily measurable in their own right, but their relationship with the effect may not always be as simple.

To illustrate this, consider how people often behave in terms of buying overseas, tourist travel. In many cases, people book their holidays and travel many months in advance of actually taking the trip. This implies that there may be a time gap between cause and effect. In other words, the exchange rate in existence at the time of the visit may not be the one that influenced the decision to make that visit several months before and, hence, the overall number of visitors at that point in time. Therefore, the influence on visitor numbers of a less than favourable exchange rate and, equally, a favourable one is likely to have a delayed effect. In the jargon, this would be known as a 'lagged relationship or effect' because of the time delay between the change in the cause and the consequent change in the effect.

Beyond these more objective, concrete, factual influences, we might also reasonably speculate that the degree of hospitality our population extends to such visitors or the quality of the experience they have when they are in our country may influence whether they want to visit or not. These, however, are nebulous terms – they do not exist as such in the real world as they are general and conceptual rather than specific and concrete. So, how do we observe and measure the quality of experience or warmth of hospitality?

We cannot do this directly, but, rather, have to do it indirectly by breaking down the concept into the 'real' things that comprise it. This is known as 'operationalisation' and is a task discussed more extensively in Chapter 5, but suffice it to say here that we would need to identify real, tangible things that would influence and indicate the presence of a higher- or lower-quality experience or better or worse hospitality.

In emphasising the importance of obtaining empirical proof to support logical theories, positivists need a mechanism to link the two together. As the deductive approach to research is the one favoured by positivists, the process begins by developing a possible theoretical explanation for the phenomena or event and then requires empirical evidence to be collected to verify, or not, the validity of this. This raises questions concerning the nature of the link between theory and reality and what empirical evidence will be required to establish whether or not this is true. What are we suggesting the nature and mechanism of the link will be and how do we decide what data is required to test this? The answer is that the positivist examines the theory and its predictions and implications in order to formulate specific relationships that the empirical data would confirm to be true if the theory is correct. These predictions are the logical consequences of the theory and are known as hypotheses. Again, we will examine the nature and role of hypotheses in greater detail in Chapter 5, but their importance to the positivistic approach to research cannot be emphasised strongly enough. For the positivist they are what the empirical aspect of the research process is designed to address and, as such, not only constitute this vital link between theory and reality but also serve to determine the structure and processes adopted to collect and analyse the empirical data. Indeed, their confirmation or otherwise is the purpose of the empirical part of the research project.

Although, as noted earlier, positivism is widely accepted among researchers from many fields as the preferred paradigm or approach to research and the development of knowledge, it is not without its critics and, as we shall see shortly, some of these reject it completely in favour of alternative approaches or paradigms. Among the criticisms of positivism is that it is largely a-contextual in nature or, to put it another way, it views people and organisations as isolated from their contexts. This is reinforced by the high levels of artificiality created by the favoured methods of the positivist, particularly in relation to experimentation.

Critics of the positivist approach also point out that researchers cannot be totally objective in the way they conduct research, that objectivity is a myth. As human beings we cannot avoid being influenced by our beliefs, values and prejudices, whether we consciously realise this or not. This challenges the impartiality claim and is reinforced by the observation that, in the positivist approach, the relationship between the researcher and the subject is one within which the former exerts much greater influence and control than the latter. It is claimed that this can distort the research process and lead to accurate (reliable) but not necessarily truthful (valid) results. For example, people who complete questionnaires can only respond to the questions asked by the researcher. This may generate accurate responses to the questions asked, but may not generate the true feelings of the respondents because they may lie outside the questions asked. Similarly, the subject taking part in an experiment has no input into, or control over, the process and content of the experiment as he or she is merely required to behave in the way the researcher wants.

Finally, it is suggested that positivistic approaches to conducting research, such as experiments and surveys, tend to gather rather superficial information compared to that elicited by means of alternative approaches. This is invariably true because the positivistic philosophy is based on what is often called 'reductionism'.

One way to think about this is via the analogy of peeling an onion. As the successive layers are peeled away, we get closer and closer to the centre of the onion until we arrive at its core. Positivists believe that this process of reducing the problem to its essential core reveals the fundamental cause–effect relationships driving the larger entity as a whole. However, it means that, by definition, many of the aspects have to be discarded so that researchers can focus on those regarded as the key ones. Clearly such an approach may have value, but it does carry the danger that the answers it delivers may be more simplistic and partial than the reality it is trying to describe and explain and, hence, be less valid as a result.

## 2.3.2 *Phenomenology*

Phenomenological, or interpretative, approaches to research place considerably less emphasis on the need to develop so-called objective research methods and more on the need for interpretation in research. This is a view based on the belief that the real world, and the phenomena and events that occur in this world, are created by the subjective thoughts, actions and interactions of people who inhabit it. In short, it is socially constructed rather than being a separate and independent entity that determines peoples' behaviour.

You should already be able to see that there are fundamental differences between positivists and phenomenologists. Indeed, they are really the antithesis of each other. The fundamental beliefs of the two paradigms – and the consequent methodologies and methods they advocate as being the most appropriate for undertaking research – are directly opposed. In the same way that it would be unthinkable for a person to simultaneously be a fascist and a communist, you cannot be both a positivist and a phenomenologist at the same time.

Phenomenology, in all its varying guises, developed as an alternative to positivism when researchers in certain fields of enquiry, such as sociology, became increasingly disenchanted with the ability of positivism and its methods to adequately explain the phenomena they were interested in. Although it was generally accepted that positivistic approaches and methods could deliver reliable results – that is, ones that can be repeated or replicated – the criticism was that they may not be valid or accurate in terms of adequately explaining real-world phenomena because of the reductionist and artificial manner in which the research is conducted. In other words, while the results may be reliable, they may well be reliably inaccurate as valid explanations.

To counter this flow, phenomenologists reject the epistemological, ontological and methodological foundations of the positivist approach and advocate essentially opposing views on each of these. Phenomenologists are interested in understanding and explaining how people make sense of the world they inhabit and are less concerned with trying to devise and use objective methods to discover deterministic relationships and general laws. By implication, context is an important element in developing this understanding because people exist and interact within contexts. Therefore, rather than trying to eliminate or control for contextual influences, they are seen as being integral to understanding. Similarly, artificially constructed situations or environments, such as those occurring in an experiment or survey, are seen to be threats rather than aids to understanding because they are partial and exclusive rather than holistic and inclusive, with the content and processes they include being selected and controlled by the researcher rather than the subject under investigation.

Not unsurprisingly, therefore, phenomenology advocates an inductive rather than a deductive approach as the most appropriate for undertaking research. This perspective suggests that a more valid understanding of a phenomena or event is likely to be derived from investigating these in their real-world contexts in the first instance than is possible by theorising about them in isolation and then collecting data on them to test the theory. As the belief is that meanings, understanding and theories can only be developed in a valid manner by studying reality first and then working backwards by analysing and interpreting the data to find patterns and relationships, phenomenology takes the opposite stance from positivism. However, this seems to imply that phenomenologist-driven research always begins with a blank sheet, at least in terms of theory. The problem with this is that, unless the research topic is absolutely unique, such a stance ignores any previous empirical or theoretical work on the issues in question and is thus in danger of possibly reinventing a wheel that is already known about! In practice, therefore, although the process may work from empirical data collection to theoretical development, the former is likely to be informed and guided by previous research findings from the literature relating to that topic.

In terms of the methods favoured by the phenomenological approach, it is clear that those advocated by the positivists – experimentation or surveys – are generally seen to be inappropriate. As we saw earlier, these methods are essentially a-contextual in nature and embody high levels of artificiality and control, which are features that the phenomenological approach rejects. Because context, realism or naturalistic enquiry and interpretation are crucially important to the phenomenological view, it should not be surprising to find that methods such as case studies and what are referred to as 'field study' techniques – participant or non-participant observation – are the type of methods preferred by phenomenologists. This is because they are more consistent with the philosophical and ontological positions taken by such researchers. As the phenomenological approach takes the recording of the complexities of the situation being investigated as its starting point in order that these may be examined, analysed and interpreted to find patterns and connections, it should not be surprising to find that these types of methods are more appropriate to collecting the type of data required for this process. In many instances, this is referred to as the building of a 'rich picture' of the complex reality being studied.

This, in turn, implies that research undertaken from a phenomenological perspective is more likely to involve the collection of qualitative rather than quantitative data. In general, this tends to be the case, but it should not be assumed that all positivistic research is quantitative and all phenomenological research is qualitative in nature. Qualitative data are collected in some positivistic studies – for example, by interviewing – and there may be elements of quantitative data involved in some phenomenological studies. In short, although it is far more likely that positivists will concentrate on the collection of hard (quantitative) data because of their amenability to measurement and statistical manipulation and phenomenologists will tend to concentrate on soft (qualitative) data because they are more capable of revealing peoples' feelings, perceptions and meanings, there is nothing inherent in the two stances that precludes the use of either type of data. Furthermore, because there are varying types and degrees of both positivism and phenomenology, it may be more useful to think of the differences in the data collection preferences between them as lying on a continuum rather than being polar opposites. In other words, while the purest forms of each would undoubtedly favour purely quantitative or qualitative data, there are variations that would advocate mixed or multiple methods and varying combinations of each type of data.

To summarise, Tables 2.1 and 2.2 illustrate the main features of, differences between and preferences within the positivistic and phenomenological paradigms. They show not only that there are clear epistemological, ontological and methodological differences between the two but also that these differences are so marked they are fundamental opposites.

However, while this is undoubtedly true, as we have noted earlier, reality tends not to be quite so black and white. Differing schools of thought do exist within each of these main types and there are variations in the form of positivism and phenomenology adopted by different groups of researchers. Put another way, you might consider this as people agreeing with the basic philosophy but having differing ideas about the most appropriate style of 'doing science' or scientific research. This is nicely illustrated by Mitroff and Kilman (1981), who discuss four types of scientist based on differences concerning the two dimensions of the type of input data and decision making they prefer.

The combination of these two dimensions produces four types of researcher:

- ◆  academic scientist (AS)
- ◆  conceptual theorist (CT)
- ◆  particular humanist (PH)
- ◆  conceptual humanist (CH).

Viewing these in a simplistic manner, we would conclude that the AS and the CH are very much the archetypal positivist and phenomenologist. The AS looks for certainty and is concerned with precision, accuracy and reliability. He or she prefers details and practical, specific, 'hard' facts and to establish these by means of controlled enquiry and, in particular, controlled experimentation.

**Table 2.1**    Key features of positivist and phenomenological paradigms

|  | *Positivistic paradigm* | *Phenomenological paradigm* |
|---|---|---|
| Basic beliefs | The world is external and objective. The observer is independent. Science is value-free. | The world is socially constructed and subjective. The observer is part of what is observed. Science is driven by human interests. |
| What researchers should do | Focus on facts. Look for causality and fundamental laws. Reduce phenomena to its simplest elements. Formulate hypotheses and then test them. | Focus on meanings. Try to understand what is happening. Look at the totality of each situation. Develop ideas through induction from data. |
| Preferred methods | Operationalising concepts so that they can be measured. Taking large samples. | Using multiple methods to establish different views of phenomena. Small samples investigated in depth or over time. |

*Source*:  Easterby-Smith et al., 1993, p. 27. Reproduced with the permission of Sage.

**Table 2.2**    Features of the two main paradigms

| *Positivistic paradigm* | *Phenomenological paradigm* |
|---|---|
| Tends to produce quantitative data. | Tends to produce qualitative data. |
| Uses large samples. | Uses small samples. |
| Concerned with hypothesis testing. | Concerned with generating theories. |
| Data are highly specific and precise. | Data are rich and subjective. |
| The location is artificial. | The location is natural. |
| Reliability is high. | Reliability is low. |
| Validity is low. | Validity is high. |
| Generalises from sample to population. | Generalises from one setting to another. |

*Source*:  Hussey and Hussey, 1997, p. 54. Reproduced with the permission of Palgrave Macmillan.

The CT is similar to the AS in that he or she has a preference for the same type of data as the AS, but the CT places greater emphasis and importance on the value of imagination and speculation to produce new, innovative insights that generate what may be called 'grand theory'. So, although the two share the same basic philosophy, they differ in what they see to be the most important purpose of doing research. The AS has a preoccupation with the specific and particular as a way of discovering a single definitive answer to an issue, while the CT is more concerned with multiple possibilities.

By contrast, the PH and CH scientists are essentially phenomenologists and adopt the beliefs, values and methods advocated by that paradigm and, in common with the AS and CT types, where they differ lies in the specific data preferences.

## SUMMARY

» What constitutes knowledge and fact is contestable.
» Different people subscribe to different views (schools of thought) concerning how knowledge and facts can be established.
» Positivism is the dominant paradigm and is a philosophical standpoint or belief that a real world of tangible phenomena exists independently and objectively, regardless of how they are perceived by people.
» The positivist researcher favours use of the deductive approach to research and also believes that truth can only be revealed by using an appropriate methodology (the scientific method) and the application of this, particularly by means of experimentation, can identify and explain cause–effect laws that are universal.
» The ability to control the research process is crucial to the positivist, so as to be able to prove cause–effect relationships, which can only be proved via empirical investigation.
» Phenomenology, or interpretivism, is an alternative paradigm based on the view that the real world is socially constructed by peoples' thoughts, actions and interactions.
» Phenomenologists advocate an inductive approach to conducting research and the use of more naturalistic enquiry methods than positivists, such as observation or case studies.
» For phenomenologists, new knowledge is developed, in the first instance, by collecting and analysing in-depth, real world data rather then testing existing theories.

## Further Reading

Clark, M., Riley, M., Wilkie, E. and Wood, R.C. (1998) *Researching and Writing Dissertations in Hospitality and Tourism*. London: International Thomson Business Press. Chapter 2.

Coolican, H. (1994) *Research Methods and Statistics in Psychology*, 2nd edition. London: Hodder & Stoughton. Chapter 11.

Easterby-Smith, M., Thorpe, R. and Lowe, A. (2002) *Management Research: An introduction*, 2nd edition. London: Sage. Chapter 2.

Finn, M., Elliot-White, M. and Walton, M. (2000) *Tourism and Leisure Research Methods: Data collection, analysis and interpretation*. Harlow: Pearson Education. Chapter 1.

Hussey, J. and Hussey, R. (1997) *Business Research: A practical guide for undergraduate and postgraduate students*. Basingstoke: Macmillan. Chapter 3.

Johns, N. and Lee-Ross, D. (1998) *Research Methods in Service Industry Management*. London: Cassell. Chapter 1.

Maykut, P. and Morehouse, R. (1994) *Beginning Qualitative Research: A philosophic and practical guide*. London: Falmer. Chapters 1 and 2.

Neuman, W.L. (1994) *Social Research Methods: Quantitative and qualitative approaches*, 2nd edition. Needham Heights, MA: Allyn & Bacon. Chapter 4.

Preece, R. (1994) *Starting Research: An introduction to academic research and dissertation writing*. London: Pinter. Chapter 2.

Saunders, M., Lewis, P. and Thornhill, A. (2003) *Research Methods for Business Students*, 3rd edition. Harlow: Prentice-Hall. Chapter 4.

Veal, A.J. (1997) *Research Methods for Leisure and Tourism: A practical guide*, 2nd edition. Harlow: Pearson Education. Chapter 2.

Wood, R.C. (1999) 'Traditional and alternative research philosophies', in B. Brotherton (ed.), *The Handbook of Contemporary Hospitality Management Research*. Chichester: John Wiley & Sons. Chapter 1.

# Chapter

## Developing the Research Proposal and Plan

### KEY CONCEPTS AND ISSUES

» *The intellectual and real-world value of a research topic.*
» *Sources of research topics.*
» *Limiting the conceptual and empirical aspects of the research topic to make it more manageable and feasible.*
» *Developing the initial research question(s), aims and objectives to focus the work and state a clear outcome.*
» *Producing a research proposal.*

## 3.1 Introduction

The 'blank page syndrome' is usually the starting point for a research project and I always hear students say, 'I have no idea what topic I want to explore.' It is difficult to think about and begin to formulate a research proposal, especially one that will be of interest to others and feasible to complete in the time available. However, the task is not an impossible one, as I hope you will begin to appreciate as you progress through this chapter.

To help you get to the point where you have a clear idea of what you are going to research, why this will be of interest and importance, how you plan to investigate it and what the desired end product will be, this chapter takes you through the process of identifying, refining and finally specifying the focus, method(s) and purpose of your research project.

In taking this journey, you will encounter issues associated with possible sources of inspiration that you may want to consider exploring to stimulate ideas on what may be interesting topics and issues to research and how to think about the intellectual and real-world value of any of them. You will also be able to think through the process of narrowing and refining initial ideas into a final format that is more focused and feasible than your starting point and has a clearly stated purpose and outcomes to be achieved at the end of the process.

## 3.2 Finding and Refining a Topic

Unless you have a long-standing interest in something particular, this is often one of the most difficult issues to resolve because there is such a wide range of possible topics to research in the context of hospitality and tourism. Students ask, 'What could I use as a topic and where do I start?' However, before addressing these questions, it may be useful to take a step back, consider the various options and ask yourself, 'Why do I want to do some research on topic x? What is it about the topic that will be interesting and motivating for me?' until something sets you thinking. The research process is a journey and one that does not always progress smoothly, so you will need a topic that will sustain your interest and curiosity until the end, otherwise it will become difficult to keep going and complete the project.

So, what might be possible sources of interesting topics? These are likely to be related either to your own personal experiences – that is, the real world – or gaps you identify from information in the public domain – that is, the theoretical or conceptual world. However, as King et al. (1994) point out, there is no particular rule governing which topic to choose for research. That said, they go on to suggest that research projects should satisfy two criteria. These are, first, that the project should pose, and address, a question that is of importance in the real world. In short, that it has some significance in terms of developing understanding, explanation and possibly prediction and is therefore not trivial in nature. Second, that a project should make a contribution to the scholarly literature relating to the research topic. Essentially, the point they are making is that the research should have value, both a practical value in the real world and an intellectual value in relation to enhancing the existing state of knowledge on the topic.

Both criteria are important, though not necessarily equally so for each piece of research, because, collectively they indicate that the work should have practical and theoretical significance. It is often not difficult to envisage what the practical implications or significance of a research topic may be as these generally will relate to some type of improvement in the real world. On the other hand, anticipating what value the research may have in terms of making a contribution to the existing body of knowledge in the field may be less clear and seem more daunting as it is often interpreted as something high-flying academics or intellectuals can do, but not the average student. The issues here are the nature of expectations and the order of magnitude of the contribution. If you were a professor at a leading university, you may well be expected to produce entirely original and ground-breaking research results, but this is not the expectation people have of an undergraduate or even a Masters-level student. Just think about the word 'contribution' for a moment. It is quite possible to make small or large contributions and both to have value. Adding something that is new, even if it is quite small, to what was known before constitutes a contribution. Table 3.1 shows some of the possible ways that such a contribution might be made.

In terms of personal interest, it could be that you have found a particular area of your course to be more interesting than others – marketing, say, or human resource management or sustainable tourism or fast food restaurants. If so, this could be a useful starting point for you. Alternatively, you may have particular career interests and selecting a topic related to these would give you an incentive to pursue and complete the work. For example, if your ambition is to pursue a career in high-quality international hotels as a rooms' division manager, a topic related to this may help you to obtain a job in this field. Alternatively, if your dream is to work in the tourism and visitor attractions field, you may wish to consider a topic related to this area. Similarly, you might want to combine an area of academic, or course, interest with one related to future job and career ambitions. For example, if you find marketing fascinating and want to work in tourism destination management, why not combine the two?

Another possible source of interest might be one based on your own experience of a hospitality or tourism organisation that you have worked in. Perhaps there was a particular problem you experienced there or a new development that took place and worked well or not. Alternatively new law or regulation may have recently come into force and you have become interested in evaluating how it has or will affect the operation of a business. The organisation may have introduced new technology or has changed the way it is structured and operates. It may have been taken over by another company that has brought in a different way of conducting business. The organisation may have had particular problems with recruiting and training casual, part-time or seasonal staff that has impacted on the quality of the product or service offered to customers. It may be a 'unique' organisation in the sense that it has been the first to introduce a new way of working, a new technology or a new type of product. In other words, where the effects of recent change or innovation are not yet known or long-standing (apparently insoluble), problems are evident, there may be scope to investigate some aspects of them.

If you are pursuing this route to identifying a topic, it might be useful to speak with other people associated with or involved in that issue and organisation. Weiers (1988) refers to this as an 'experience survey'. It is essentially an exploratory exercise, conducted in a relatively unstructured manner, to 'surface' ideas, views and so on. It simply involves having conversations with a number of people associated with, and probably affected by, the situation, in an attempt to obtain a range of perspectives regarding the nature of the issue or problem,

**Table 3.1**    Ways in which research may make a contribution to the literature

| *Type of issue* | *Example* |
| --- | --- |
| Choose a hypothesis seen as important by scholars in the literature for which no one has completed a systematic study. Evidence found to support the hypothesis, or not, will make a contribution. | This might be something like 'increased levels of inbound tourism in developing countries help to stimulate economic growth in these countries'. |
| Choose an accepted hypothesis in the literature that we believe might be false or hasn't been adequately confirmed and investigate it. | This could be something along the lines of 'The speculation that the banning of smoking in public places, such as bars, pubs and restaurants, will result in a decline in business'. |
| Attempt to resolve or provide further evidence for one side of a controversy in the literature or perhaps demonstrate that the controversy is unfounded. | For example, an ongoing debate in hospitality is the conflict between the views that, on the one hand, hospitality has unique features not found in other types of business and, on the other hand, that it does not. |
| Identify unquestioned assumptions in the literature and design research to evaluate these. | The commonly held assumption that 'High levels of labour turnover in hospitality/tourism businesses are due to low pay' could be explored. |
| Argue that an important topic has been overlooked in the literature and undertake a systematic study to address this gap. | An example of this would be my research into critical success factors (CSFs) in hospitality businesses because, although CSFs had been researched in many other contexts, there were no systematic studies on this in a hospitality context. |
| Show that theories or evidence designed for some purpose in one body of literature could be applied in another to solve a problem. | An example of this would be the SERVQUAL studies, which were developed and tested in other service industry contexts, but the researchers claimed that this model could be used in any service business context. |
| Take a study conducted in one empirical context and repeat it another. | This might be a study conducted in another industrial context, such as banking or retailing, or in another country or culture. |

*Source:* Adapted from King, G. et al., 1994, pp. 16–17

the possible cause–effect mechanisms and probable answers or solutions. In some instances, they may give you vital raw material that will enable you to focus and structure the research project.

A good example of this process is provided by Brotherton and Watson's (2000) piece of case study research that sought to identify if a company's senior and public house managers had shared views regarding what was most critical for successful public house operations. Here, the senior managers' views and priorities were established in the exploratory part of the work. It was then a relatively simple matter to incorporate these into a questionnaire, asking the public house managers what level of importance they placed on each. Then the two sets of results were compared to ascertain the similarities or differences in views between the two levels of management.

In another unpublished student research project, the individual concerned wanted to determine whether or not the factors that the managers of fast food restaurants believed were most important to their customers' satisfaction were regarded as such by the customers themselves. To do this, initial conversations with the restaurant managers surfaced the factors they deemed important and these were then incorporated into a questionnaire for the customers, asking them to indicate how important each was to them. Again, by comparing the two sets of results, the similarities and differences could be identified.

Turning to sources in the public domain, here we are talking about information made available to the general public in one form of media or another. This might be the printed word – books, journals, magazines, newspapers, trade publications and so on – or audio or visual in nature – television, film, radio, DVD – or a combination of the two, such as multimedia material available on the Internet. However, whichever media format it appears in, it essentially reports what is and what is not known about the topic in question and helps to make people aware of the debates, points of view, differing interpretations, controversies and so on relating to the area. Therefore, the media in general is often a useful source of stimulation or even possibly inspiration when you are thinking about what a suitable topic might be for your research project.

As the writers/producers – be they academics, journalists or practitioners – of this type of material are invariably experts within their respective fields, they are likely to point out what is known and what is not, what is questionable or contestable, where evidence exists and where it does not, whether there are different perspectives being taken on the issue or issues, and so on. All of this can be helpful when you are trying to identify unanswered questions and gaps in the existing knowledge on the topic. Indeed, in some cases, the authors may indicate the key questions and issues that need further research. We shall return to consider many of the issues relating to the literature, in its broadest sense, when we consider the literature-reviewing stage of the research process in more detail in Chapter 4, but it takes place after the topic, aims and objectives have been formulated, so it is much more focused in nature than the kind of initial explorations being suggested here. At this point in the process, the published literature is purely used as a source of ideas to identify the broad topic for the research project.

By looking at this material, your interest and curiosity may be sparked in varying ways. For example, at the time of writing, television news reports have indicated that avian, or bird, flu exists within certain countries. This raises questions such as how is it going to affect tourism to those countries and what is the relationship between people's health concerns and their willingness to travel to certain destinations? Similarly, we also read in the newspapers that low-cost airlines are extremely successful in helping to increase the volume of international air travel while, at the same time, environmental groups tell us that the carbon emissions this additional travel is generating are helping to speed up the process of global warming and climate change. So, are low-cost airlines a positive factor in helping to open up new tourism destinations and develop visits or volume to them or are they, in the longer term, likely to contribute heavily to climate change, which, in turn, may make some of these destinations less attractive?

Once you have carried out these kinds of explorations and identified the broad topic for your research project, the next stage is to refine and focus this into something that is more realistic and feasible. In most instances, the initial idea will be something quite general and potentially large in scope. For example, your initial topic might be as broad as 'marketing in the hospitality industry' or 'new product development in tourism'. If you think about either of these for a second, you will be able to see that their breadth is potentially enormous and, given the time and resources you have to complete the work, this makes them unrealistic and not feasible. Therefore, you need to make the topic more manageable, but how?

The first step is to recognise that this type of broad research topic has two components. They are the conceptual and contextual aspects. Let us take the 'marketing in the hospitality industry' topic to illustrate this.

The 'marketing' aspect is the conceptual component of the topic and the 'hospitality industry' part the context within which it is to be explored. Because of their scope, both of these must be refined to produce a manageable project. To do this, it is useful to ask yourself a series of questions about each of them and try to make them more specific. So, for the context, you might begin by asking, 'Which sector of the hospitality industry do I want to use to explore marketing? Am I more interested in hotels or restaurants or contract food service?' If you choose hotels, you might then ask, 'Is it corporate, chain or independent hotels I'm interested in? Is it upscale, exclusive, mid-market or budget hotels that I would like to focus on?' If it is restaurants, you may ask, 'Do I want to concentrate on fast food operations, fine dining or public house restaurants? If I chose one of these areas, would it still be too broad? Would I have to limit it further, say to one particular company or brand, such as McDonald's, or perhaps to one location – fine dining restaurants in London, for example?'.

This process should enable you to produce a context that is more focused and realistic than that of your starting point. So, for example, we might move from 'marketing in the hospitality industry' to 'marketing in UK budget hotels'. This considerably reduces the contextual scope of the project because it eliminates all the other sectors of the hospitality industry and other types/grades of hotel from the context of the study. This means that it is more realistic and manageable than before. Indeed, we may even decide to limit it further to something like 'marketing in the two UK budget hotel market brand leaders' or even just 'the market leader'.

However, even though this contextual focusing principle is sound, you need to be aware that, as the scope narrows, it has an influence on the type of research design that is then most appropriate to investigate it. If the context is 'marketing in UK budget hotels', it is likely that the most appropriate research design is a survey, probably using a mailed or electronically distributed questionnaire. If, however, it is limited to the market leader or the two brand leaders, it is more likely that a single case study or comparative case study design will be used. In turn, this could imply that a standard questionnaire is not the most appropriate way to collect data from the companies concerned and it may be necessary to interview the marketing managers in each and use company documents to obtain the information required. This may raise issues of access and confidentiality and could be a high-risk choice.

The key point here is that the refining of the topic is ultimately not a discrete and isolated part of the research process as a whole. In common with many aspects of the research process, it is, rather, something that requires trade-offs to be made to produce an acceptable balance between the alternatives. In this sense, and because it takes place at the beginning of the process, there is a need for some forward thinking to take place. For example, if you either do not want to undertake a single, or even comparative, case study project or you feel that there may be problems with being able to get the information required to complete such a project, then this needs to be taken into account when the contextual aspect of the topic is being refined.

So, refining the context is important in helping to make the project more manageable, but it is only half the story. We still have a conceptual part to address, as 'marketing' is extremely broad in scope. For example, in our UK budget hotels context, we might concentrate on pricing and sales volume issues, the effects of promotional activities, the effectiveness of alternative distribution channels, the relative merits of different forms of advertising, marketing to different segments of the market, segmenting the budget hotel market and so on. Again, the principle here is the same as that related to the context – the general field is too broad to be feasible unless the context is reduced to a very small unit. If the context were to be a case study of a single company, then it could well be feasible to investigate all the aspects of that company's marketing. Conversely, if the context is defined in a wider manner – say, all UK budget hotels – then to try and investigate all the marketing policies and practices across this broader context would be complex and very time-consuming.

It would be reasonable to conclude from this that there is an inverse relationship between the breadth of the context and the concept. If the context is narrowly defined, in terms of its scope and scale, then there is room for the conceptual element of the research to be wider and more inclusive. Largely because of practical and pragmatic concerns – namely, the time and resources available to conduct and complete the research and how easy it is to gain access to the people or organisations you need to acquire information from – it is generally advantageous to define the context in such a way that you can deal with it satisfactorily within the constraints you face. This really means that you have to think about and make a judgement on the degrees of size (scale) and variability (scope) you can realistically cope with in the time and resources you have available. Other things being equal, this usually means that limits or parameters have to be placed on both of these to make the project feasible.

However, there is not necessarily a simple linear relationship between these considerations. Although, in general, it is true that reducing the context in scale and scope tends to be beneficial for successful completion, if it is reduced to a single or only a few entities, then access becomes a key issue. If you decide to concentrate your research on one organisation – perhaps because you have worked there and are familiar with it – it is absolutely critical that you are as sure as you can be that the information you need to complete the research will be made available to you before you take this option. Just think about this for a moment. If you decide on a project that involves sending out questionnaires to conduct a survey, then the context is wider and more variable but the risk of non-response is being spread. If only half of your sample of, say, 100, complete and return your questionnaire, you have 50 completed questionnaires to work with. Even if the response rate is far lower than this – say only 30 are returned, for example – you may well have enough data to complete the work. On the other hand, if you are dependent on one or two key people in the case study organisation being able and willing to give you their time and release possibly commercially sensitive company documents to you, this is potentially much riskier because they may change their minds, leave the company, have their superiors tell them that the information cannot be released and so on. In short if, for whatever reasons, your key sources of information fail to deliver, then you will have enormous problems.

Therefore, if you intend to focus your project on a very limited context and, hence, information sources, you must be as sure as you can be that the information you need will be available to you once the project starts. To do this, it is vital that you explain to your key sources, in as much detail as possible, what the project is designed to achieve and what specific information you will require from them to complete it. Being too general or vague about both of these at the beginning may cause potentially insoluble problems later.

Experience suggests that many people who are willing to help will readily say yes to a student asking for assistance with a general topic, but, when they are later faced with requests for the release of detailed information, they may decide that it is not possible for a variety of reasons. What they may have agreed to in general or in principle at the outset they may find impossible to deliver on when the detailed request is made.

So, once the topic has been refined somewhat into a more manageable form, the key question or questions that need to be answered can be developed. Taking the examples we have used above, we might now be in a position to phrase our topic as follows: 'The impact that promotional activities have on occupancy levels in UK budget hotels'. Here, the conceptual aspect now has a clear focus – on the promotional aspects of marketing – and the contextual element is clearly limited to one type of hotel operation. Together, these act to screen out a potentially huge amount of other information and concepts. Now we only have to deal with the literature relating to promotion and budget hotels and collect real-world data from the latter.

To reinforce the benefit of this, compare our final formulation of the topic with the one we started with – 'Marketing in the hospitality industry'. It should be obvious that this would be much more difficult to address as it is less specific and larger in scale and scope than the final one. In addition, because it includes such an enormous range of conceptual and contextual considerations, such a topic has huge breadth but very little depth. To adequately cover the breadth, very little detail could be included for each part. Given that, whatever the specific requirements of the research project, there are always constraints or limits on the reporting of the results, such as a maximum word limit for an undergraduate dissertation of, say, 10,000–12,000 words, then, the greater the breadth of material and issues that have to be included, the less room there is for any in-depth analysis of them. In this situation, it is likely that those assessing or evaluating the work will find it to be predominantly descriptive and trivial or superficial in nature as a result. Clearly, attracting such a judgement is to be avoided, for obvious reasons.

## 3.3 Refining the Research Question(s)

Once you are armed with the refined topic, it is possible to focus the research project a little more by formulating the key question(s) it will address or answer. Bearing in mind the need to retain the idea of conducting a focused and purposeful enquiry, it should be self-evident that the research question(s) should be limited in number. There may only be one or, at the most, two or three. The issue is how do we move from our topic to the research question(s)? There are various ways that this might be achieved.

Perhaps the most obvious way to initiate this process is to begin by reading the literature on the topic to identify if there are existing theories or hypotheses related to it that could be applied to, and tested within, the context of the topic. For example, for our budget hotels and promotion topic, we might begin by reading some of the general marketing literature on promotional activity to see if there are any general theories or models that we could apply and test within the context of budget hotels. Alternatively, we might examine the literature on budget hotels and find that marketing managers or others have made claims regarding the effectiveness of certain types of promotional activity and want to research this to discover if there is evidence to support these claims. We might find that someone else has undertaken a study on our topic in another country and could then consider whether or not the results would be the same if this were repeated in the UK. Similarly, we might find a study on our topic that was conducted some time ago and now, because the contextual conditions have changed, this needs to be updated to see if its results and conclusions are still valid.

This initial exploration of the literature does not constitute a critical review of the literature (discussed in Chapter 4) but is more of an initial scan to help us identify possible ways forward in the focusing of the intended project. Some authors (see Sekaran, 2000) refer to this as the initial or preliminary information-gathering stage of the research process. In this sense, it is less concerned with a detailed analysis and understanding of the literature in the field and more with becoming aware of, and sensitised to, the possibilities it may reveal.

Another source of possible inspiration lies within our own thinking or imagination. This may help to generate different ways of looking at a particular issue. For example, hospitality and tourism businesses invariably have a visible customer interface and an invisible backroom operation, but many other types of service business have a similar structure – banks, supermarkets and so on. Are the visible and invisible elements of these businesses the same as, or different from, those found in a particular kind of hospitality or tourism business? Are the organisational and operating structures of a hotel and a supermarket – and, therefore, management issues – the same or different?

## 3.4 Developing Aims and Objectives

At this point you may ask, 'If we have the research question(s) the project will be designed to answer, isn't that enough? Why do we need an aim and objectives as well?' The answer is, even though the question(s) provide a focus for the research and, at least to some extent, give an indication of what the project will be trying to achieve, they are not formulated in what might be referred to as 'output' terms. To illustrate this, consider the question we formulated previously – 'How, and to what extent, do price promotions affect occupancy levels in UK budget hotels?' Though it encapsulates the issue, it does not define what the end product, or aim, of the research project will be. To formulate this, we need to convert the question into another format. In this case we might do this by converting it into the following aim: 'To determine the strength and mechanism(s) of the relationship between price promotions and occupancy levels in UK budget hotels'.

This enables us to answer the research question but it gives an additional degree of focus to help guide the design of the research project and how it is conducted. The work will focus on quantifying the strength of the implied cause–effect relationship between price promotions and occupancy and also on discovering how this relationship actually works – that is the mechanism involved.

One thing that you should note concerning the conversion of the question(s) into the aim is the change in terminology from a type of general query to wording that is positive and ends-related in nature. The aim, unlike the question, defines more specifically what the research will achieve. Thus, here we are saying that we will 'determine' rather than ask 'how and to what extent'. We define the desired end product of the process, which will make it easier for us, and of course others, to judge whether this has been achieved or not.

The purpose of the work is now to do or produce something quite specific, not just answer a less detailed question. Hence, aims should always be written in the form 'To ... '. This makes it clear that the purpose of the work is to be action-orientated and produce a specific output. The action verb that immediately follows this declaration may vary but it needs to specify the nature of output that is desired and, presumably, regarded as feasible. It may be to 'identify', 'state', 'determine', 'compare', 'analyse' or 'evaluate', for example.

The action verb used in the aim is seen by some to indicate the level of intellectual or academic treatment that the subject of the research is to receive from the researcher. It is often thought that intentions to 'identify' or 'determine' something indicate the pursuit of a lesser purpose than ones to 'analyse' or 'evaluate'. This may be true, but it is not always the case. Indeed, it can be misleading if the remainder of the aim is not taken into account. A consequence of this is that sometimes you may feel that you have to use the higher-level verbs – 'analyse', 'evaluate' – in your aim to indicate that it will be sufficiently academic in nature. You may even be exhorted by a tutor to do this.

Using this logic, our aim above could possibly be seen as rather simplistic and unambitious, perhaps even not at the intellectual level required for a final year undergraduate dissertation. However, to do so would be far from the truth. To determine the strength and mechanism of a relationship between price promotions and occupancy would be a demanding task in its own right. It would certainly not be an unambitious or easy task to accomplish. If, on the other hand, the aim was 'To determine the types of price promotion used by UK budget hotel companies', this would be quite a low-level, descriptive activity with perhaps little value as it would produce trivial outcomes that were probably already known before the work began. Similarly, as we saw in Chapter 1, an aim with the purpose of 'Determining the critical success factors for UK budget hotel operations' is appropriate and worthwhile because, although academic and industry commentators may have already speculated on what these might be, no one had collected the empirical evidence to test these speculations before. Thus, achieving the aim would add something new to the existing body of knowledge in this area. Indeed, to see how this was actually achieved, see Brotherton (2004).

One key aspect to bear in mind when thinking about the nature of an aim for research is the existing state of knowledge relating to the topic and research question. If it is relatively limited, it may be appropriate to design a piece of research that will be more exploratory and descriptive rather than analytical or evaluative. Knowledge tends to develop in small steps, so, if it is very limited within the area chosen, there may be great value in work that provides a more comprehensive and developed view of the issues. Conversely, if the topic resides within an established field of research work, it is unlikely that additional description would add anything of value to this existing body of literature.

Having made clear what the overall purpose of the research is – the aim – we are now in a position to work backwards from it and specify what we need to do in order to achieve this end result. This involves determining the steps or stages and tasks that will be required to achieve the aim. These are known as the objectives and, collectively, they should equate to the aim. In other words, if we achieve all the objectives, then we will achieve the overall aim.

To establish the objectives, we need to ask the question, 'What must we complete or achieve to ensure that the aim can be achieved?' Taking the aim from our example above – 'To determine the strength and mechanism(s) of the relationship between price promotions and occupancy levels in UK budget hotels' – we now need to consider what would be necessary to achieve it and, once again, specify these things in action-orientated terms. So, for example, we might ask ourselves questions such as, 'What type of information will be needed from the literature and the real world?' 'How are we going to identify and collect this information?' 'Which procedures and techniques will be required?' 'When will each task have to be completed?' 'Can we undertake some tasks simultaneously or will they have to be completed consecutively?' and 'Who will we need assistance and/or support from to do this?'

As there are many different ways of expressing objectives, with some emphasising process stages rather than more specific content and differing preferences of individuals and institutions, it is difficult to give definitive advice on the exact type of approach and wording that should be used to formulate objectives. That said, any objective should be action-orientated, specific, achievable and clearly be making a contribution to the achievement of the aim. Exhibit 3.1 provides an example of an aim and its associated objectives for a project that illustrates these features.

---

### Exhibit 3.1    *Specifying the Aim and Objectives for a Research Project*

*Aim*

To evaluate the critical success factors (CSFs) for cruise line operations.

*Objectives*

1   To conduct a literature review to identify the nature of CSFs in general and in relation to cruise line operations.
2   To develop a theoretical framework/conceptual model of the CSFs from the literature review and produce associated hypotheses.

*(Cont'd)*

3   To collect empirical data from appropriate cruise line organisations and/or individuals.
4   To analyse the empirical cruise line operations data and test the study's hypotheses.
5   To produce conclusions and recommendations for further research into cruise line operations.

## 3.5 Putting the Research Proposal Together

There are differing views on what should and should not be included in a research proposal and the format that should be used to present it. Similarly, your institution will undoubtedly present you with what is required and in what format for the proposal you have to develop. However, whatever the specifics of these, a research proposal is a statement of intent and should include the following.

◆   *A title* This will not necessarily be the same as the aim of the project and is not critical at this stage as it can be changed later on if necessary.
◆   *An aim and objectives* These indicate the overall purpose, desired outcome and stages required to achieve the aim.
◆   *An introduction, background or rationale for the research* This explains and justifies why the issue(s) to be researched are important, how your work will develop from what is known already and how it may provide a contribution to advancing this knowledge;
◆   *A research plan indicating what you plan to do to achieve the aim* This may or may not include some indication of timings for the start/completion of these activities, but it should always include as much detail as possible on the overall approach and the methods and processes to be used for the data collection and analysis. Again, at this early stage, this may be somewhat speculative, but it can be changed later on when more is known.
◆   Some references should also be included to indicate that evidence exists to support the statements you have made regarding the importance of the work and the methods and processes you have chosen to undertake it.

The key question to ask when putting the proposal together is, 'Could anyone pick up this proposal and actually do the research?' In other words, is it clear enough for anyone to understand, is it feasible given the likely constraints and resources available and does it have sufficient details to enable someone to go ahead and start the research? Think of the proposal as a brief you are giving to someone to actually do the work.

# 3.6 **Ethical Considerations**

It is increasingly common for research proposals or plans to include an indica-tion of any ethical issues and considerations the conduct of the research may raise. Indeed, showing that these have been considered and that conducting the research will not give rise to any significant ethical implications may be required as a prerequisite for the approval of a research proposal. It is likely that your institution will have research ethics policies, procedures, structures and documentation to ensure that any research conducted within the auspices of the institution, including that for undergraduate dissertations, is designed and conducted in an ethically acceptable manner.

So, what are ethics or ethical considerations and how do these relate to the research process? Ethics is concerned with moral values, principles and actions, such as honesty, integrity, transparency, obligations to others, responsibility and trust. In short, behaving in the 'right' way. Research ethics are therefore concerned with the moral principles that are used to inform the planning, design, conduct and publication of research. Ethics is not just an issue associ-ated with the implementation of the research design in terms of collecting the data, but one to be taken into consideration throughout all the stages in the process, not only to ensure that the dignity, rights and welfare of any human particpants are protected but also that the work is designed and implemented in an honest manner.

In the UK, one of the leading research councils – the Economic and Social Research Council (ESRC) – has produced a 'Research Ethics Framework' con-taining six key principles of ethical research that it would expect to be addressed in a research proposal (ESRC, 2005: 3). They are as follows.

- ✓ **Research** should be designed, reviewed and undertaken to ensure integrity and quality.

- ✓ **Research** staff and subjects must be informed fully about the purpose, methods and intended possible uses of the **research**, what their participation in the **research** entails and what risks, if any, are involved.

- ✓ The confidentiality of information supplied by **research** subjects and the anonymity of respondents must be respected.

- ✓ **Research** participants must participate in a voluntary way, free from any coercion.

- ✓ Harm to **research** participants must be avoided.

- ✓ The independence of **research** must be clear and any conflicts of interest or partiality must be explicit.

Therefore, any research proposal should contain a consideration of ethical principles such as these within its component parts. In short, it is incumbent on the person writing the research proposal to demonstrate that he or she has considered the extent to which the project may be ethically compromised in any of these respects. Often this does not require lengthy explanation or justification, although it may be required for contentious projects. Normally, inclusion of a short statement or series of statements that demonstrate the proposer has thought through any possible ethical implications raised in the proposed research will be sufficient.

Key issues to consider and state would be the potential benefits from the research and the ethical risks it may give rise to. In particular, issues associated with the integrity of the research design and possible risks to participants, including those that may affect their wider context, such as family, community, employer organisation and so on, need to be addressed. More specifically, these areas are likely to involve consideration of the expected quality and accountability (how it can be verified) of the research, how voluntary, informed consent (where possible and feasible) from the participants will be obtained and how issues of confidentiality, privacy and data protection will be addressed.

Depending on the extent of the ethical implications identified in the proposal, it may require anything from a light touch, an expedited approval process if these are minimal to, if they are more significant, a more rigorous approval process conducted via a research ethics committee. If your institution requires you to complete an ethics form to submit with your proposal for approval, then some of the ethical issues will be outlined in this. However, it may not cover ethical aspects of the overall research design and these may still need to be dealt with in the proposal. To give an indication of the issues this type of form may require you to address, see Exhibit 3.2, which contains a checklist taken from the ESRC's ethical framework, referred to above.

---

### Exhibit 3.2    A Checklist for Ethical Issues

1   Does the study involve participants who are particularly vulnerable or unable to give informed consent (children, people with learning disabilities, your own students)?

2   Will the study require the cooperation of a gatekeeper for initial access to the groups or individuals to be recruited (students at school, members of a self-help group, residents of a nursing home)?

3   Will it be necessary for participants to take part in the study without their knowledge and consent at the time (the covert observation of people in non-public places)?

4   Will the study involve the discussion of sensitive topics (sexual activity, drug use)?

5   Are drugs, placebos or other substances (food substances, vitamins) to be administered to the study participants or will the study involve invasive, intrusive or potentially harmful procedures of any kind?

6 Will blood or tissue samples be obtained from participants?

7 Is pain or more than mild discomfort likely to result from the study?

8 Could the study induce psychological stress or anxiety or cause harm or negative consequences beyond the risks encountered in normal life?

9 Will the study involve prolonged or repetitive testing?

10 Will financial inducements (other than reasonable expenses and compensation for time involved) be offered to participants?

11 Will the study involve the recruitment of patients or staff through the NHS?

*Source*: ESRC, 2005, p. 36

If you are able to answer 'no' to these questions, then it is likely that your proposal will only require a light touch approval process. If the answer to any is 'yes', then you would need to describe how these ethical issues will be dealt with in the research as it would then be necessary for a research ethics committee to give their approval.

## SUMMARY

» To identify a suitable research topic, think about what you are interested in, speak with others and be aware of current controversies.

» From a general idea, begin to narrow the conceptual and contextual aspects down to make it more focused and feasible.

» Get a suitable focus in terms of a question to answer or an aim and objectives to achieve.

» Think about what you will need to do and how you are going to do these things to produce the desired outcomes.

» Put all your ideas together into a proposal and ask yourself if it is clear and whether it would be sufficient for anyone to be able to pick it up and then do the work.

» Do not forget that you will need to address the ethical issues your proposed research may give rise to.

## Further Reading

Blaxter, L., Hughes, C. and Tight, M. (1996) *How to Research*. Buckingham: Open University Press. Chapter 2.

Clark, M., Riley, M., Wilkie, E. and Wood, R.C. (1998) *Researching and Writing Dissertations in Hospitality and Tourism*. London: International Thomson Business Press. Chapter 3.

Flick, U. (2002) *An Introduction to Qualitative Research*, 2nd edition. Thousand Oaks, CA: Sage. Chapter 5.

Gill, J. and Johnson, P. (1991) *Research Methods for Managers*. London: Paul Chapman. Chapter 2.

Jankowicz, A.D. (1991) *Business Research Projects for Students*. London: Chapman & Hall. Chapters 2 and 3.

Johns, N. and Lee-Ross, D. (1998) *Research Methods in Service Industry Management*. London: Cassell. Chapter 3.

Orna, E. and Stevens, G. (1995) *Managing Information for Research*. Buckingham: Open University Press. Chapters 2, 5 and 6.

Preece, R. (1994) *Starting Research: An introduction to academic research and dissertation writing*. London: Pinter. Chapter 8.

Saunders, M., Lewis, P. and Thornhill, A. (2003) *Research Methods for Business Students*, 3rd edition. Harlow: Pearson Education Ltd. Chapter 2.

Sekaran, U. (2000) *Research Methods for Business: A skill-building approach*, 3rd edition. New York: John Wiley. Chapter 4.

Sharp, J.A. and Howard, K. (1996) *The Management of a Student Research Project*, 2nd edition. Aldershot: Gower. Chapters 2 and 3.

Veal, A.J. (1997) *Research Methods for Leisure and Tourism: A practical guide*, 2nd edition. Harlow: Pearson Education. Chapters 2 and 3.

# Chapter

## Sourcing and Reviewing the Literature

---

### KEY CONCEPTS AND ISSUES

» *The nature of the 'literature'.*
» *What is a literature review and why is it necessary?*
» *Searching and sourcing the literature.*
» *Accessing and obtaining the literature.*
» *Critically evaluating and reviewing the literature.*
» *The role and placement of the literature review in deductive and inductive studies.*
» *Literature and research design relationships.*
» *Writing the literature review.*

---

## 4.1 Introduction

In this chapter, we will explore the searching, sourcing, accessing and reviewing of the literature element of the research process. The body of literature existing on a particular subject, topic or question essentially represents what is already known about it. Put another way, it is the existing body of knowledge. It is extremely important, when conducting a piece of research, to be critically aware of what this is as it helps to indicate where your research could/should go in order to add something to what is already known. By obtaining, reading and reviewing the existing literature, you become more aware of what is and is not known, who the key researchers in the field are, what methods, techniques and procedures have been used and how this knowledge can be used to help you develop your own ideas. It also ensures that you do not 'reinvent the wheel' and produce trivial work by investigating things that are already known.

In addressing such issues as what constitutes the literature, sourcing, searching and accessing it, why a review of it is necessary, how this should be approached, structured and written, I have taken the view that what is more important to you is the development of an understanding of the principles underlying these issues and why they should be regarded as important to you within your research project. I have also tried to indicate why certain key aspects of the literature review will be seen as important by the people who are going to read and mark your research project. What I have not done is provide detailed information on, and references to, information sources and how to record, analyse and review the literature. The reasons for this are that you are either likely to be aware already of the databases and other sources available for searching for literature in your institution or, if not, you could be very easily by talking to the library staff, and you are also likely to have received guidance notes from your tutors on the specific requirements they have for this. Of course, another reason is that the space available within your text as a whole will be limited. If you need a much fuller explanation and further help on these issues, Fink's (1999) book, solely on literature review, would be one to consult.

## 4.2 Why is a Literature Review Necessary?

Although, as we shall see shortly, the purpose and positioning of a review of the existing literature on a particular subject or topic may vary depending on the stage of a research process, one of the main reasons for conducting it is to demonstrate that you are aware of and have examined the current state of the knowledge relating to the topic you have chosen for your research project. As the vast majority of research topics within a particular field are likely to have been considered to some degree by previous research studies, be they conceptual or empirical in nature, there will invariably be some published literature relating to the topic you have chosen to pursue. In some cases, the quantity of this literature can be enormous. In others it may be rather sparse. In general, it is probably reasonable to say that the newer and more original the topic, the less likely it is that it will have been studied previously by others, so less literature will have been published on it and the reverse will be true for subjects that have been a focus of interest for several years.

Earlier in this book, it was stated that research is conducted to contribute to an increase in the knowledge relating to a particular topic or field of study, to add something new to what is known already. To achieve this and make the research effort worthwhile, logic dictates that we must be aware of this knowledge if we are to add something new to it. If we do not, then we may be guilty of doing over again what somebody else has done perfectly well or, alternatively, producing a piece of research that is trivial and really has little, if any, value. So, we might say that one of the purposes of conducting a literature review is to protect ourselves from the potential criticism of producing trivial work. If we ignore the current state of knowledge and simply produce research findings that repeat those that already exist within the published literature, then we would expect others to tell us that this has been a waste of time because what we are telling them is nothing new. Again, logically, if we are to design a study that will possibly contribute something new to what is known, then we must be aware of what that knowledge is to ensure that the study is innovative in some way.

This highlights another purpose of the literature review: it helps us to design our research study. To take the state of knowledge on a particular topic beyond what is already known, we need to address questions and problems that currently do not have adequate answers or solutions. In this sense, undertaking the literature review helps us to build on the existing knowledge in a logical manner. It also gives us an opportunity to explain and justify the topic we have chosen, the questions or problems we are trying to address and that the approach we are taking to do so is appropriate, relevant, important and valid. Therefore, if we identify unanswered questions in the existing literature, differing interpretations of the same issues, such as controversies, or other gaps in the knowledge relating to issues that have not yet been explored, then we have the rationale we need to conduct our study.

Similarly, this analysis helps us to build a bridge between what is currently known – the literature – and what it is hoped will be added to this knowledge in the future – the results of our study. As most advances in knowledge occur via relatively small, incremental additions to or revisions of existing knowledge, analysing the literature is important as it helps to establish a continuity in the development of knowledge. Put another way, it also helps you to demonstrate that your findings and conclusions do indeed add something new to what was known before. Furthermore, having a good understanding of the current state of play provides clues, and sometimes raw material, to help you focus and design your study. At the very least, a review of the literature indicates the types of approaches, processes, instruments, analytical techniques and contexts that have been used in previous studies. Beyond this, you will also become aware of the conceptual and theoretical positions previous studies have adopted. This means that you do not have to start with the proverbial 'blank sheet'.

If you are lucky you may find a ready-made research design within the literature that you can use in your study. This is not to say that you can simply plagiarise previous work. It goes without saying that doing so is unacceptable. However, you need to be aware of the difference between plagiarism and replication because the latter is common, quite acceptable and may help you to develop a fairly robust design for your study. Although plagiarism has many forms and connotations, essentially it is cheating as you are copying someone else's work and attempting to pass it off as your own.

Replication is different from plagiarism. Although it does involve an element of copying – because you are literally repeating something done before – there are two important differences. First, there is an explicit recognition of the fact that someone else conducted the original work. Second, there is some variation on the original. If this were not the case, then there would be little point in doing it. Let us look at some examples to clarify these important distinctions.

Many researchers studying the issue of 'service quality' in the hospitality and tourism fields (see, for example, Brotherton and Booth, 1997; Frochot and Hughes, 2000; Knutson et al., 1990; Lee and Hing, 1995; Saleh and Ryan, 1991; Stevens et al., 1995) have undertaken studies designed to assess the applicability of an instrument known as SERVQUAL, which was originally designed to measure the level of service quality experienced by customers in other types of service business environments.

The purpose of these studies was to test the extent to which the SERVQUAL concept and instrument could be applied to hospitality and tourism environments or, put another way, to answer the question of whether or not it could be regarded as a concept and an instrument that could be used successfully across all types of service business without having to be modified to fit particular contexts.

This approach is also relatively common where a study has been conducted in one country and the researcher asks the question, 'Would the results be the same in another country?' Personally I have conducted this kind of study twice in my research (Brotherton and Burgess, 1997; Brotherton et al., 2002). In the first of these, a study to identify the academic research interests of hospitality companies conducted by other researchers in the USA was repeated in the UK to see if the results would be the same. In the second, a study conducted in the UK to identify the critical success factors in UK corporate hotels was repeated in Holland, again to ascertain if the factors regarded as critical in the UK would also be regarded as such in Holland.

Even in circumstances where the methods used in previous studies do not appear to be suitable for your study, this does not mean that they will not have some value. As Bell (1993: 34) puts it, 'they may give you ideas about how you might categorise your own data, and ways in which you may be able to draw on the work of other researchers to support or refute your own arguments and conclusions'. So, even where existing material does not fit your plans closely enough for you to use it, either in its original or a modified form, it is still likely to be useful as it can help shape your thinking about how you might proceed with your research. This is not only the case in terms of how you might design and conduct the study but also in relation to how you might analyse the data you collect. For example, you may find that previous researchers have tended to use questionnaire surveys to collect their data and have employed particular statistical techniques to analyse these. Not only will this give you some ideas about how you might resolve these issues in your work but it may also help you to see that planning what to do for each stage of the research process should not be done in isolation because decisions made at one point will usually have implications for a later stage. For example, the way that a questionnaire is designed and the type of questions it contains will determine the type(s) of data that it will collect. In turn, the use of certain statistical techniques requires the existence of particular types of data. Therefore, the type of data analysis you intend to conduct should be thought about at the same time or before the questionnaire is being designed.

Up to this point in the chapter, there has been an implicit assumption made regarding the role, timing and purposes of the literature review. If you have spotted it, then well done. If you have not, the assumption has been that the research to be conducted will have taken a deductive approach. As deduction works from what is known to what is unknown and tries to test the validity of the known theory in the research project, the review of the literature must occur before the new research is conducted. However, as you know, if an inductive approach is adopted, then matters proceed from the unknown to the known, from reality to the development of theory. In this latter case, at least in principle, the collection of empirical data comes before the review of any literature and the drawing of conclusions. Therefore, the literature review is positioned differently and has a different purpose in the inductive research process. At best, the review may be conducted alongside or at the same time as the empirical data are being collected. This is often known as a 'grounded theory' approach to research (Glaser and Strauss, 1967) as the development of theory is said to be grounded in, or derived from, the collection and analysis of the empirical data. In other instances it happens after the data have been collected and serves as a comparator for the data and the themes emerging from the analysis of these data. One important point to make here is that induction and how a qualitative study is conducted should not be seen as synonymous in relation to the literature review. By this I mean that it is possible to conduct a qualitative study using a deductive approach, in which case the literature review would precede the data collection process.

## 4.3 What is the Literature?

Before considering the types and forms of literature, it is perhaps worthwhile at this point to briefly comment on what is meant by 'the literature' relating to a particular topic or field. In essence, this phrase is used to refer to the collective body of knowledge relating to a particular context. In short, it is all that is known and, indeed, unknown about a topic or field. So, when people talk about the 'body of literature' or a 'extant literature' or about making a contribution to 'the literature', they are referring to the current state of knowledge about a particular topic.

In the vast majority of cases this literature will be text, including figures, tables, diagrams and pictures, and will be printed and published in books, journals, magazines, newspapers and so on. Of course, the same or similar material may be published electronically on websites or other types of storage device.

Regardless of its form, the important characteristic is the fact that it is in the 'public domain' and, therefore, potentially available for everyone to access. However, in reality, there are always some restrictions on the availability of published information. The most obvious of these is the ability to pay the price of obtaining or accessing the material – to buy the book, subscribe to the journal and so on. This will not generally be an issue for you, as your institution will have paid to obtain books for its library or the subscriptions required for a hard or electronic copy of a journal. Similarly, some information published on the Internet will only be made available if a fee is paid. That said, a great deal of the information available on websites can be freely accessed.

Although texts published either traditionally or electronically are likely to be the dominant form of literature you will use for a literature review, it should not be forgotten that there are other forms of information that can be included within the literature relating to a particular topic or field. Depending on the nature of your research project, it may have no, little or great relevance to your literature review. This information tends to be that which is produced in an audio and/or audio-visual format – radio and/or television programmes, film media on tape, CD or DVD, artwork, advertising images and so on.

It is generally accepted that there are three main types or categories of information:

♦  primary
♦  secondary
♦  tertiary.

There is some variation in the research methods literature concerning the definitions and, hence, what should be included in the primary and secondary categories. Primary information is that which is collected for the first time from the real world – namely, it is new, original and empirical in nature. Thus, information obtained from questionnaire surveys, interviews or observations would be referred to as primary information. This is the type of information you will most likely be seeking to collect during the empirical phase of your research project.

Secondary information or data is essentially that originally collected by someone else, either an individual or an organisation, for their specific (primary) purpose(s), but which can be utilised for a second time in the current project. This really constitutes the substantive body of literature pertaining to a given topic or field of enquiry available in the public domain. In addition to books, periodicals (academic, trade or professional), reports, newspapers, website information and so on, it may also come in the form of unpublished dissertations or theses held in libraries, government or quasi-government bodies, publications, conference proceedings and company reports, to name just a few sources.

Tertiary information is essentially processed and summarised secondary information that has been distilled into a reduced form to facilitate the identification of the secondary literature that exists and what this may contain.

Therefore such sources as indexes, catalogues, abstracts, bibliographies, databases, encyclopaedias and so on constitute tertiary information. These can be a shortcut to identifying the literature that exists within a field and, depending on their format, may be searchable using keywords or phrases to speed up the searching process.

## 4.4 What is a Literature Review?

It is common for academics to refer to the literature review as a 'critical review' of the existing literature, but what does this mean? It does not mean providing a simple regurgitation or restatement of what is contained in the literature. Neither does it mean doing so with the addition of a few linking comments from yourself. Consider the discussion in Exhibit 4.1 before we explore these issues further.

---

### Exhibit 4.1    When is a Literature Review a Literature Review?

Manuel is a final year undergraduate student on a BA Tourism Management course and his dissertation supervisor (Dr Alistair Brown) has asked him to come and see him in his office to get some feedback on the draft literature review he submitted a week ago.

'Hello Dr Brown, I hope you have some good news for me', Manuel said when he arrived for the meeting.

'Come in, Manuel,' replied Alistair, 'I have certainly got quite a lot to say to you.'

'Oh dear,' thought Manuel, 'I don't like the sound of that!'

Alistair began, 'First, Manuel, can you tell me what your understanding is of what a literature review should be?'

Manuel replied, 'Well, I think the idea is to record what is known about the topic to show that I know this and to help me formulate appropriate questions for the research.'

'OK, that's true,' Alistair said, 'but there is a bit more to it than that. I've read your draft and, although you have been very thorough in covering the breadth of the literature relating to your topic, it is too descriptive at present, with very little critical analysis or comment.'

'I thought you might say that', Manuel said, with an impending sense of more work to do! 'I know we have been told that the review should be critical,' Manuel continued, 'but I'm not sure how to do that, can you help me please?'

'No problem, that's what I'm here for, Manuel', Alistair said, helpfully. 'Let me try to help you think about this. First of all, think about the relationships between the issues of who, what, why, when and how in relation to the literature.'

Manuel looked even more confused.

*(Cont'd)*

Alistair continued, 'At present, you cover most of these in your review, but in a descriptive and isolated manner. You tell me who has said what, when texts were published, how they arrived at their conclusions and even, sometimes, why. However, what is missing is the underlying analysis of any similarities or differences between the previous studies, a recognition of the philosophical roots of the different authors, whether or not there are any gaps or omissions in the literature you've reviewed, what the strengths and weaknesses of the studies are and how valid and reliable the methodologies used and results obtained might be.'

'Wow,' Manuel gasped, 'that sounds really difficult, I'm not sure I can do that.'

'Okay,' Alistair said, 'I know you can and I'm going to talk you through one part to show you that it is not as difficult as you seem to think.'

'Okay, that's great', Manuel said, unconvincingly.

'So,' Alistair began, 'Let's look at the section on customer satisfaction. Here you say Jones (1999) found in his study that facilities for children were not regarded as being as important as other factors by the questionnaire respondents, but Tolmey (2002) obtained different results from his questionnaire.'

'Yes, is that not being critical?' Manuel asked.

'No,' Alistair replied, 'You are merely reporting a difference without offering any suggestions as to why this was the case. For example, were the two studies conducted at the same time of year, were they undertaken in the same type of tourism business, did they have similar sample sizes and compositions, were the questionnaires administered in the same way?'

'Ah, I see what you mean', Manuel replied. 'In the first study, a large proportion of the sample were women and family visitors, but in the second they were mainly student coach parties visiting the centres. Also, in the Jones study, the questionnaires were left on the restaurant tables for the visitors to complete, but, in Tolmey's study, a team of interviewers went around to interview the visitors and complete the questionnaires. So, I guess that the different results might have occurred because of differences between the samples and the ways the questionnaires were implemented.'

'Excellent, Manuel – now you're getting the hang of it,' Alistair said. 'If you look at the literature in that way, then you are going to get much more depth into your review and be able to identify and critically comment on the quality and significance of the previous work.'

'Thanks, Dr Brown', Manuel said, gratefully. 'I see exactly what you mean. The next version will be much better and looking at it that way should also help me to decide what approach I should take in my empirical research.'

'Exactly, you really have got the hang of it now. I'll look forward to seeing the next version, Manuel', Alistair said, pleased that Manuel now understood what he needed to do.

So, Manuel's supervisor makes the point that merely restating, listing and describing previous work does not indicate that the reviewer has engaged sufficiently with the literature. Such an approach is really quite superficial and likely to attract significant negative criticism and comment.

For a review to be regarded as critical, there must be evidence of engagement with the literature. This demands more than regurgitation because it involves an element of processing. When you engage with the literature, you study it in depth because you examine it in detail in an attempt to develop a greater understanding of its relevance, validity and significance. This is exactly what Manuel's supervisor was pushing him to do. Alistair wanted him to demonstrate that he had developed an appropriate degree of insight in relation to the sources he had referred to. In the example, Manuel moved on from simply listing and describing previous work to a position where he was beginning to evaluate it by considering the extent to which it might be seen as robust and credible or flawed.

## 4.5 Sourcing, Searching and Accessing the Literature

Before you can conduct a literature review, you obviously have to identify what relevant literature exists. This means that, in the first instance, you need to identify possible sources of the literature. The most obvious source is the library, particularly for books, but other sources, such as the Internet in general and other online databases, bibliographies and so on, may be as, if not more, fruitful in terms of speed and ease of access. Most institutions now have subscriptions to electronic journals and subject-specific and/or more general online databases and you should check which of these you are able to access at the earliest opportunity. In addition, many publications, such as newspapers and magazines, have their own websites that can be searched for electronic copies of articles.

Once the potential sources of material have been identified, the next stage in the literature reviewing process is a literature search. Depending on the nature of your topic and research aim/objectives, the scope and scale of the literature that might be relevant could be quite limited or vast. Assuming that you have followed the previous good advice to make sure that your project has a suitable focus, the potential breadth and volume of material that would be regarded as relevant to your study should be limited. However, even where you have done this, there are some questions and issues that will have received a large amount of attention from previous researchers and the volume of literature will reflect that.

To help you cope with some of these issues, in an ideal world, you should know exactly what you are looking for before you start the literature search. The problem is, invariably, that this is unrealistic because you probably will not know what literature exists before you start searching to find it. That said, there are some things that you can do to make your life easier. Even if you cannot know exactly what you are looking for at the outset, you can place some limits or parameters on the search to potentially limit the volume of 'hits'. Intuitively, you probably know and practise this already. For example, if you are looking for something on the Internet and enter a term or terms into a search engine such as Google, if your terms are quite broad you are likely to get many thousands of results, but if you repeat the search with more specific terms the volume of hits will be reduced.

The same principles apply to searches of online databases, library catalogues, bibliographies and so on. One way to begin to limit the potential terrain for the search is to qualify or delimit your search terms. For example, if your project is investigating service quality in hotels, then instead of simply entering something like 'service quality' as the search term it may be preferable to enter 'service quality+hotels', as this will limit the number of hits to those that focus on service quality literature specifically related to hotel businesses. If your study is limited to the UK or the USA or any other particular country, then you could also add this to the search string. As you make the search more specific and limited in scope then you can expect there to be fewer hits, but they are also more likely to be relevant. Conversely, if you find that by limiting the search terms this generates only very few references, you can always widen these.

One way to expand or limit your searching of Internet sources, particularly databases, indexes and abstracts, is to use what is known as Boolean logic. This is not as complicated as it may sound! What it does is expand or contract the search terms. For example, if you were conducting a keyword search for material on recruitment, selection and interviewing, you could enhance your chances of finding material connected with all these keywords by formulating the search so that it will only find material containing all three. By entering the search term 'recruitment AND selection AND interviewing', the search is only going to deliver in its results material containing all three of these terms. Alternatively, if you wanted to widen this search to find material with any one of these three terms in it, then you could formulate your search term with 'OR' instead of 'AND' between the keywords. This would then identify material containing at least one of these three terms.

Where the spellings of keywords differ in UK or US English, such as 'behaviour' and 'behavior', you can use 'AND' to ensure you pick up both. However, there is a shortcut for this known as entering a 'wild card'. So, in this case, you could enter 'behavio?r' and this would pick up material with different spellings of the word. Also, to capture variations relating to a particular keyword, there is another alternative to using a string of variations connected by 'AND'. This is known as 'truncation' – using a chopped-down version of the keyword. By taking the basic stem of the word and adding an asterisk, this will produce results relating to the different variations on this stem. So, for example, the search term 'motivat*' would pick up related keywords, such as motivation, motivational, motivating, motivate and so on.

Computerised searches may also be conducted and broadened or constrained using other search criteria. For example, if you know the names of the most important authors of the material you are interested in, you can search using their names. Similarly, many databases and indexes allow searching to take place for a specific year or a range of years which, again, can help you to widen or limit your search. Alternatively, if you know the journals that are most likely to contain the type of information you are looking for, then it may be possible to specify that you want to search for the keywords within a particular journal.

There are also other ways to limit and/or focus a search. If you are only interested in literature published in English, then you may want to specify this at the beginning. If you do not specify a time period for the search, then, potentially, you may get hits going back many years or decades. Sometimes this is necessary, but often it is sufficient to limit your search to more recent sources. It is difficult to suggest a definitive time period to use because this varies according to the nature of the research topic and its purpose but, in many cases, identifying the literature published over the last 20 years is likely to be more than sufficient. This could always be extended at a later stage if the sources reveal, through the references contained in them, there were important studies produced at earlier dates that are likely to be relevant to your study or, if such a extended time range delivers too large a number of hits, you can instead limit the range further as described above.

Nevertheless, although broadening or limiting the range of your search can be useful, it will not help you to identify the material you need if you have used inappropriate terminology in the search terms. As we saw earlier, the spelling of terms can, and does, differ in UK and US English. In addition to this, different terminology can be used for the same things in the UK and USA. For example, in the UK, it is common to refer to the 'hotel industry', but this is known as the 'lodging industry' in the USA. In the UK, we talk of 'fast-food restaurants', but these are known as 'quick-service restaurants' in the USA. The same issues can arise in the context of conceptual terms. In the literature, some authors use the term 'critical success factors' (CSFs), but others use 'key success factors' (KSFs) to refer to the same thing. Also, because jargon and terminology change over time and differ from one country to another, we need to be careful how such words are used in search terms. For example, some countries distinguish between their hotel and tourism industries, but others do not – they include the hotel industry within the tourism industry. Today, it is common to use terms such as 'downsizing', 'delayering' and 're-engineering' in relation to organisational change, but in the past terms such as 'restructuring', 'streamlining' and 'reorganisation' were used to refer to such activities. Furthermore, because we are so familiar with the use of abbreviations and acronyms, we may write these as our search terms without thinking. They may, or may not, relate to the formulation of the keywords in the database, index or website. So, using 'UK' or 'US' instead of the spelled out versions of these terms may give rise to problems, as may using 'WTC' instead of 'World Tourism Council'.

Another issue to consider is the type of material to search for. As noted earlier, the literature is represented in varying forms and media, but not all of these will be equally relevant or valuable for your particular purposes. Similarly, not all of them will be equally trustworthy or credible. For example, you may expect that material published in an academic journal is more likely to be objective and accurate than that in a company's own publicity literature or a newspaper. Also, remember that there is always a time delay between when work has been completed and when it is written up and published. This is at its shortest for the most frequently published media, such as those that are daily, weekly, or monthly, and at its longest for books, where the text may have been written a year to two years before it is actually printed and published. Even in the case of academic journals, the peer reviewing and publication processes papers go through before they actually appear in issues can be quite extended, possibly as long as those associated with books.

Although a generalisation, it is probably fair to say that one of if not the best type of material to concentrate on in the first instance is that found in academic journals, followed by books. Frequent publications, such as newspapers, magazines, trade journals and so on, do have the advantage of containing very contemporary, up-to-date material, but it is subject to less scrutiny than that found in academic journals and can be influenced by other, subjective, pressures of a commercial and/or vested interest nature. It is also likely to be less detailed because of the pressure for space in such publications. By way of contrast, the material contained in academic journals will normally have been subjected to review and scrutiny by other academics in the field before being accepted for publication and thus will be quite detailed because, in general, the authors of this material will have been required to make clear the aims, objectives and purposes of their work, provide a critical review of the literature, detail and justify the methodology they have adopted in the study, explain, as fully as space allows, the instruments and procedures used to collect and analyse the data and discuss the importance and significance of the findings. This means that the material is going to provide you with a lot of detail and has a high degree of credibility.

Finally, after you have searched to establish the literature available, assessed what is relevant for your purposes and acquired it, you must think about the importance of keeping full and accurate citation records for all the material you have sourced and acquired, regardless of whether or not you are sure that all of it will be cited in the final work. The information required for these purposes is detailed in Chapter 11. Some degree of forward thinking at this point about such details can help to save pain and time later, because if you get into the habit of making sure that all the information you may need for citation purposes is recorded on handwritten notes, photocopies or printed versions of electronic documents you will not be caught out when writing up your project.

## 4.6 Evaluating and Reviewing the Literature

We saw earlier in this chapter that it is necessary for you to engage with the literature in order to review it appropriately and that the review should demonstrate insight. These require evaluation to take place, but what does this mean?

Evaluation is concerned with making judgements. Of course, we can all make subjective and fairly superficial judgements and we do so every day, but they may have little or no basis in fact and should more properly be regarded as personal opinions. Evaluation is more objective, organised and criterion-related.

To illustrate the difference, if I asked you what you thought of two different cars, you might say that one looked sportier than the other or safer or more comfortable and so on. On the other hand, if I asked you to evaluate the two cars against each other, you would probably ask me how and on what basis? In other words, you would be asking me to provide you with some basis for making the comparison, some common denominator that you could use to compare the features and performance of the two cars. In short, you would be asking me to provide you with a framework or criteria that you could use to do this in an explicit and objective manner. So, for example, I might give you a checklist to use for this containing criteria such as petrol consumption, 0 to 60 miles per hour acceleration time, the boot capacity, the braking distance to a stop at 60 miles per hour, the number of airbags in the car and so on.

Translating this into the context of a literature review for a research project, we might think of comparing and contrasting the literature in terms of:

♦ the philosophical stance taken by different studies – that is, whether it was positivistic or phenomenological;
♦ the research approach and design adopted – that is, whether it was deductive or inductive and/or was conducted using a survey or case study;
♦ the type of data collection instruments and processes used – that is, whether closed or open questions were asked and if they were implemented at a distance (posted or e-mailed) or directly (people interviewing respondents face to face);
♦ how the samples were determined, what the sizes and compositions were and if they were adequately representative or biased;
♦ the techniques used to analyse the data;
♦ whether the conclusions derived from the findings appropriate were valid or not.

This may appear to be a lengthy and difficult task, and in some respects it is, but you are expected to produce a critical review of the literature and this is what is required to do so. However, not only will this effort produce a review that is much more acceptable than a trivial, descriptive one, it does not necessarily require more time and words. Because you are looking for patterns, themes, consistencies, irregularities, gaps, omissions, strengths, weaknesses and so on in the literature, you do not need to include as much descriptive detail in the review as you would if you were outlining all the studies. In this sense, you may write the same amount of words, but the structure, approach and content will differ. In short, you should include less detail in terms of 'what' the literature says but more about 'why' and 'how' and the quality and credibility of the work.

At this point, it is also worth mentioning that there is, or certainly should be, a connection between how you approach and organise the evaluation of the literature and the structure that the written review will take. This, again, is a case of different tasks in the process having implications for each other. In the following section, we consider how the written review might be organised and structured and identify some alternatives in these respects. These have implications for how the evaluation might be organised and conducted. In short, if you plan to organise the write-up of the review using particular sections, it would be wise to think about using a similar structure to evaluate the literature, otherwise you may find that you have quite a bit of work to do to fit the evaluation into the write-up structure. This is one of the many parts of the research process where a degree of forward thinking can help you to connect the sequential stages as smoothly as possible and reduce the amount of extra work you will need to do if you do not work in this way.

## 4.7 Writing the Literature Review

Having processed the literature, all that remains is to write up the review. As you will know by now, the purpose, format or style that this may take will differ depending on whether the research process takes a deductive or inductive approach. In the same way, the timing, placement or positioning of the review within the process will also differ. Normally, if the research is to be conducted by means of a deductive process, the literature review will appear in the final written document as a separate section or chapter (see Chapter 11 for more on this). Indeed, as we have seen previously, one reason for choosing a deductive approach is that there is a substantial body of literature in existence, from which established perspectives, theoretical frameworks and models and methodologies can be identified and reviewed to help focus and shape your own research questions and methodology.

Where an inductive approach is used, the review may be presented at the end of the study, where it is likely to be used as something to compare and contrast the empirical data with. Here, the review does not direct and guide the empirical research process, but instead provides assistance to help connect the theoretical perspectives emerging from the empirical work to any literature that does exist on the issues. Remember, the purpose of deductive research is to test existing theory, while inductive research seeks to build new theory.

Taking the review in a deductive study first, which is likely to be the favoured approach for most of the research work conducted for undergraduate or postgraduate dissertations, the main questions are; 'How do you organise and structure the writing of the review?' and 'What style should be used to write it up?' Really, there are no definitive answers to these questions because the nature of given bodies of literature and research studies varies enormously. That said, there are perhaps certain principles that you should bear in mind when writing this type of review. We have already established that it needs to be critical and evaluative rather than merely descriptive. It should illustrate that you are knowledgeable about the previous work in the field; help you to identify key assumptions, questions, issues, gaps and omissions in the current state of knowledge; and inform your decisions concerning what data to collect, how these might be analysed and the methods and procedures that might be the most appropriate to do this.

In the next chapter, we will be exploring how the 'product' of this literature review provides vital raw material to help design the conceptual and methodological details for the proposed research and, thus, connects existing and new knowledge in a logical and systematic manner. To provide suitable raw material for this purpose, the review needs to be written in such a way that it becomes possible to identify the key concepts and methodologies in the existing literature.

So, how can this be done? Cresswell (1994) proposes an approach structured on identifying the key factors relating to cause and effect and what relationships are suggested to exist between the two sets of factors. As we shall see in Chapter 5, these are known as the independent (causes) and dependent (effects) variables. His model indicates that the review should begin with an introductory section, informing the reader about the organisation of sections and which are contained within the review. This type of introduction should be present whatever specific approach or format is adopted in what follows it. After this, Cresswell (1994) suggests that a section reviewing the literature on the causes, or independent variables, should be present and then one reviewing the effects, or dependent variables. Once these have been established, the next question is either 'How are these connected?' or 'What is/are the cause–effect mechanism(s) or relationship(s) between them?' Therefore, a section dealing with these issues is required next before the review is concluded, with a summary section to highlight the major themes and so on.

Although the logic of this is sound and it may be possible to organise and structure your review accordingly, it is not always that easy to organise the material in this way. If your research topic or question has a number of subdivisions or components, it might be difficult to write the review in this format. Also, this structure does not automatically make it easy to identify and compare and contrast the philosophies and methodologies underlying previous work.

A somewhat easier approach may be to structure the review into sections, such as:

♦ introduction;
♦ key questions or issues addressed;
♦ dominant philosophies and approaches;
♦ main themes and methodologies, gaps, omissions and controversies;
♦ summary (the current state of play).

Alternatively, you may wish to use more of a 'content' basis to structure the review. By this I mean using major subdivisions within the field. These may be few or more prevalent depending on the nature of the research question(s) and the literature base. For example, in my research on critical success factors (CSFs) in hospitality businesses, the literature could be divided into two main categories – that relating to CSFs in other organisational contexts and that concerning CSFs in hospitality organisations. However, it could also be further subdivided into more specific categories within each of these two broad areas. In the case of the hospitality CSFs literature, it could be broken down into studies concerned with different types of hospitality business (such as hotels, restaurants, pubs and so on), or geographically (North America, Europe, Asia-Pacific), or by the business function forming the context of the study (information technology systems, food and beverage contracts and so on). The point here is that there are usually many ways to structure and organise a written review of the literature, some of which are appropriate for certain studies and not others.

In the previous section, we identified that, when evaluating the literature, some degree of forward thinking regarding how the writing of the review might be structured could prove to be useful for helping to structure the approach to the evaluation. However, it may also be the case that, in the absence of this, the way in which the evaluation evolves will tend to indicate an emerging structure for the written review, as patterns, themes, connections, relationships, controversies and so on become evident.

In terms of what style of writing is appropriate for the review, this is dealt with more extensively in Chapter 11. However, in common with the imperative to make the review critical and evaluative rather than merely descriptive, there is a need for a more discursive style to be used in the review. If the evaluation has identified commonalities and divergences, agreements and disagreements, patterns and themes in the literature, as it should have done, then these should be reflected in the way the review is written. In turn, this implies discussion rather than statement and a flowing text rather than one broken up into a lot of discrete blocks. The reader needs to be able to follow the story being told and you need to lead him or her through it to its conclusions. Think of this like an upside-down pyramid. As the story unfolds, from its broader beginnings to a much more specific and focused end, you should lead the reader from the background context at the beginning, through the main themes, processes and actors, to a clear identification of the most important elements at the end.

Again, although dealt with more fully in Chapter 11, it is worth mentioning here that there are certain academic writing conventions you need to follow when writing the review. As you will be referring extensively, either directly or indirectly, to the published work of other people, it is important to recognise and record this in the text by using, correctly, the referencing system recommended by your tutors. This will avoid any problems of you committing, intentionally or otherwise, plagiarism and suffering the penalties associated with this. It is also wise to remember that what you are writing about in the review is objective 'evidence'. It may be tempting sometimes to insert your own personal, subjective opinions, but this should be unnecessary if you have conducted the evaluation properly as they will be embodied in the evaluations that you have made.

## SUMMARY

» The 'literature' may be comprised of various types of published information, including printed media, such as books, journals, periodicals, magazines and newspapers; electronic media, such as e-journals and books, websites, DVDs, CDs, and other forms, such as video, film, audio recordings and so on.

» Different forms or types of literature may have greater or less credibility.

» A literature review enables you to demonstrate that you are aware of, and understand, the existing knowledge relating to your research topic or question. It also enables you to demonstrate that you have engaged with it by evaluating and reviewing it in a critical manner.

» It can help you to decide what type of study – new, replicative, comparative – may be appropriate and/or feasible in the light of what is known already from the literature.

» It also helps to form a bridge between what is already known and what you plan to add to this by carrying out your research. In this sense, within the context of a deductive study, it can help to inform your decisions regarding the formulation of the conceptual framework and hypotheses to be investigated in the empirical part of your research and the data collection and analysis methods, techniques and procedures that might be adopted.

» In an inductive study, it is used as a resource to assist the data analysis and interpretation.

## Further Reading

Bell, J. (1993) *Doing Your Research Project*, 2nd edition. Buckingham: Open University Press. Chapter 4.

Blaxter, L., Hughes, C. and Tight, M. (1996) *How to Research*. Buckingham: Open University Press. Chapter 4.

Clark, M., Riley, M., Wilkie, E. and Wood, R.C. (1998) *Researching and Writing Dissertations in Hospitality and Tourism*. London: International Thomson Business Press. Chapter 7.

Fink, A. (1999) *Conducting Literature Reviews: From paper to internet*. Thousand Oaks, CA: Sage.

Hussey, J. and Hussey, R. (1997) *Business Research: A practical guide for undergraduate and postgraduate students*. Basingstoke: Macmillan. Chapter 4.

Jankowicz, A.D. (1991) *Business Research Projects for Students.* London: Chapman & Hall. Chapter 8.

Johns, N. and Lee-Ross, D. (1998) *Research Methods in Service Industry Management.* London: Cassell: Chapter 3.

Orna, E. and Stevens, G. (1995) *Managing Information for Research.* Buckingham: Open University Press. Chapter 3.

Preece, R. (1994) *Starting Research: An introduction to academic research and dissertation writing.* London: Pinter. Chapter 4.

Saunders, M., Lewis, P. and Thornhill, A. (2003) *Research Methods for Business Students*, 3rd edition. Harlow: Pearson Education. Chapter 3.

Sekaran, U. (2000) *Research Methods for Business: A skill-building approach*, 3rd edition. New York: John Wiley. Chapter 4.

Sharp, J.A. and Howard, K. (1996) *The Management of a Student Research Project*, 2nd edition. Aldershot: Gower. Chapter 4.

Veal, A.J. (1997) *Research Methods for Leisure and Tourism: A practical guide*, 2nd edition. Harlow: Pearson Education. Chapter 5.

# Chapter

## Developing the Conceptual Framework

**KEY CONCEPTS AND ISSUES**

» *The conceptual framework.*
» *Constructs, concepts and variables.*
» *Correlation and causation.*
» *Hypotheses.*
» *Theories and models.*
» *Operationalisation.*
» *Measurement and scales.*
» *Validity and reliability.*

## 5.1 Introduction

In the previous chapter we explored the issue of 'what is already known' by considering what is involved in carrying out the literature review relating to a research topic. We saw that the output from the literature review constitutes the raw material for formulating the conceptual and methodological approach to the empirical aspect of the research we plan to conduct. In the same way, it also helps us to explain and justify why the design and implementation decisions we are about to make will be appropriate and valid – because they will be based on our objective review of the best evidence available. Therefore, we will be addressing two sets of issues in this chapter. First, the conceptual framework to adopt for a study, which will specify the main factors, or variables, involved in the issue(s) and question(s) to be researchd, how and why these are related or connected and what predictions (hypotheses) can be made and tested on the basis of this. Second, how to explain the methodology that will be used to achieve this.

## 5.2 **The Conceptual Framework**

To explore the issues associated with creating a conceptual framework will involve us in considering questions such as what is it, why is it necessary, where does it appear in a research study, what does it do and what does it have to do with concepts, constructs, variables and hypotheses? Taking each of these questions in turn, we will begin to explore the nature, purpose(s) and roles of the conceptual framework within the research process.

### 5.2.1 *What is it?*

The conceptual framework is sometimes referred to as a theoretical framework or a model. However, it is not necessarily the same as either of these, as you will see later. Essentially, the conceptual framework is a structure that seeks to identify and present, in a logical format, the key factors relating to the phenomena under investigation. Depending on the nature and purpose(s) of the research project, the conceptual framework may be correlational or causal in form. A correlational framework would be one designed to postulate or suggest possible connections between two or more factors. For example, it might be suggested that there will be a correlation between food hygiene standards and food hygiene qualifications or that cost-reduction programmes will be associated with different levels of profitability. Similarly, a more complex example might suggest that a range of different factors is associated with a particular phenomenon. Consumers' decisions to purchase a particular product or service could be connected to their income, job security, personal tastes, its accessibility, the extent to which it is perceived to be good value, the availability of competing products/services and so on.

On the other hand, a causal framework would be one designed to be more specific about the nature and direction of the suggested relationship(s). Here the conceptual framework is used to present a causal – cause–effect – linkage between factors. Using the examples above, we could change each of them into a causal statement by amending how they are stated. We might say that *if* more people obtain food hygiene qualifications, *then* food hygiene standards will rise or companies that implement cost-reduction programmes will experience higher levels of profitability. Note here that the words '*if*' and '*then*' are italicised in the above statement. The 'if ... then ...' form of expression is a standard way of expressing causal relationships because such a statement can be tested – that is, we can arrive at a conclusion that confirms the statement is either true or false. In other words, the hypothesis is either supported by the evidence (verified) or it is not (rejected).

## 5.2.2 *Why is it necessary?*

A research study without a conceptual framework would be like a body without a skeleton! The conceptual framework is necessary to provide a logical and coherent structure for any research study, whether it informs its design in a deductive approach or integrates its results in an inductive approach. In most, if not all, research work, there are two main aspects – a review of existing literature in the field and an empirical investigation. The conceptual framework is the essential link between these two aspects as it serves to establish a logical connection between the existing body of knowledge and the new knowledge your research is trying to generate. Thus, it creates continuity between what has gone before and what is to come.

## 5.2.3 *Where does it appear in a research study?*

This depends on the type of approach that is taken to designing and conducting the study. If an inductive approach is taken, where the empirical data are collected during the early stages of the study, the conceptual framework will not be developed until later in the process. In this case, the conceptual framework is a product, or outcome, of the analysis applied to the empirical data. Thus, it emerges from this analysis to assist you in establishing any logical links between the interpretation of reality and any existing literature in the field. On the other hand, if a deductive approach is adopted, then the conceptual framework performs a different role and is established much earlier in the process. Here, it is derived from the literature review undertaken during the early stages of the research project. It is this review that informs the nature of the conceptual framework to be used for the empirical part of the research investigation. Therefore, in this case, the conceptual framework is the synthesis of the critical review of the literature and, as such, identifies the key concepts, constructs and variables relevant to the study's empirical investigation.

## 5.2.4 *What does it do?*

As you will have gathered by now, the conceptual framework has a different role to play in inductive and deductive research. In the former, it is very much a 'product' of the empirical investigation, while, in the latter, it is an essential 'input' into the design of the empirical work. This means that its purpose in inductive and deductive research is different. In induction, its main role is to provide a logical and coherent framework to interpret the empirical data and develop a theoretical understanding of the phenomena being studied. In this sense, it is an 'integrative' mechanism, designed to surface and articulate the underlying concepts, dimensions and variables within the empirical data from which a theoretical explanation for the real world observations can be developed.

In deductive research, the conceptual framework is used in a more disaggregated manner to test the hypotheses it contains. Here, the framework is broken up into its constituent parts in order that the postulated linkages and relationships may be expressed as hypotheses that, in turn, are then tested in the empirical investigation. Therefore, in this approach, the framework is a major influence on how the the empirical work is designed and conducted – that is, the decisions made regarding the methods and processes to be used to collect and analyse the data.

## 5.2.5 *What does it have to do with concepts, constructs, variables and hypotheses?*

Concepts, constructs and variables are the building blocks for the conceptual framework. These effectively help to identify the key dimensions and elements relating to the phenomena being studied and facilitate their measurement. Given the potentially enormous number of individual items or factors that could be included in any conceptual framework, there is a need for these to be grouped or categorised into more manageable entities. Hence, concepts are collections of associated events, objects, conditions, situations and so on that are aggregated together in order to make life simpler. In this sense, they do not exist in the real world, but are abstractions created by people to simplify the complexities of the real world and, at least in theory, make understanding and communication easier. However, as you will see later, this is not always as straightforward as it might appear.

Constructs are often confused with concepts, but they are not synonymous. Constructs are more abstract than concepts and used to group related concepts together. Thus, constructs perform the same role in grouping related concepts together as concepts do in grouping more specific factors together. Therefore, the role of both constructs and concepts in developing the conceptual framework is essentially the same. They are mechanisms that help to structure the complexity of the individual elements relating to the phenomena in question. In short, they help to develop a logical and hierarchically ordered structure for the framework. For example, 'quality' is an abstract term, so, to define it, reference has to be made to specific, real factors. Quality itself, in common with many other abstract notions, may be a construct or a concept. We might refer to the concepts of product and process quality to capture the ideas of tangible and intangible aspects of the tourism or hospitality experience. In turn, we might combine these two as conceptual components of a broader construct, such as service quality, to refer to the totality of the experience a consumer has.

Variables are derived from constructs and concepts and tend to be more tangible, observable and specific. Grouping related items together into concepts or constructs may assist conceptual clarity and understanding, but it does not help to measure the effect, relationship or association between the specific elements in the framework. To do this, the constructs and concepts need to be converted, translated or operationalised into specific and tangible items that can be measured as directly and unambiguously as possible. This is the role of variables in the conceptual framework.

## 5.3 Constructs and Concepts

Constructs and concepts can be easily confused and used, incorrectly, as if they were the same thing. One way to distinguish between the two is to see a construct as something larger and more abstract than a concept or, alternatively, consider that constructs are made up of groups of concepts that are narrower in scope and less abstract in form. Another way of putting this would be to say that a construct is a broader, more abstract, generalisation than a concept. For example, if we took a very broad, generalised term such as 'customer satisfaction', we might imagine that there would possibly be quite a range of factors relating to, or potentially influencing, the degree of satisfaction a customer feels or experiences. Among them may be concepts such as the quality of the product or service they receive, the friendliness of the company's staff they interact with, whether they perceive the purchase to be good value for money or not, the extent to which the product or service met their needs and wants and so on. Similarly, as you probably know, the construct of 'personality' is comprised of personality types, which are concepts, such as introverts and extroverts.

So, a construct is something we 'construct' to represent a combination or collection of other things that can be used to communicate the meaning of this grouping. In this sense, it is a form of communication shorthand that enables us to communicate and share meanings in an economical manner. Although concepts are used in the same way, they are closer to the real world and less extensive in the range of things that they are used to represent. Hence, the very broad term 'personality' would be a construct and the somewhat more limited term 'extrovert' a concept.

Both constructs and concepts help us to simplify a complex world because we can group together related things or items to convey a quite complex idea more simply. In general life and conversation, this usually does not create problems and is a positive benefit, making communication easier and more economical. However, because the meaning of a construct or a concept depends on the nature and extent of the real, tangible things it represents or is associated with, the degree to which the meaning of the abstract term is shared depends on the extent to which different peoples' interpretations of what this means are the same. The extent to which constructs and concepts can be used as an aid for communication depends on the extent to which people share the same definitions of them.

In many general instances, this is not an issue because we learn the meanings of these from a young age as a natural process of our development and socialisation. However, where more specific language codes are used, such as the jargon associated with academic disciplines or particular industries or professions, there may be constructs and concepts that are not common in everyday language and communication. In addition, there may also be some that are commonly used in the latter, but, when used in the former, have different connotations or meanings within the more limited and specific context of their use. Therefore, there is invariably a need, within a research context, to make clear how the construct or concept is defined and what it is being used to represent – that is, what you mean when you use it.

To give you an example of this, I have conducted quite a lot of empirical research into critical success factors (CSFs) in hospitality businesses (see, for example, Brotherton, 2004a, 2004b) using questionnaires. However, because the meaning of the term CSFs is one that can be interpreted differently by different people, asking them a series of question about it is potentially problematic. To try and avoid this, the questionnaires contained a definition of what I meant by the term CSFs on the front page and the respondents were asked to read this before answering the questions that followed in an attempt to ensure, as far as was practicable, that they all had the same understanding of the term CSFs before responding to the questions about it.

As constructs and concepts are abstract inventions, they do not exist in the real world and cannot be directly seen or measured. Also, because they are collections of associated things, they are not unitary (single) elements, but combinations of, potentially, many elements. Therefore, to use them in the empirical part of a research project, you need to convert or translate them into more specific and concrete things. This is generally known as 'operationalising' the concepts or, sometimes, as writing the operational definition for the research and is a task we shall examine later in this chapter. Before we get there, however, we need to explore another aspect of the conceptual framework that is used to accomplish this translation. It is the specification of the variables associated with the concept(s) to be used in the framework.

## 5.4 **Variables**

There are four main types of variables that can be found or included in a conceptual framework:

- ◆ independent
- ◆ dependent
- ◆ intervening
- ◆ moderating.

Before we consider each of these, in terms of what they are and the function(s) they perform within a conceptual framework, read the discussion in Exhibit 5.1

as this may help you to develop a clearer understanding before encountering some of the jargon associated with them.

---

### Exhibit 5.1    *What are These Things Known as Variables?*

Bill is Assistant General Manager at the Eldorado theme park and has worked in the tourism industry for ten years, since gaining a Higher National Diploma qualification when he was younger. He is currently studying, on a part-time basis, for an MA in tourism management at the University of Rutland. Penny, the General Manager of Eldorado, has a BA and an MA in tourism management and is keen to help Bill fulfil his potential and gain the MA qualification.

During their regular weekly meeting, Penny has noticed that Bill has seemed less confident than usual and, at the end of the last meeting, asked him, 'Is there something wrong Bill? You seem to be distracted in some way. Is there anything I can do to help?'

Bill was a little embarrassed, but replied, 'Well, yes, there is something I'm worried about and you probably can help, but I have been too embarrassed to ask you because you might think I'm stupid for not understanding it.'

Penny laughed, 'Come on Bill, we've known each other long enough for you to know that won't be the case.'

'Okay,' said Bill, 'It's to do with my MA course. We have just started the Research Methods module and the tutor gave a lecture last week on conceptual frameworks and variables that went straight over my head. I'm a practical man, not some academic theorist, so when you get someone rambling on about independent, dependent, intervening and moderating variables and how important these are for doing research, not only does it scare me rigid but also I don't understand the jargon.'

'Ah, I see,' said Penny, 'Well, the good news is it's not as bad as you think and the bad news is that you are going to kick yourself when I explain it because you do know what these are but not in the terms that the academic used. Okay, you can look at me sceptically, but I'll prove it to you. Do you remember last year, when we had the problem of our marketing effort not delivering the extra numbers of visitors we wanted?' Bill nodded. 'And,' Penny continued, 'I asked you to investigate this for us to find out why?' Bill nodded again. 'How did you explain what was happening to me?' asked Penny.

Bill replied, 'Well, I said that, although the extra marketing spend and effort should have led to a higher number of visitors, the fact that our marketing messages tended to create some less than positive impressions of the park among potential visitors and our competitors launched their campaigns around the same time diluted the effect our messages might have had.'

'Exactly,' said Penny. 'Well, let's just think about what you've said for a moment. Getting more visitors was seen to be dependent on increasing the marketing spend and effort, but that relationship didn't materialise in the way we expected

*(Cont'd)*

it to because of the other factors you identified. So, let's translate that into "varia-blespeak". The marketing spend/effort we can change separately – independently – of the number of visitors we have. We can manipulate or control this, but we can't control its effects – that is, how many more or fewer visitors it generates, agreed?'

'Agreed', said Bill.

'So,' Penny continued, 'which is the independent variable and which is the dependent variable?'

'That's obvious,' Bill retorted.

'Because the number of visitors is, at least to some degree, dependent on or influenced by our marketing effort, that must be the dependent variable and the thing we can change independently of it is our marketing spend/effort, so that must be the independent variable.'

'Spot on, Bill,' Penny exclaimed.

'You see, I told you that you knew what they were and you do. Now let's address the others. You said that our competitors' marketing campaigns diluted or reduced the effect our marketing effort had on increasing visitor numbers. So, what type of variable is that?'

'I guess it was a moderating variable,' Bill replied nervously, 'because it wasn't something that happened as a direct consequence of our extra marketing effort, but had an impact from outside of the relationship between extra effort and visitor numbers.'

'Same again, Bill,' Penny said, 'you've got it in one.'

'Okay,' Bill said, now more confident, 'so the unintended, more negative per-ceptions our messages created must be the intervening variable in this scenario because they occurred as a result of us activating the campaign and intervened to alter the relationship we expected between the extra effort and higher visitor numbers.'

Penny smiled and said, 'Absolutely. So, do you need any more tuition on this?'

'No thanks,' Bill said. 'You were right, I did know it all along. I just got confused by the different terminology and jargon.'

'That's right,' Penny replied, then went on to say mischievously, 'so you created a conceptual framework that identified and included all the key variables, speci-fied the nature of the relationship between these, hypothesised what the nature and direction of the cause–effect mechanism was between the independent and dependent variables, identified other variables that acted to alter this prediction and stated how and why it would work.'

Bill laughed and said, 'Now, wait a minute, I'll be thinking of myself as some sort of genius soon!'

So, as Bill discovered in our little scenario, you probably know what these vari-ables are in a less systematic and jargonised, but more intuitive, real-life con-text. Think about your own experiences as a student. The category of degree you aim to achieve depends, at least in part, on how much time and effort you put into your studies. You would probably see this relationship as one where more time and effort should lead to a better class of degree. What you may also find is that one unexpected consequence of doing this is that you become happier and more confident in your knowledge and abilities and this, in turn, might help you to obtain an even higher class of degree than you predicted. However, on the other hand, your ability to put more time and effort into your studies might be constrained – moderated – by the need to undertake part-time work to help supplement your finances.

## 5.4.1 *The dependent and independent variables*

Does this sound familiar? I guess it will do, so let's put it into a more academic format by restating it in terms of the jargon associated with variables. The thing that depends on all the others is the level of degree you aim to achieve. Therefore, it is the dependent variable. It is the variable you are most interested in as all the others are things that are likely to influence this end. The amount of time and effort you put into your studies, we have suggested, will influence, if not determine, the level of degree you are likely to obtain and it is something that you can change or manipulate separately from the final outcome. So that is the independent variable – it can be changed on its own or independently of the others.

## 5.4.2 *The intervening variable*

The intervening variable is something that happens as a direct consequence of a change in the independent variable and has an effect on the expected relationship between it and the dependent variable. That effect might be known and expected before the empirical part of the research has begun or may not be until after the effect of changing the independent variable on the dependent variable is known. This effect may be to enhance or lessen that which the independent variable has on the dependent variable. In our case, the effect is positive, it is a beneficial consequence, side-effect or spin-off because the extra time and effort spent on study create more self-confidence and belief, which, in turn, generate a 'greater than expected' outcome – gaining a higher class degree.

## 5.4.3 *The moderating variable*

Similarly, a moderating variable is one that moderates the expected relationship between the independent and dependent variables. Once again, it might be positive or negative in nature. In our example, it is negative because having to work to earn money may mean your ability to spend more time and effort studying is limited in some way. In the same way that an intervening variable may or may not be evident before the investigation begins, in some situations the moderating variable may be identifiable from the beginning and in others it only becomes evident when the expected independent–dependent variable relationship does not materialise from the evidence and needs to be explained by identifying what is moderating or affecting it.

## 5.4.4 *Expressing relationships between variables*

There are various ways that we can express such suggested (postulated) relationships between the variables. A simple narrative statement, such as that shown in Exhibit 5.2, may be used. Alternatively, we might express it in diagrammatic form (see Figure 5.1). Another option would be to express it as a logical function. For example, we could state that, other things being equal or held constant, the class of degree (D) we expect to get would be a function of (f), or depend on, the amount of time (T) and effort (E) we are prepared to devote to this, giving us the equation $D = f(T,E)$.

---

### Exhibit 5.2    *Stating the Relationship Between Variables*

If I were to increase the amount of time and effort I spend on studying (independent variable), then I would expect to get a higher class of degree (dependent variable). In addition to this, as a consequence of me putting more effort into studying, I might obtain an even higher class of degree because I will be more self-confident (intervening variable), but this predicted relationship may be affected by the fact that I have to spend some time working to earn extra money (moderating variable).

---

To widen this type of formulation somewhat, we could adopt what Clark et al. (1998) refer to as a 'mapping sentence'. This seeks to combine the independent, dependent and what they refer to as the 'subject' variables. The latter are characteristics of the sample to be used in the research that are sometimes also referred to as categorical variables. These are characteristics of the sample – different views, behaviour, opinions and so on – that can act to change the expected relationship in some way. Using our degree example, we might express this as follows. A student (male or female) who (works part-time or does not work part-time) will obtain a higher class of degree if he or she (puts more time and effort into studying), but this relationship may be also affected by (he or she developing more self-confidence and belief as a consequence of studying more). So, for example, we could explore the influence of the categorical variable of gender to investigate if any relationship existed between the class of degree obtained by males and females. Similarly, we could compare the class of degree obtained by students who worked more or less and/or put more or less time and effort into studying.

Therefore, if we want to explain something, whether just a suggested association between two or more things or a predicted cause–effect relationship, we

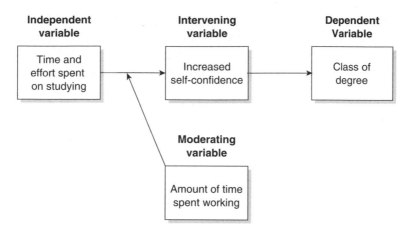

**Figure 5.1** Stating the relationship between variables

need to identify the variables involved in that relationship. However, it is not always possible to identify all the four main types of variables before the research is completed and the results of the empirical study are known. The two variables that are most problematic in this respect are the intervening and moderating variables. In some situations, it is possible to identify and specify one or both of these and include them in the study's conceptual framework before the empirical work commences. Where it is reasonable and logical to speculate about a set or chain of events that can be articulated before the relationship is tested, this can be done. For example, it is well known that when governments or businesses change things, such as public expenditure or taxation, marketing spending or product prices, time lags can affect the incidence and timing of the expected effect on the dependent variable(s) in question. In short, the effect(s) of the change do not occur instantaneously or even within a short period of time after they have been made.

In the tourism industry, currency fluctuations and tourism volumes travelling to alternative destinations are a good example of this time lag effect. As many people make their travel or holiday plans and book well in advance of the actual trip, the currency exchange rates in existence at the time of booking or prior to it are those most likely to influence decisions about country of destination when people are choosing between more and less expensive places. Even if currency fluctuations after booking mean that the destination chosen now becomes more expensive and others less so, it is highly unlikely that the customer will cancel the original booking and book the one that is now cheaper because there are financial penalties for this type of cancellation. Also, once the original decision has been made, there is invariably a great reluctance on the part of customers to change because they are also psychologically and emotionally committed to the decision.

However, there are many other situations where either possible intervening or moderating variables or both are not obvious at the outset. Such variables only become so when the results of the study are available and the expected relationship between the independent and dependent variables has not materialised or is somewhat different to that predicted. In such cases, the variables are identified as a consequence of the study and may be used to explain unexpected or unpredicted outcomes. An example of this is given in Exhibit 5.3. The extract in it indicates that the ability of licensed house managers to exert direct control over the factors influencing the success of their pubs' operations became evident after the data had been analysed and, further, suggested that, using this controllability variable, these factors could be classified as operational or strategic in nature.

---

### Exhibit 5.3  Identifying Moderating Variables via Data Analysis

A preliminary analysis of the phase 1 questionnaire results suggested that it might be possible to subdivide the critical success factor (CSF), critical skills and competencies (CSC) and critical performance measures (CPM) items into the categories of *People*, *Products* and *Processes*. However the factor analysis[*] conducted on the phase 2 results did not support such an ex ante contention as the factors generated by this procedure did not correspond with such a categorisation. The factor analysis results for the CSF items could be interpreted in two different ways. First, the CSFs placed into Factor Two – namely, Location, Size and Range of Products – may be seen to be concerned with the 'physical' nature of BASS Taverns' provision, with those placed into Factor One more concerned with the 'human' aspects. However, this is an interpretation we reject because we would expect such a categorisation might reasonably place CSF 1 (Quality of the Tavern's Premises) in the 'physical' rather than the 'human' category. Thus a more robust way of interpreting these results may be to regard the CSFs placed in Factor Two to be those largely outside of the individual Licensed House Managers' (LHMs) control and hence more *strategic* in nature, whereas those in Factor One are subject to local control and are more *operational* in character.

*Source*: © Brotherton and Watson, Shared Priorities and the Management Development Process: A Case Study of Bass Taverns, Tourism and Hospitality Research, 2000, *The Surrey Quarterley Review*. Reproduced with permission of Palgrave Macmillan.

[*]*Factor analysis* is generally known as a 'data reduction' technique and is explained further in Chapter 9. It is a statistical technique used to explore the extent to which the data can be grouped together into separate categories (or factors) to represent different dimensions of the concept(s) being investigated.

The two variables, or sets of variables in some cases, that must be identified before a deductive study can be conducted are the independent and dependent variables. Without these it would be impossible to test the theory and associated hypotheses. Of course, in the case of an inductive study, these would be identified as a consequence or product of the data analysis. As we have seen already, the dependent variable is the main subject of the study – it is the thing that we are most interested in or the outcome we are trying to explain. It, in turn, is a product, outcome or effect of something else and, therefore, to explain it, we have to identify what causes it and why. A good analogy here is that of a doctor diagnosing a patient's illness or condition. If you go to the doctor with some symptoms, you would expect the doctor to tell you what the reasons are for these and prescribe some treatment to cure them. To do this, the doctor would need to know what things could cause the effects you can see or feel and why these could cause them. In short, for the doctor to provide an appropriate diagnosis of the problem and prescribe appropriate treatment, the possible cause(s) of the effect(s) must be known and the mechanism(s) or relationship(s) between them must also be known.

The number of possible relationships between variables is limited to three. Variables may be related in a positive, negative or inverse manner. Where a positive relationship exists, the two move in the same positive direction, and vice versa for a negative relationship. For example, the more people are willing to eat out in a particular location, the greater the number and/or sizes of restaurants that will be opened – that is, the increase in the size of the market stimulates existing businesses to expand and new ones to open, and vice versa where fewer people eat out.

Where an inverse relationship exists, the variables move in opposite directions. For example, the more restaurants put up their prices, the fewer people will want or be able to afford to eat in them, and vice-versa.

## 5.5 Theories and Models

According to Cooper and Schindler (1998: 47) a theory 'is a set of systematically interrelated concepts, definitions, and propositions that are advanced to explain and predict phenomena (facts)'. In short, it helps us to understand, explain and predict what has happened, what is happening and what will happen. Furthermore, if we can understand, explain and predict, we may also be able to control what does happen. In this way, theories help us to interpret the real world and guide our thinking and actions. We all use theories in our everyday lives, although very often we do this implicitly or even unconsciously as they are embedded, whether we realise it or not, in the way we think and act. They are the generalisations we make about the things we observe or experience and how they are connected or related in order to understand, make decisions and predictions.

There can be a tendency to see theory and fact as opposing forces, but this view does not recognise the interdependency of the two. For a theory to be useful, it must be able to explain and predict. The better it can do that, the more practical value it has. In the same way, to be effective in a practical situation requires an understanding of how the underlying forces operate – that is, we need to have a theoretical understanding of them and their relationships. Where a theory does not adequately explain and provide a sound basis for action in a real world situation or environment, it does not mean that a theoretical understanding is worthless, just that a better theory needs to be developed.

As our understanding of the world around us progresses, new theories replace older, less useful, ones or existing theories are revised and improved to fit the real world better – often by making them more universal or general rather than being limited to particular time periods or contexts. Indeed, the most useful theories are those that are not limited to the existence of specific conditions. These are often known as general theories or sometimes universal laws because they are equally valid and applicable across time and space. Those having a more limited applicability tend to be referred to as context- or condition-specific theories because their value is limited to certain contexts or the existence of certain conditions.

Models or theoretical models are sometimes confused with theories. Although they are related, they are not the same thing. While the role of theory is explanation, the role of models is to represent the logic of the explanation. Such representation of theories may be descriptive, explanatory or designed to simulate the processes the theory is about. In other words, the model may be relatively simple, revealing the structural relationships between its components, or slightly more developed, in that the nature of these structural relationships is explained, or more complex still, with the processes associated with the relationships being simulated.

## 5.6 Hypotheses

As we have seen so far in this chapter, theories, models and conceptual frameworks help to link together the constructs, concepts and variables associated with the issue(s) we are seeking to address in our research. What a hypothesis does is state what the logical implication(s) of the theory and so on are if the theory is correct or valid. In other words, a hypothesis expresses a prediction of what we would expect to find if the theory proves to be sound. Given that 'good' theories are not only able to explain why things occur but also predict outcomes, we need a mechanism that allows us to test whether or not the theoretical explanations and predictions can be supported by evidence from the real world.

This mechanism often takes the form of a hypothesis or series of hypotheses. We could view a hypothesis as a type of 'educated guess' about a problem's solution. We know the theory and what this suggests or implies should be the case, but we need a link to be able to test it to see if it is true. Alternatively, we might see this as us having suggested or asserted that there will be certain relationships between the concepts in our conceptual framework and/or theoretical model, but which we cannot confirm at this point in time because these assertions have not yet been tested. Either way, the common denominator here is the idea of being able to test the guess or assertion. Therefore, we need a statement that can be tested and that is the role of the hypothesis.

Depending on the extent to which the theory we are dealing with has been developed previously and/or our ability to be more or less specific in wording the hypothesis, we may be looking to test an association, connection or a more definite cause–effect relationship. Hence, our hypothesis might be tentative or prescriptive in how it is written. Similarly, we may or may not know or be able to logically speculate about the direction of the relationship between the two or more variables in our hypothesis. All of this means that we can have hypotheses that are either correlational or causal in nature and correlational hypotheses may be directional or non-directional in form.

By definition, a causal hypothesis will be directional as we are specifying and testing a cause–effect relationship. A correlational hypothesis is one suggesting or postulating a connection or association of some kind between at least two variables. For example, the theory may suggest that there is some relationship between the amount of money paid to employees and the volume of effort they are prepared to put in to their work. If this was to be specified in a non-directional form, then we would simply hypothesise that the two are connected in some way – that is, we would use the wording of the previous sentence. On the other hand, if we could be more specific about this, we might be able to specify it in a directional form, such as, in companies where employees are paid more, the volume of work they produce seems to be higher. Here we are suggesting a directional relationship in the way the hypothesis is written – that is, where there is higher pay, employees seem to work harder, but this is still only an association, in the sense that the two seem to appear together and our guess or hypothesis suggests that one might come before the other.

However, to turn this into a causal hypothesis, we would have to state it in more definite terms. For example, if employees are paid more, then this will increase the volume of work they do. The key words here are 'if' and 'then' or, put another way, given the existence of one thing, the other will occur or happen. Here we are specifying that a change in the causal, independent variable(s) will definitely create the effect in the form of the dependent variable. In other words, that the effect will follow the cause. For us to be able to specify this type of hypothesis, we need to consider whether or not we can meet what are called the three conditions for causality. This may sound complicated, but it is really quite logical and simple. The first condition is that what is regarded as the cause must happen before the effect, otherwise it could not be regarded as a potential cause. This is known as the 'temporal' or time condition. The second is that there are not any other possible cause(s) of the effect. If there are other variables that can cause the same effect, either in conjunction with the one we are specifying or independent of it, then the cause–effect relationship specified in our hypothesis would only be, at best, partially true and, at worst, false or erroneous. This is known as the elimination of alternative causes condition. The third is that the condition of covariation can be met. This simply means that both variables, or sets of variables, in the cause and effect categories vary together – that is, when prices change, there is always some change in consumer demand for the product or service.

So, we might hypothesise that having a 'happy hour' in a bar, when drink prices are lowered, will lead to either more customers visiting the bar and/or existing customers buying more drinks during this period than they would otherwise. This would clearly satisfy the temporal condition – prices are lowered before the rise in demand occurs – and the covariation condition – both prices and demand change or covary.

The only problem we might encounter here is that it may be difficult to eliminate other possible causes of the rise in demand beyond that of the reduction in drink prices. In other words, would the rise in demand have happened anyway or for some other reason if we had not changed the drink prices? This is possible. To test for this, we could operate the happy hour for a period of time and then stop it to see what effect these changes have on demand. If demand drops back to the level, or very near to it, that existed before we started the happy hour, then this may give us some evidence to strengthen the belief in the cause–effect relationship between drink prices and quantity purchased.

Finally, both correlational and causal hypotheses can be stated in negative or positive terms. The literature in general refers to these as the 'null' and 'alternate' forms of the same hypothesis. This means that one of the two ways of stating the hypothesis will be confirmed by the research data. The null form would state that the independent variable (cause) does not have a relationship with or effect on the dependent variable (effect). The alternate form states the reverse – that is, the independent variable does have a relationship with or effect on the dependent variable. These are the only two possible outcomes for a hypothesis – either the two sets of variables are related in some way or they are not. Therefore, if the results of the research confirm the truthfulness or validity of one of these and suggest it should be accepted on the basis of this evidence, then the other must automatically be rejected. Either form can be used, as they are the reverse of each other, but it is common for the null form to be used in many research studies because the sceptical proposition that there is no connection or causal relationship between the variables is one favoured by the scientific method.

## 5.7 Operationalisation

In compiling our conceptual framework, we have brought together theoretical insights, relationships and predictions, identified the key constructs, concepts and variables required to formulate the framework and considered the hypotheses derived as a logical consequence of the framework, which will be tested in the empirical part of the research. We also referred earlier to the need for abstract and intangible constructs and concepts to be converted or translated into something more concrete and tangible to help us collect empirical data in order to measure it. This is known as operationalising the concepts or, alternatively, as creating an operational definition or series of definitions of the concept(s). Whatever form an operational definition takes, the basic purpose is the same: to establish explicit and unambiguous meaning and assist in the empirical measurement of the concept(s) concerned.

One way to think about this is to consider what you would need to do to 'operationalise' (put into practice) an idea or concept someone expresses to you. The idea or concept is likely to be fairly general and lack details. It is rather like a skeleton without flesh. To put the idea or concept into practice, therefore, you would have to translate the principle into practical terms. For example, the concept underlying the TGI Fridays' restaurant experience may be expressed as something like 'the provision of casual, informal dining that entertains and provides good value for money'. Sounds like a great idea, but what are the implications of this in terms of the type of restaurant, colour schemes, decor, service style, menu items, presentation of the menu, the type of staff needed, type of server–customer interaction and so on? All of these aspects would have to be considered in order to develop an operational plan to deliver the concept, because they would all need to work together to deliver an experience consistent with the concept.

Similarly, think about the concept of budget or low-cost travel or hotels compared to those of a full-service airline or hotel operation. The end products are different because the concepts underlying the operations differ. The two forms of hotel or travel provision are designed to deliver different types of customer experiences.

While this is quite easy to see and understand where the concepts are very different, it can be less clear where the concepts are similar. Indeed, even when dealing with the same concept, different people may interpret what this means in operational terms in differing ways. So, one company's view of the type and style of provision that should reflect the idea of a budget airline or hotel brand may differ from another's.

This all means that it cannot be assumed everyone will translate or operationalise a concept in the same way that you do. The meanings associated with a concept cannot be assumed to be constant and consistent for different people, organisations or cultures. In short, *you* may know what you mean when you use or refer to a particular concept, but how can you be sure that other people will interpret this in the same way? One way to solve this problem is to make your definition explicit rather than implicit – that is, to provide an operational definition.

We saw earlier in this chapter that abstract concepts are collections or combinations of things associated with a concept and the sum of their components.

To operationalise them, we need to subdivide them, breaking them down into their constituent components. Because they are comprised of related categories or groups of components, this allows us to identify the major 'subheadings' included under any conceptual heading. These are commonly known as the main 'dimensions' of the concept. For example, if we take the concept of consumer demand, we can say that all the factors likely to influence this could be placed into the two main dimensions of price and non-price factors. The former is self-explanatory, but the latter could include such things as peoples' income level, their tastes, fashions, the prices of complementary and/or competing or substitute goods, marketing and promotional messages and so on.

Figure 5.2 illustrates how the concept of 'quality' can be divided into two main dimensions of 'product quality' and 'service quality'. It would be logical to assume that any assessment or judgement of the overall quality of, say, a restaurant meal experience would be influenced by the quality of both the physical and service aspects of the experience. However, the terms product and service quality are still abstract and, potentially, variable in terms of how people perceive and give meaning to them, so any attempt to use them to collect data, by asking people to rate the quality of the restaurant product and/or experience, may be flawed. Therefore, we need something else that is potentially less ambiguous and easier for people to respond to. These are known as 'indicators' or 'elements' of the dimension. They are specific, tangible occurrences or attributes of the dimension and it is these that we use to formulate the question we put to people. So, as Figure 5.2 shows, if we want to collect data from restaurant customers to obtain their judgements on the quality of the food product they have received, we need to ask them questions about the taste of the food, its freshness, the portion size, its presentation and so on. These are much more specific and concrete things for people to consider and respond to than simply 'product quality' and so are far less likely to generate widely differing interpretations of what they mean or refer to on the part of the people answering questions.

To put this another way, if I asked you to give me your opinion or judgement of the quality of the food product you had received in a restaurant, I'm sure that you would be able to give a response or answer to this question, but how would you be able to do so? You would probably think about some or all of the specific considerations mentioned above or perhaps even add others as you formulated your judgement. Although you could give me an answer, the problem for me would be that I would not know what you used as a basis for it and whether or not this was the same as that of the other people who had answered the question.

In these circumstances I would not know, and could not claim, that all the answers had been consistent and given using the same definition of the term. This would mean that there would be some, perhaps considerable, doubt over the reliability of this data as a whole. The point here is the one made earlier,

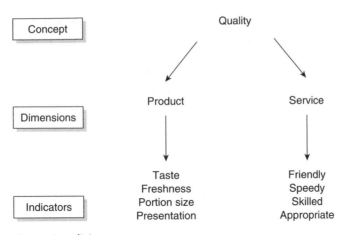

**Figure 5.2**   Operationalising a concept

that, if the definition is made as explicit and tangible or concrete as possible, then the likelihood of different people interpreting this in different ways will be reduced. In turn, this should make the whole set of answers as reliable as possible.

Before we consider the major types of empirical research designs that can be used to plan and organise the collection of the empirical data in Chapter 6, we need to explore the issues associated with developing valid and reliable measures because it is important to realise that the quality of the data to be collected using any of these designs will, in large part, depend on the quality of the preparation for doing this and an important part of that preparation relates to the issues explored in this chapter. If the conceptual thinking and planning – in the form of identifying the underlying theory, the associated concepts and variables, how these are connected, what predictions can be made and what is required to operationalise them – are not give adequate consideration, then what follows – the empirical part of the project – will be more difficult and probably less valuable than it could have been. In other words, if the foundation for the empirical research is not constructed well, then everything built on top of this may be less than robust.

## 5.8 Measurement and Scales

Once the variables relating to the constructs and concepts to be explored in the empirical part of the research have been identified and operationalised, the next task to be faced is the development of valid and reliable ways to measure them. This necessitates a consideration of the type of measurement scale that might be most appropriate for collecting the data and measuring the variables in the desired manner. However, before we consider the main types or levels of measurement scales, there are two conditions that should be met by any type of scale.

The first of these is known as the condition of 'collective exhaustion'. This means that the content of the range or scope of the scale should be sufficient to collectively exhaust any other possible responses. In everyday language this means that it covers all the possible answers. This may sound complicated, but it is really quite straightforward. For example, a scale containing response options for only three-, four- and five-star hotels would not be collectively exhaustive unless the sample was restricted to these three categories of hotel as there are other types of hotels, such as those with two or no stars or using grading criteria or symbols other than the star rating system. Similarly, a scale relating to the age of the respondents that only had the categories 18–30, 31–40 and 41–50 would not be collectively exhaustive as there could be respondents younger than 18 or older than 50.

In some cases, as we will see later in this section, where the range of potential variation in the variable is very large, a more open-ended way of collecting the data may be used to avoid having to have a huge range of possible response categories to cover all the possible options. Where this is not the case, the age categories problem above could be solved by adding two other catch-all categories to each end of the range – under 18 and over 50. In the hotel star-rating case, we could solve the problem by adding a category of 'other (please specify)'.

The second condition is known as mutual exclusivity. Again, this is simpler than it may sound. It means that the categories used in the scale should not overlap. The importance of this is that a person responding to the question cannot then give the same response to more than one of the items in the scale. For example, if a question asked, 'How many times have you flown on a budget airline in the past six months?' and gave the options of none, 1–5, 5–10, 10–15 and more than 15, there would be a potential problem. Because the 1–5 category overlaps with the 5–10 and the 5–10 category overlaps with the 10–15, if there were people who had flown five or ten times, then they could indicate this in two different categories, but we would not know how many people who had flown five times had ticked the 1–5 or 5–10 boxes or, indeed, how many who had flown ten times had indicated this by ticking the 5–10 or 10–15 boxes.

Once again, there is a simple way to avoid this problem – make sure that the response options or categories are separated. So, in our example simply changing the categories to 1–5, 6–10, 11–15 would make them mutually exclusive. Then, people who had flown five or ten times could only record this in one of the categories, so the problem has been eliminated.

It is generally accepted that there are four basic types and/or levels of measurement scale:

- nominal
- ordinal
- interval
- ratio.

## 5.8.1 *The nominal scale*

This scale is used to name, group or classify either respondents' characteristics or substantive answers into different groups or categories. In the jargon, it places the values of the attributes into separate groups or categories and, because of this, is sometimes known as the basis for measuring 'categorical' variables. This means that the values used to measure the variable will be contained in a range of mutually exclusive and collectively exhaustive categories used in the scale.

This is a relatively simple type of measurement scale because all we can deduce from it is that the members of a particular group or category share at least one thing in common. For example, they are all male or female, single or married, burger or pizza restaurants, museums or theme parks. If the question relates to a more substantive aspect, it would mean that they buy or don't buy the product, have travelled on a budget airline between one and five or six and ten occasions in the last six months, have visited the tourism destination before or have not.

Despite its simplicity, questions using the nominal scale can generate useful information on the characteristics of the respondents included in the sample that will allow you to describe the composition of the sample – a feature that we shall see is important in Chapter 8 when we consider sampling issues. This information can also be used to explore possible differences between categories of respondents when the data are analysed. We shall consider this in more detail in Chapter 9, but, to give you an idea of how useful it might be, we could combine our age categories with those relating to how frequently people fly with an airline to establish whether or not there is any connection or relationship between peoples' ages and the numbers of flights they go on. If we found that people between 18 and 30 were far more likely to fly than those younger or older, we might then choose to target marketing campaigns at this age group. That said, the type of data provided by the nominal scale is limited in terms of the extent that we can manipulate or analyse it using statistical techniques. In itself, nominal data are only amenable to calculating either the frequency (the total) and/or the percentage of the responses in each category, but they can still be used to explore possible associations between variables. This, again, is something that we will return to in Chapter 9.

## 5.8.2 *The ordinal scale*

The second type or level of measurement is the ordinal scale. This is used to place the attributes of the variable into some form of order – from highest to lowest, more to less, top to bottom, best to worst and so on. For example, you might use this type of scale to ask questions about peoples' perceptions, their experiences, behaviour or intentions or to elicit a judgement about a product or service. It could also be used to ask companies how they rate themselves and their competitors on a range of factors, such as service quality, price, brand recognition, standardisation or customisation of service delivery, accessibility of unit locations and so on.

This type of information can be valuable, but there is an underlying issue with ordinal data. The distances between the orders or levels in the scale tend to be viewed as being equal, but this assumption cannot be substantiated. Intuitively, you might be tempted to think that the gap between 1 and 2 and 2 and 3 in an ordinal scale represents the same amount of difference, but this may not be the case. For example, if you asked someone who had visited a range of tourism destinations to rate or rank these destinations from best to worst, the basis on which they would make these judgements would not be known to you. They might decide in their own minds that the destination ranked as the best, or number 1, was far and away the best compared to that recorded as number 2, but that the one recorded as number 3 was only very slightly less desirable than number 2.

## 5.8.3 *The interval scale*

The third type of measurement scale is the interval scale. This is widely used in both academic research and life in general and you will probably be quite familiar with it, even though you may not realise it is called an interval scale. This scale has a standard interval between the range of points in the scale and the interval usually has a value of one. In addition, the nature of each point in the scale is defined and this allows the magnitude of the difference between each point to be measured. If this sounds complicated, don't worry, it is not, as you will see.

You are likely to be familiar with what are often referred to as three-, five-, seven- or nine-point scales that range from, say, terrible to excellent, from totally disagree to totally agree or never to always. Regardless of the specific form the scale takes, the principle is the same – it provides a range of possible 'defined' responses or response options to a question or statement from totally negative at one end to totally positive at the other. The important word here is 'defined' because this enables you to know the nature of the opinion or judgement that has been made relating to the number it corresponds to in the scale. This is something we noted above will not be known in the case of an ordinal scale because the intervals are not defined for the respondent who is putting things into a rank order between say one and five or one and ten.

The agree/disagree type of interval scale is commonly known as a 'Likert' scale and defines the points, in a five-point scale, as follows – totally disagree, disagree, neither agree or disagree, agree, totally agree. This form requires people to respond to a statement because it asks them to indicate the extent to which they agree or disagree with it. Where you want to ask a question, rather than provide a statement, and ask to what extent the respondent believes something is important or not important, then the points would take something like the following form – not at all, not very, fairly, very, totally.

Although the wording of the response options differs in these two examples, they both provide a balanced range of points for the person to express their agreement or disagreement with the statement or opinion of the importance or unimportance of the factor. They do this because they have an equal number of negative and positive options and one in the middle that is neutral. This allows the person to express either a totally or strongly negative or positive opinion or one that is indifferent or neutral. To obtain greater detail in the positive or negative responses – known as more precision – the scale would be extended to a seven-, nine- or even greater, point scale because this would allow more negative or positive options to be included.

## 5.8.4 *The ratio scale*

The ratio scale is a more open-ended scale. It normally has a zero starting point and, at least theoretically, could extend to infinity. As it is open-ended, it does not contain categories, groups, ranks or points in the same way that the scales we have looked at above do, so it collects what is often referred to as ungrouped, unclassified or raw data. This invariably means that ratio data have to be grouped or organised after they have been collected whereas the other scales group the data as they are being collected. This is not necessarily a detrimental feature because it provides more flexibility to group the data in different ways after collection, but it is often easier, where feasible, to build this organisation of the data into the scales used to collect them.

The ratio scale is generally used where the variable is known or expected to vary continuously across a range and frequently where the full range of variation is not known or could be quite extensive, as discussed above. For example, asking nominal scale questions about how many part-time and full-time staff are employed in the companies a questionnaire is sent to could be problematic if they range from small to very large because the range of categories that would need to be provided would be large. In these circumstances, it would be more economical to use a ratio scale to obtain the exact numbers and group these data afterwards.

## 5.8.5 *Selecting an appropriate scale*

So, the scales each have their advantages and uses and which one you choose use is a matter of judgement and relates to the type of data you need to collect. However, there are certain issues that should be borne in mind when making this choice. First, it is generally not a good idea to select a scale that is more involved than the one that will collect the data you need as this tends to make the writing of questions and input of data for analysis more time-consuming.

Second, however, as we will see in Chapter 9, the use of certain types of statistical analysis techniques require you to have collected certain types of data. This means that you need to do a little forward thinking and consider what you intend to do at the data analysis stage, letting this inform your choice of measurement scale(s) for collecting the necessary data.

Finally, the two considerations above give rise to a tension between the use of simpler and more complex scales because the first suggests that you adopt a more economical approach, while the second suggests that you use the more statistically powerful scales to open up more data analysis options later in the process. The balance to be struck between these two is one that needs some thought. My comment on this would be that it is always possible to do less, in analysis terms, with richer data, but you cannot do more with the more basic kind of data. Therefore, it may be advisable to aim higher rather than lower when thinking about which scale to use, especially in the case of substantive questions.

## 5.9 Establishing Good Measures

Whichever scale or scales are used in developing an instrument to measure the variables, the measures used should be as good as possible. This means that they should be as accurate or valid, as precise and as reliable as you can make them.

Accuracy or validity is concerned with the extent to which the measure(s) conform with, or actually measure, the truth. This means that they should be able to provide data that measures what it is supposed to measure and gives an accurate reflection of reality.

Precision is concerned with the amount of detail to be included in the measure. A measure that is very precise will be able to provide very fine detail – that is, one that is able to measure in millimetres would be more precise than one only able to measure in centimetres. Alternatively, a nine-point interval scale would provide more precision than a three-point scale.

Reliability refers to the consistency of the measure when it is used over time or in different contexts. If a measure is highly reliable, then it can be used across a wide range of contexts and time periods because it will produce 'stable' measurements. However, a reliable measure may not necessarily be an accurate or valid one. It is quite possible for consistent measures to be obtained but for them to be consistently inaccurate or invalid. Similarly, a measure may be valid, but not reliable as it may measure accurately but is not able to achieve this consistently across different contexts or time periods. Therefore, you should not see validity and reliability as being the same thing.

The key questions here are how do you know if your measure is valid and reliable and how do you choose the level of detail or precision? There are certain issues you can consider regarding these aspects when designing the measure before it is used and there are others used to test the validity and/or reliability of the measure after the data have been collected. In terms of validity, the basic principle is to try and ensure that the measure actually measures what it is designed to measure. To do this, it must be logically consistent with the operational definition of the variable(s) and cover all the aspects of the concept(s) you wish to measure.

## 5.9.1 *Determining validity*

To demonstrate that a measure is valid, there are different tests of validity that you can use, ranging from the more subjective to more objective, evidence-based confirmations. The simplest, and weakest, argument to use to convince others that a measure is valid is known as 'face validity'. This is similar to the idea of accepting something at face value – it looks or seems to be okay. However, this is a subjective judgement and so others may not see things in the same way. Also, it means any claim that the measure is valid cannot be supported by any kind of objective evidence or testing.

'Content validity' addresses the issues referred to above of logical consistency and coverage. In other words, to claim that a measure has content validity, you would need to demonstrate, perhaps by logical argument, that the measure consistently and completely represents the concept being measured and covers the full range of meanings of the concept.

'Construct validity' depends on the quality of the operational definition used in the research design – that is, how adequate (in terms of coverage) and appropriate (in terms of value) it is. This can be established by means of convergence – a process known as 'convergent validity'. This may involve comparing the results obtained from your measure with those previously obtained from another, established, measure for the same construct(s). If the two sets of results are the same or sufficiently convergent, then this would provide evidence for your measure having the property for convergent validity.

Another way of trying to establish the construct validity of a measure could be to claim 'discriminant validity'. This refers to the extent that it is possible to separate or discriminate between the concept you are measuring and others in the theory it relates to. If this can be done, then it indicates that the measure is measuring the target concept and not any others. In other words, the measure is not confusing the measurement of the concept by including items that measure aspects of other concepts – it is only measuring what it is intended to measure and nothing else. This might be claimed via logical argument prior to the collection of the data and/or after the data have been collected by using an appropriate statistical test. For example, a test known as factor analysis (see Chapter 9) could be used to do this.

In circumstances where the measure is seeking to use a criterion to differentiate between groups that are known to be different or predict something that, it is hypothesised, it should be able to predict, 'criterion-related validity' might be used. There are two types of criterion-related validity corresponding to these two situations. First, 'concurrent validity' would be used to validate a measure designed to differentiate between groups that are known to be different. This may involve the use of another independent measure, for which data already exist, to compare the results from your measure with those from the other to ascertain whether they correlate sufficiently or not.

Second, 'predictive validity' would be used to claim that your measure is valid in being able to predict the effect of the criterion in the future – that is, the criterion is measured after a passage of time.

## 5.9.2 *Determining reliability*

The reliability of a measure can be claimed in two main ways before the measure is used. First, by adopting a previously used and proven measure. If previous research has been undertaken and the researcher(s) concerned has been able to prove the reliability of the measure(s) they have used, then your measure can be claimed to be reliable on the basis that evidence already exists to indicate that the measure is reliable and yours is the same.

Second, you can go through a process of testing or trialling your measure before you actually use it to collect data for the project. This essentially means repeating the use of the measure in a series of tests or trials to establish whether or not it behaves in a consistent manner.

However, whether you are fortunate enough to find an existing measure you can use or have the time to engage in testing or trialling your newly devised measure, you can only really confirm the reliability of the measure used in your specific research context after it has been used.

There are various procedures and tests that can be implemented to determine how reliable your measure has been. If it has been used to collect qualitative data and designed to help you make judgements based on observations of, say, audiovisual material, text or pictures, there is an obvious danger of subjective bias if you are the only person making the judgements, because only one person is interpreting the data by applying the measure. Other people analysing the same data with the same measure may come to differing conclusions. This is known as the 'equivalence' problem and one way to address this would be to use what is know as 'inter-rater reliability' testing. This simply means using more than one person, independently, to apply the measure and produce the results or make the ratings. If the results obtained from two or more independent raters are the same, then the measure would be regarded as reliable, the opposite being the case if the reverse were true.

To establish the stability aspect of a measure's reliability requires that the measure be repeated over time. This is commonly known as the 'test, retest' method. It is similar to the pre-usage testing or trialling process referred to above, but here it is conducted within the context of the research project itself rather than as a preoperational trial. This method is commonly used in laboratory experiment contexts, but may be more difficult to employ in other circumstances. For example, to repeat a postal questionnaire survey may be very time-consuming and expensive and there would be no guarantee that the same people would respond a second time.

One widely used technique for establishing the internal consistency of multi-item measures (those using a number of items relating to each concept for the subject to respond to) is called 'split-half' reliability. This is used for quantitative data and seeks to establish the extent to which the pattern of responses to a given set of items correlates – that is, the greater the degree of correlation there is between the items in the set, the greater the internal consistency, or reliability, of that set of items. We shall explore this further in Chapter 9, but note here that the most widely used test to establish this is known as Cronbach's Alpha Coefficient. Given that a perfect correlation between two or more items would have a value of 1.0 and items not correlated at all would have a value of 0, it is not hard to see that the closer the value is to 1, the closer, or better, the correlation is and, hence, the greater is the internal consistency of the items.

## SUMMARY

» Developing a conceptual framework helps to synthesise the literature review and inform the empirical research design to effectively link the conceptual and empirical aspects of the research project.

» The conceptual framework may be correlational or causal. In the deductive approach, it precedes the empirical work, but, in the inductive approach, it is an outcome of the research process.

» The conceptual framework brings together in a logical manner the constructs and concepts that the research is concerned with and enables key variables to be specified.

» The four main types of variable are the independent, dependent, intervening and moderating variables.

» Hypotheses are derived from the conceptual framework. They can be correlational or causal in nature and expressed in positive (alternative) or negative (null) formats to suggest that a relationship exists or does not.

» To measure the constructs, concepts and variables in the conceptual framework, they have to be translated or operationalised from abstract – intangible – to concrete – tangible – indicators.

» Any measures based on the four basic types of measurement scale – nominal, ordinal, interval and ratio – should be as accurate or valid and precise or reliable as possible.

## Further Reading

Babbie, E. (1992) *The Practice of Social Research*, 6th edition. Belmont, CA: Wadsworth Chapter 7.

Buttle, F. (1999) 'Measurement', in B. Brotherton (ed.), *The Handbook of Contemporary Hospitality Management Research*. Chichester: John Wiley. Chapter 12.

Carmouche, R. and Kelly, N. (1995) *Behavioural Studies in Hospitality Management*. London: Chapman & Hall. Chapter 11.

Clark, M., Riley, M., Wilkie, E. and Wood, R.C. (1998) *Researching and Writing Dissertations in Hospitality and Tourism*. London: International Thomson Business Press. Chapter 5.

Cooper, D.R. and Schindler, P.S. (1998) *Business Research Methods*, 6th edition. Singapore: Irwin/McGraw-Hill. Chapter 2.

Davis, D. (1996) *Business Research for Decision Making*. Belmont, CA: Wadsworth. Chapter 6.

Finn, M., Elliot-White, M. and Walton, M. (2000) *Tourism and Leisure Research Methods: Data collection, analysis and interpretation*. Harlow: Pearson Education. Chapter 2.

Hussey, J. and Hussey, R. (1997) *Business Research: A practical guide for undergraduate and postgraduate students*. Basingstoke: Macmillan. Chapter 5.

Preece, R. (1994) *Starting Research: An introduction to academic research and dissertation writing*. London: Pinter. Chapters 2 and 3.

Sekaran, U. (2000) *Research Methods for Business: A skill-building approach*, 3rd edition. New York: John Wiley. Chapters 5 and 8.

Veal, A.J. (1997) *Research Methods for Leisure and Tourism: A practical guide*. Harlow: Pearson Education. Chapter 3.

# Chapter

## Choosing the Empirical Research Design

**KEY CONCEPTS AND ISSUES**

» *Choosing the most appropriate research design and being able to justify your choice – theoretical and practical considerations.*
» *Designs for quantitative and qualitative data.*
» *Issues of validity, reliability and credibility.*
» *Survey, experimental, observational, case study and comparative research designs.*
» *Control and artificiality versus freedom and naturalistic enquiry.*
» *Dealing with the potential for error.*
» *Implementation and process issues and choices.*

## 6.1 Introduction

In this chapter we will consider the main types of research design that are available for you to choose from to plan and organise the collection of the empirical data you need to answer your research questions or test the hypotheses you have previously established. None of the alternatives is perfect or equally applicable to all research questions and projects – they each have strengths and weaknesses. In making the decision as to which one to use for your purposes, there will be both logical, or methodological, and practical, or pragmatic, considerations to take into account and you will need to be able to explain and justify the choice that you make. This is important because the way you choose to collect your empirical data is a key indicator of how appropriate and robust your method has been. Put another way, if you were asked to judge whether someone's conclusions were sound or flawed, you would need to consider whether the method they had used to arrive at those conclusions was sound or not. Alternatively, if you wanted to build a house, you would want to have sound foundations to build it on, otherwise it might fall down! The same is true in research projects. If you want others to have confidence in the validity and reliability of your research findings, then you must convince them that the method you have used to generate those findings has been appropriate.

To illustrate this, consider the discussion in Exhibit 6.1 before you go any further.

---

### Exhibit 6.1   Which Empirical Research Design Option should we Choose?

The members of the senior management team of the Travel Delight tour operating company are having their weekly team meeting to discuss how to proceed with a possible major investment in new information and communications technology. John Deeside, the Managing Director of the company, is a very intelligent and experienced man who did not go to university when he was young. In his hand-picked team are Patrick Hampshire, the Finance Director, who has a PhD in physics; Shirley Rutland, the Human Resources Director, who has a MA in anthropology; Dominic Cornwall, the Marketing Director, who has a BA in business studies; Carla Sussex, the Operations Director, who has a BA in tourism management; Bill Somerset, the IT Director, who has a PhD in information systems; and Sophia Kent, the Public Relations and Communications Director, who has an MSc in psychology.

'Okay', said John, starting the meeting, 'this is a big project and one we can't afford to get wrong because it could either make or break the business. So, we all feel that updating our IT and communications system is a good idea, but we don't know if it will work in the way we expect or deliver the improvements we want. At this stage we are really guessing and hoping, but that's not good enough to commit $20 million to! I, and the Board, need some hard evidence before we can consider going ahead. That's where you guys come in. Let me hear your ideas and I'll see if I'm convinced.'

Patrick makes the first contribution: 'Well, if we really want to have some hard and credible evidence, we need to set up a controlled experiment to test our hypotheses and establish the cause–effect relationships and mechanisms.'

'Yes, I agree in principle,' Sophia chipped in, 'but we're not in a situation where we can set up a controlled laboratory experiment – it would be too expensive, time-consuming and difficult to implement and, anyway, it might also be too unrealistic in terms of the real context we're dealing with. So, what I would suggest is that we set up a programme of interviews with employee and customer groups to discuss and get their feedback on what we are planning. That would enable us to capture the perceptions and concerns of the key players and take these into account when designing and implementing the new system.'

'Possibly, but, on the other hand, what we could do,' Dominic suggested, 'is put together a questionnaire survey so that we could ask a representative sample of the employees and our customers what their views, concerns and priorities are in relation to this type of technology. That would give us data on, and an insight into, what the key issues might be.'

'Interesting, if different, views so far,' said Patrick. 'What do the rest of you think?'

Shirley ventured, 'One way to get a real insight into how people are going to react to changes in technology and the way things work would be to go into the situation(s) these are going to impact and observe how the employees and customers currently interact with how we are doing things now. This would give us an idea about how they perceive the current situation, how relationships work now and what are seen to be the norms.'

'That would be useful,' Carla added, 'but it wouldn't tell us how the employees and customers might react to the changes we are planning. So, what I would suggest – perhaps in addition to what Shirley has proposed – would be an approach that would enable us to get an understanding of the current situation, introduce changes in technology in one or two areas of the business and then evaluate the effects and impact of those with a view to rolling the technology out across the company later when we've learnt what the issues and problems might be.'

Finally, Bill got the chance to have his say: 'This sort of change is never easy, is it, but, so far, we seem to be concentrating on the users and interfaces. As important as these are, they really are secondary to the architectural and technical aspects of the system. If we don't get these aspects right, it won't work anyway. So, I suggest we concentrate on modelling and trialling the system in miniature to begin with to make sure that it's set up right and works well, then we can consider some of these other ideas.'

'Wow,' exclaimed Patrick, 'I knew this was not going to be easy, but you guys have really given me some things to mull over. What has come out of this is that we need to give this some considerable thought over the coming weeks before we make any decisions on how to proceed. Perhaps we could start by formulating and agreeing what our aims and objectives are for introducing the changes, as this will enable us to specify what information we need to achieve these and then that might give us a clue about what may be an appropriate way to gather the information we need to make a final decision.'

This discussion reveals a real, practical, managerial problem that needs some form of research-related activity to help the management team arrive at a considered, evidence-based decision. However, the route they could take to achieve this end may vary according to the ideas put forward because there are different approaches, ways or designs that can be adopted to collect data and arrive at conclusions. Some of these may be more or less preferable depending on the circumstances, but they all have their advantages and disadvantages. In short, none is perfect and none is totally useless. Therefore, the reasons behind any decision concerning which one to select – and, by implication, which ones to reject – need to be considered and articulated in relation to the purpose(s) of the exercise itself – that is, the decision needs to be explained and justified. The point is that the way in which data are collected is one consideration lying behind whether or not other people will see the process adopted to arrive at the findings and conclusions as having sufficient credibility to give them confidence in the outcomes that flow from this.

In selecting which design to use, a key issue is whether or not you will be able to justify your decision in the methodology section or chapter of the project or dissertation. If you can do so, then you will probably have thought the alternatives through and are able to present a good argument to justify your choice. If you cannot, then you will have made the decision on the wrong basis and could be in trouble!

This does raise the question, however, how can you justify your decision? The basic principle to be considered when answering this question is fitness for purpose or, in other words, is the chosen design the most appropriate one to enable you to collect the data required to answer the research question(s) or test the research hypothesis? If you are following a deductive process, you will have developed, as a product of your literature review, your conceptual framework and associated hypotheses (remember Chapter 2) as the basis, or raw material, for informing your choice and the implementation of the empirical research design to be adopted. Therefore, you should be able to demonstrate a logical and consistent connection between these two elements in your methodological explanation and justification. In short, you should be able to show that your empirical design choice is the most appropriate for achieving your research purposes, as defined in the conceptual framework.

The other source of evidence, in addition to this argument of logical consistency, is previously validated methodology. By this I mean evidence from prior, published research studies conducted by other researchers who have investigated similar phenomena using empirical research designs and data collection methods or procedures that have proved to be successful and robust. If others have previously demonstrated that particular approaches have been found to be valid and reliable, then their work can be used as evidence to support your choice of design.

To help you think this decision through, the rest of this chapter explores the alternative designs available to conduct the empirical data collection phase of a research project.

## 6.2 **Experimental Research**

Experimental research designs are derived from the historical legacy of what have been viewed as the 'best' ways to implement the scientific method within the physical and natural sciences. Indeed, the adoption of the positivist philosophy, deductive approach and experimental method is the hallmark of traditional scientific enquiry in these fields. In terms of the method experimentation, particularly laboratory experimentation, is seen by many, though not all, as the ideal design for conducting empirical research. This gives rise to the questions why is this the case and, if it is, should you seek to use experimentation as the favoured design for your empirical work? The reasons for experimental designs being seen as ideal are that they facilitate 'controlled enquiry' in terms of the manipulation of the inputs, conditions and processes and valid and reliable measurements of the data or output. An experimental situation, particularly in a laboratory, enables the researcher to control everything and thereby eliminate anything that could contaminate or confound the process. In this sense, it is often the method most capable of meeting the conditions of causality that we discussed in the previous chapter and, hence, is the most suitable for testing hypotheses to demonstrate cause–effect relationships and mechanisms (see Jones, 1999).

As a consequence of this, other empirical research designs often used by researchers taking a deductive approach to their research – particularly surveys and comparative/replicative methods – tend to adopt the same or very similar principles to those of the experimental method. The problem associated with them, however, as we will see later in this chapter, is that, because they are not implemented in as highly controlled conditions as experiments are, the ability to control and manipulate is more limited and therefore the potential for error to occur is greater.

Regarding the second question above, not all phenomena, issues or questions can be addressed easily by using experimental designs and they are the very antithesis of the phenomenological/inductive school of research, which rejects not only the philosophy and approach underlying the experimental method but also the manner in which it is put into practice. As experimentation is invariably conducted in either a totally artificial environment (the laboratory) or one that is quasi-artificial (an experiment set up in the real world) within which the researcher exerts a high degree of control and manipulation, it is argued that this artificiality compromises the validity of the work because it is contrived and unnatural. In the case of laboratory experiments, internal validity – that is, accuracy and truthfulness within the boundaries or parameters of the laboratory conditions – is considered to be high, but these conditions are, in themselves, contrived and artificial and may not be transferable to the real world. Conversely, where experiments are conducted in the real world, external validity – that is, accuracy and truthfulness within the real-world conditions in which the experiment takes place – is said to be high because these are occurring in more, but not totally, natural conditions. Nevertheless, because the extent and degree of control that are possible under these conditions are reduced, there is a greater potential for errors to arise, which, in turn, may compromise the internal validity of the results.

Therefore, whether you should choose experimentation as the method for your research or not will depend on whether it is the most desirable and feasible way in which to answer your research questions and hypotheses or not. Of course, this raises another question – how do I decide whether it is the most appropriate and feasible way or not? This is not an easy question to answer in a few words, but, if your research is going to adopt an inductive approach or is exploratory in scope, is not being conducted to establish cause–effect relationships, requires data to be collected from a wide variety (particularly in geographical terms) of people or organisations, or is concerned with phenomena that are not easy to simulate and control, then it is likely that an experimental design will not be the most desirable or, indeed, feasible method for your purposes. On the other hand, if your project does demand that the cause–effect relationships and mechanisms be explored or it is conducted in a limited and controllable environment or is concerned with testing or tri-alling new principles, practices or products, then use of an experimental design may be appropriate.

There are numerous types of experimental research designs, ranging from the simple to the more complex and powerful, but because this type of design is one that is rarely applicable to most undergraduate or postgraduate research issues and questions in hospitality or tourism – often for practical reasons of time and resources available to undertake the research – a detailed considera-tion of these designs is not included here. If this is the design you require, how-ever, then excellent sources to consult for more detail and guidance are Jones (1999) and Sekaran (2000). Both of these deal with the design considerations and Jones also includes examples of, and references to, the application of exper-imental designs to published research studies conducted in hospitality.

However, regardless of whether you intend to adopt an experimental design for your empirical research or not, the basic principles of experimental research design are useful to know if you intend to take a deductive approach for your project because, as stated earlier, other designs utilising this approach have been developed using and adapting the principles of experimentation. As dis-cussed previously (Chapter 5), before we can proceed to the stage of collecting empirical data using the deductive approach, we need to identify and opera-tionalise the concepts and variables we wish to measure, specify the relation-ships between them in the conceptual framework and develop hypotheses to enable us to test these proposed relationships. This is what an experiment is designed to do within a predetermined and controlled environment.

To conduct an experiment, the researcher exerts a considerable degree of control over its inputs, format and processes to try and ensure that any poten-tial errors are eliminated or, at the very least, minimised so that valid results can be obtained. Similarly, publishing the details of the method(s) used facilitates future, independent testing of the reliability of the measurement instruments as others repeat, or replicate, the experiment. Although the ability of the researcher to exert the same degree of control within a survey or comparative research is more limited than it is for experimentation, this does not mean that these designs do not exhibit similar or equivalent characteristics to those used for experimentation as they are modified to fit the different contexts and conditions under which these designs are implemented.

This will become evident in the sections that follow on these designs, but, to illustrate this point, consider what is involved in designing and conducting a questionnaire survey. As well as all the conceptual and measurement considerations and decisions made by you as the researcher, the survey design also involves making decisions concerning the selection of a sample to give the questionnaire to, the writing of the questions, the method to be used in implementing or administering the questionnaire and, finally, the recording methods and analysis of the data obtained from the questionnaire – all of which are under your control as the designer and implementer of the survey.

Furthermore, given that you will want to make these decisions to help generate as much valid and reliable data as possible, your ability to 'design in' as much control over the content and processes involved to minimise potential error will be important. So, although the context of a survey is different from that of an experiment, many of the principles involved in the design and implementation of research based on both of these are essentially the same – it is the extent to which these can be achieved and how they are addressed that differs.

Finally, there can be a tendency for students of hospitality or tourism management to take the view that experimental research is okay for physicists, chemists, biologists, geneticists and other laboratory scientists in white coats, but it is not relevant to people preparing for a career as managers in the hospitality or tourism industries. While this is true in the sense that you are not envisaging a career as a laboratory scientist, it would be wrong to assume that you will never encounter the experimental method in these industries. One obvious application lies in new dish and menu development, where experimentation is commonly used to develop and refine such new products. Another lies in testing out new ideas or concepts that are as yet unproven. For example, the cost of launching a new product format, rebranding or making process or system changes can be very significant and potentially disastrous if they fail.

Therefore, it is common for companies to set up experiments – although they are perhaps more frequently referred to as 'test units', 'trials' or 'pilot operations' – to establish whether or not a change will work before it is applied to the whole organisation. Similarly, where companies believe that changes in work practices, customer flow management or organisational restructuring will be beneficial, but would be disastrous if that belief was unfounded, they may use the experimental approach to test the beliefs first by making the changes in one part of the organisation to see if the evidence supports the belief or not. This is akin to talking about testing a hypothesis.

## 6.3 Survey Research

Survey research is a very common and popular form of empirical research design that is widely used by academics, commercial research organisations and companies. For example, you may have heard of polls conducted by organisations such as IPSOS MORI or Gallup reporting the level of support for a political party or predicting election results as they are commonly featured on television news programmes or in newspapers. Similarly, such programmes, in their coverage of topical issues, frequently refer to the results from a survey conducted on a particular newsworthy topic, such as health or the environment.

Hospitality and tourism companies and organisations also conduct surveys to gather information on issues that are important to them. For example, many companies have some form of customer feedback or satisfaction survey questionnaire that they use to collect data on the customers' experience of the product or service. These are often left in a hotel room, placed on restaurant tables, given to customers on a flight, mailed out to tourists after they have returned home and so on. Companies may also use surveys to obtain feedback from employees to ascertain how happy and satisfied they are.

Whatever the specific form and purpose of a particular survey, it is essentially a technique to communicate with and collect information from a 'representative sample' of individuals or organisations, mainly using verbal or written questioning (Lucas, 1999). The key words here are 'communicate', 'representative sample' and 'questioning'. The issue of what a representative sample is will be considered in more detail in Chapter 8, but the principle of this is that, in most cases, it is not possible to survey the entire population of individuals or organisations, often for reasons of time and cost, so a sample is selected from the overall population and the answers derived from this sample are then generalised back to the population as a whole.

This may sound complicated, but it is not, at least in principle. For example, for an organisation like Gallup to predict the voting intentions of, say, 40 million voters in the UK, it may only need to conduct a survey, usually by telephone, using a sample of around 3000 people. As long as the characteristics of the sample mirror those found in the voting population as a whole, it should be sufficiently representative for the results obtained from the sample of 3000 people to be generalised to the voting population as a whole and, hence, for the election results to be predicted. On the other hand, if the sample was not sufficiently representative of the voting population as a whole, then, when the survey results from this sample are expanded, or extrapolated, to the population, the prediction based on these would turn out to be wildly wrong. In short, error in the sample selection is magnified when the results are generalised back to the wider context. From this it should be clear that the issue of sample selection for a survey is critical if generalisation and prediction are desired, as they invariably are, from the survey results.

So, we have to get the size and composition of the sample right for a survey, but the other key issue is asking the sample respondents the questions. We all know that a survey questionnaire asks us to answer or respond to the questions or statements it contains to give its authors the information they require, but what is often forgotten in this process is the fact that the questionnaire itself is a communication vehicle. In some senses, this is obvious as it communicates the questions to the potential respondent, but communication is not always as successful as we would like or anticipate and there is the potential for both manipulation and/or error.

Communication is a two-way process. The sender of the message has to make the meaning as clear and unambiguous as possible so that the receiver understands it in the way it was originally meant and then he or she can respond appropriately to close the loop. The problem is that this process does not always work in the way we had hoped or anticipated. I am sure that you will have experienced situations where misinterpretations and misunderstandings have occurred when you have tried to communicate, either orally or in writing, with someone else, even though you may have felt that your original message and its meaning were entirely clear.

Similarly, it is possible to manipulate the communication process by phrasing questions or statements in such a way that they lead the respondents' perceptions in the direction you want in order that they give you the answers you want. Once again, we will consider this and other issues relating to the writing of survey questions and questionnaire design in more detail in Chapter 7. However, it is worth making the point here that a survey has to be carefully planned and constructed if it is to be regarded as a sound vehicle for collecting empirical data and for the results obtained from it to have credibility.

A survey may be appropriate for your research project, but, in common with all the other possible designs discussed in this chapter, it is not necessarily better than others and should not be regarded as an automatic choice. Surveys have their advantages and disadvantages, as do all the other designs. Perhaps the main advantages of surveys are that they can be relatively quick and easy to design and implement compared to other empirical design options. Surveys also, if designed and conducted properly, can deliver reliable results and the nature of the data obtained from questionnaires is frequently, although not always, amenable to statistical manipulation, which, in turn, can make objective comparisons easier to achieve.

The main disadvantages are that the survey interview or questionnaire is a contrived and artificial situation. As the survey respondents can only respond to the questions they are asked and, in many cases, only in the format prescribed in the questionnaire, this places parameters on the nature and type of response that can be given. Also, peoples' responses to survey questions tend to reflect what they are prepared to say, or reveal, about their true feelings on the issue and not necessarily what they really feel or believe. These issues together raise questions concerning the validity of the data collected.

Surveys can be used for many research purposes, but most of them can be grouped under one of two headings – replication and new studies. Where previous studies have used survey methods to obtain data and you intend to repeat or replicate one of them in your study, there are often good reasons to choose the same method, instrument and procedures as the original work. As you will see later in this chapter, such a project would be essentially comparative in nature – that is, you want to repeat the study to compare the results of your study with those of the original and it is easier to do this when the methods used in the two studies are either identical or very similar. This would be the case whether your study was being conducted to update the original work that had been undertaken some time ago and was now regarded as not being representative of contemporary conditions or you wanted to repeat a study originally undertaken in another industry, country or cultural context within the hospitality or tourism industry. For example, a survey of the most important influences on hotel guest satisfaction may have been conducted in the USA and you want to repeat it in the UK to see if the hotel guests in each country have the same views, or a survey on museum visitor expectations may have been conducted 20 years ago and you want to update the results.

Alternatively, a survey of banking customers may have found that they could be grouped into certain segments according to their age and lifestyle and you want to undertake a survey of airline passengers to see if the same segmentation applies to that context, or you want to explore the tourism attraction preferences of independent travellers in Spain in your project and have found a previous survey that addressed the same issues in a study conducted in Greece, so you are interested to know if the findings from the Greek study are the same as yours.

Although it is not always possible to exactly replicate the original survey questionnaire, because of differences in terminology or issues that have changed over time, it is usually possible to produce an alternative version that is equivalent, but not exactly identical, to the original. In the case of 'new' studies, a survey might be used to explore a gap, or gaps, in previous work that has been identified in the process of conducting the literature review on the topic or to take a new angle or perspective on the same issues.

Surveys can be used for descriptive or analytical purposes, though they tend to be more commonly used for the former than the latter. An analytical survey would be one concerned with the collection of data to test hypothesised cause–effect relationships and ascertain the mechanisms underlying such relationships. So, for example, although questions may be asked to determine the what, when, how often and how many aspects of peoples' behaviour or actions, an analytical survey would also want to ask the why questions as well. These would be absent from a descriptive survey as its purpose would be to identify the characteristics of the sample and relate these to their preferences, attitudes or actions to ascertain similarities or differences. Another way of distinguishing between these two types would be to see the descriptive survey as essentially one that is designed to obtain and record facts, whereas the analytical survey is more concerned with producing explanations.

Either of these types of survey could be conducted on what is known as a cross-sectional or longitudinal basis. Which is chosen is simply an issue of time. A survey conducted on a cross-sectional basis is one undertaken at a particular point in time and, therefore, the effects of changes in context, conditions, attitudes, preferences, behaviour and so on over time are not taken into account. A longitudinal study, however, explicitly incorporates the effects of time as the survey is repeated at intervals and the results from successive implementations are compared to assess the impact of change over time.

One, albeit imperfect, way to think about the difference between the two is to consider the cross-sectional survey as a still photograph that captures an image at one point in time and the longitudinal one as a film or video that follows evolution or development over time.

A survey can be implemented in various ways. These are sometimes described as directly, semi-directly or indirectly, but I prefer to think of these alternatives as either direct – face-to-face interviewing – or 'distributed' – where the questionnaire is sent, or distributed, to the potential respondents by either postal, telephonic or electronic means. It is the telephone survey that others regard as the semi-direct method of implementation because the person asking the questions does have some real-time contact with the respondent, as opposed to the respondent merely receiving a written questionnaire in the post or accessing it electronically. It is not direct because the two are not physically in the same location and it is mediated by the telephone.

Your choice of survey implementation method is likely to be dictated by considerations of time and cost, which, in turn, are frequently determined by the geographical dispersion of the survey sample. Where the sample is dispersed over a wide geographical area, the time and cost involved in travelling to all the locations where the respondents are likely to be prohibitive, so a distributed method is likely to be more suitable. On the other hand, if the sample respondents are limited geographically to one or a number of locations close to you, then it may be feasible to use a direct, face-to-face, interviewing method of implementation.

There are no major advantages per se to using either a direct or distributed strategy to implement a survey, but there are implications for the design and content of the survey questionnaire. We shall consider these issues further in Chapter 7, but they revolve around the communication issue of questioner–respondent interaction. Where a survey is distributed by one of the means identified above, there is no direct contact between the two parties, which means that any ambiguity and potential for different interpretation must be eliminated from the questionnaire before it is used. If the recipient does not understand what is being asked, how to respond or is confused by the wording of questions or other instructions in the questionnaire, there is no opportunity for any of these issues to be clarified by the questioner. On the other hand, although it is good practice and desirable for even questionnaires used in direct contact with the respondent to be as free as possible from such contaminating errors, it is possible to interact with the respondent to explain or clarify any uncertainties and so on. However, there is then the potential, if it is not done consistently and carefully, for this to influence or bias the nature of the responses.

In common with all the research designs, surveys are not perfect and there are various sources of error that can arise to potentially contaminate the data obtained from a survey questionnaire. Errors can occur in the sampling strategy and procedures used to determine and select the survey sample. We will explore this subject more in Chapter 8, but let us look briefly at the sorts of errors the can occur now so that you can bear them in mind before you progress too for in the design of your project.

First, if the sample is selected in anything other than a random manner or the random selection procedure is not applied correctly, then bias may be designed into the sample itself.

Second, systematic (non-sampling) errors can exist. These are usually associated with problems in the questionnaire. For example, if a question can be interpreted in different ways by the respondents, then it will be virtually impossible to tell which interpretation has been used by which respondent to guide their responses and, as they have effectively been responding to a different question, this effect will invalidate the data relating to that question – all the data collected on that question will be useless. Therefore, as you might imagine, this is a pretty serious problem. To avoid it occuring, it is usually recommended that the questionnaire is tested, or trialled, before you implement it, but more advice on this is given in Chapter 7.

Third, errors can arise from respondents. For example, the non-response form of error can be a major problem. This can happen simply because questionnaires are not completed and returned by the respondents, or when questionnaires are returned but some of the questions have not been answered by all of the respondents. A simple example will illustrate the nature of this problem.

If you mailed out questionnaires to a sample of 100 companies and only 50 were completed and returned, the response rate would be 50 per cent. Not only does this reduce your actual sample to half the size you originally determined that you needed but it also raises the issue of how to know if the 50 companies who did not respond would have responded in the same way to the questions as the 50 who did. The fact is that you cannot know, which begins to threaten your ability to generalise from the results. As you have probably surmised, there is an inverse relationship between a survey's response rate and the degree of non-response error. In other words, as the response rate increases, the level of non-response error decreases and vice versa. Therefore, the key to reducing the non-response error is to try and obtain as high a response rate as possible.

There are various tactics outlined below that you can use to try and achieve this, but none are foolproof.

- Make the questionnaire as easy and quick to complete as possible.
- Ensure that a date for completion and return is clearly communicated to the respondents.
- Include a 'selling' message with, or in, the questionnaire to motivate the receiver to complete and return it.
- Offer some form of inducement, such as a copy of the results.
- Provide a reply-paid envelope to eliminate there being a cost involved in returning the questionnaire.

However, all of these tactics only serve to possibly improve the initial response rate. Once you have passed the return deadline and not all of the questionnaires have been received, there are other things you can try to improve the final response rate. For example, it may be possible, if you have the information, to contact the respondents who have not returned their questionnaires by telephone to remind and/or encourage them to do so. Alternatively, you could send out another copy of the questionnaire to those who have not returned theirs with a message exhorting or encouraging them to complete and return it.

Another source of non-response error can occur where the sample is self-selected. In other words, the respondents choose to complete the questionnaire for various reasons of their own. A good example of this type of problem is often to be found in situations where companies leave questionnaires out for their guests or customers to complete if they choose to do so or they issue questionnaires to their customers but leave it up to them as to whether or not they complete these.

The customer feedback/satisfaction questionnaires seemingly so beloved of hospitality, tourism and other businesses are a prime example of this. Often hotels will leave this type of questionnaire in their guest bedrooms, restaurants may place them on their tables and holiday companies may hand them out to passengers on their return flights. In each of these cases, but particularly the first two, the people most likely to complete the questionnaires will be those who are either very happy or very unhappy with their experience because they wish to praise or complain about it. Thus, the sample obtained as a result of a survey organised in this way is likely to be highly biased and the data are very unlikely to be representative of the views of the hotels' guests or restaurants' customers as a whole. In short, it is really rather a pointless exercise. The message here is clear: if you choose to place or leave your questionnaires in a location for people to pick up and complete or ignore, then you have no control over the selection and composition of the sample and cannot justify claims that the sample is representative. You will recall from earlier in this chapter that it is absolutely crucial for a sample to be representative if you want to generalise from the survey's results.

In the case of questionnaires that are returned but not every respondent has answered all the questions, you have to make a judgement as to whether the level of response to individual questions is sufficient to regard the data as credible or not. There is no easy rule for doing this, but, if from 50 question-naires returned, only five respondents answered question 10, then you might reasonably conclude that, with a 90 per cent non-response rate to this question, it would not be sensible to draw conclusions from this data. On the other hand, if, of the 50 questionnaires, 30 respondents had answered question 10, then this 60 per cent response rate may well lead you to the opposite conclusion.

The issue here is one of representativeness. If more than half of the respon-dents have answered the question, you may well feel that this is likely to be more representative of the sample as a whole than if only, say, 10 per cent answered the question. Therefore, the key to making the decision to include and use data on individual questions where not all the respondents have answered them is how confident you feel about being able to claim, and justify, that the amount of data you have is sufficient to be regarded as representative of the sample as a whole.

Response bias is another potential source of survey error. This arises either as a consequence of deficiencies in the questions asked or from the behaviour of the respondents. Where questions are worded in ambiguous terms and can be misunderstood, then errors will probably arise. Similarly, where respon-dents, for some reason, decide to provide answers that misrepresent or delib-erately falsify their true feelings on an issue, the validity of the data becomes questionable. This begs the question, why would they want to do this?

It is thought that where questions are asked about issues that are potentially sensitive to respondents, the responses they give may be contrived in some way to protect themselves or perhaps portray them in a more favourable light. For example, if a company is asked to rate itself in terms of the quality of its products compared to those of its competitors, it is likely that the person responding on behalf of the company will wish to portray his or her company in a favourable light, so might not give a true or accurate answer. Similarly, if a person is asked questions that are associated with his or her self-image, then these too could well attract biased responses.

Finally, errors can creep into the administrative aspects of survey implemen-tation. Where a direct implementation strategy is used, with more than one interviewer conducting the survey interviews, it is possible that the interview-ers will behave in different ways when presenting the questionnaire to respon-dents. Some may offer additional information or explanations, others may not, some may prompt the respondents and others not. Whatever the nature of the differences, they contaminate the implementation process because the bases on which the respondents are providing answers differ and this makes it problem-atic to aggregate and compare their responses.

It is also possible for interviewers to cheat when completing questionnaires. It has been known, particularly in commercial research situations where inter-viewers are paid, for them to cheat by completing the questionnaires themselves!

The remedy for interviewer error, of the unthinking helpfulness kind, is to ensure that the interviewers are well briefed and trained before the process begins to try and make certain, as far as is reasonably possible, that they all implement the questionnaire in the same manner. To reinforce this, instructions to the interviewers can be written into the questionnaire – 'do not provide any additional explanation for these questions', 'only ask the question as it is written – do not add anything to this', 'do not prompt the interviewee' and so on – to try and ensure that they all behave in the same way.

Once the survey has been completed and the questionnaire data are available for processing, errors can arise in keying this data into computers for analysis. This can be as simple as pressing the wrong key or two keys together when entering the data. Therefore, once the data have been entered, it is good practice to review the data sheet, or its equivalent, to check that there are no rogue entries that should not be there.

## 6.4 Comparative Research

Although all research involves comparisons of various kinds, the difference between comparative research designs and others that include varying amounts of comparisons is that the former has a specific comparative purpose from the outset – it is a central part of the rationale for conducting the research in this way, not just a byproduct of its design. It is overt and explicit rather than implicit.

Even though research conducted using one of the other designs discussed in this chapter may reveal similarities and/or differences when its data are analysed, the difference between them and a comparative research design is that the latter is specifically used to address one or other of these similarities or differences. In short, it is a design used to discover and explain differences or similarities between phenomena in either a spatial or a temporal context – that is, between different spatial entities, such as companies, industries, countries and so on, or between different time periods, such as today and ten years ago.

Such comparative studies can help to test the extent to which a theory can be generalised across different time periods and/or contemporary contexts. For example, comparative research designs might address questions such as the following.

♦ Can a theory of consumer behaviour developed in the context of the American domestic tourism industry be applied to the same industry in China?
♦ Are the factors that determine the volume of air travel today the same as those ten years ago?
♦ Why do some hospitality companies seem to have very low levels of staff turnover when others have very high levels?
♦ Why are some tourism companies very profitable while others in the same line of business are not?
♦ Why do some female managers in the hospitality industry achieve high managerial positions but others do not?

In each of these cases, a comparative research design would be suitable to try and identify the answers to these questions or reasons for these differences.

There are two basic approaches that can be taken when designing comparative research. First, the positive approach, which is concerned with identifying similarities in the independent variables associated with a common outcome or dependent variable. For example, we could ask, in those companies that have very low levels of staff turnover (the common dependent variable), are there similar reasons evident (independent variables) to explain this? In other words, are the same outcomes in different situations caused by the same things?

Second, there is the negative approach, which involves explaining different or divergent outcomes by identifying the major, common reasons for these variations. For example, using the same context as above, we might identify companies with very different levels of staff turnover (the outcome or dependent variable) and ask why this is the case – that is, what common independent variables may explain this difference? In this approach, the aim is to try and identify the main or most influential independent variables contributing to the different outcomes, then explain why these same variables can generate different outcomes. In this example, it may be due to varying abilities on the part of the companies to pay sufficient wages or salaries or to motivate their employees sufficiently. The issue here is how well the companies perform in relation to the same independent variable that influences the outcome – that is, the underlying cause of different levels of outcome is the same, but, where performance regarding this variable is good, the outcome is more positive and vice versa. The same principle would apply if the study were comparing individuals or groups.

Because comparative research inherently deals with different contexts or time periods, one of the key issues in designing any form of comparative research is that of equivalence. With either spatial or temporal differences in the research context, conceptual and/or measurement differences are likely to arise. This gives rise to a major problem in making direct and valid comparisons between different contexts because, to make valid comparisons, a common denominator is required. For example, the way in which tourism, the tourism industry and tourism expenditure are defined – and, hence, measured – in different countries differs, making direct comparisons of the tourism statistics these countries produce problematic. Similarly, if we wish to track changes in tourism arrivals to a country over time, we may be faced with the problem that the definition of a 'tourist arrival' and the way statistics on this have been collected and analysed could have changed during the time period we want to look at.

The point here is that, to make valid comparisons, we need to be able to compare like with like or as close to this ideal as possible. This does not mean that we need to seek out identical entities – because, by definition, there would not be any differences between them – or, at the other extreme, entities that are totally different in every way – they would have no similarities at all, so there would be no basis for making comparisons. It is the entities between these two extremes, possessing both differences and similarities that are sufficiently similar to be regarded as being equivalent, that are interesting.

This is not a context issue because, often, we will want to study very different contexts, but one that is conceptual in nature and concerns measurement. It becomes most problematic when the research contexts include different countries, cultures and languages – cross-national/cultural or international studies – and less so when the context is more limited and homogeneous – companies within the same line of hospitality or tourism business (Brotherton, 2003).

In the former contexts, because of such influences, the same concept can have very different connotations and meanings in each context, which has the effect that there is no common denominator or reference point to make the comparisons with. This means that making valid comparison is very difficult as there is a lack of conceptual equivalence – that is, we are not comparing like with like.

In the latter contexts, because of the relative homogeneity of the situation, there is likely to be a shared or common denominator to make comparisons with, making it less problematic.

One way to illustrate this issue is to consider the simple example of measurement. Where the concept and practice of measurement are the same – that is, the same system and calibrations are used across the contexts, then a common denominator exists. However, where one context uses, say, imperial measurements and another uses metric ones, there is no common denominator and, to establish equivalence, one set of measures has to be converted into the other. The same is true in the case of different currencies, where the exchange rate between them establishes equivalent values. To have a common denominator in this case would require all currencies to be expressed in terms of their value relationship to one currency. In many instances, this is achieved by expressing different currency values and volumes in US dollars, as this provides a common currency to facilitate comparisons between countries.

These observations should indicate to you that comparative studies undertaken on an 'intra' (within), as opposed to an 'inter' (between), contextual basis are less likely to face such equivalence issues. So, studies designed to compare companies within the same line of business or individuals performing the same job in similar companies would be easier to design, in terms of conceptual and measurement equivalence, than would studies designed to compare service systems in fast food restaurants and banks (see Brotherton, 2000). However, this should not be taken to mean that studies designed to compare different contexts are to be avoided. Indeed, there is often great value in comparing issues, practices and problems in hospitality or tourism contexts to those found in other types of industry because any similarities found across different contexts could help to make the theoretical explanations for the phenomena more general and less context-specific. Indeed, the greater the variations between the contexts used for comparative purposes, the greater the ability to generalise from similar results obtained from them. By contrast, where the contexts are very similar, similar results may be transferable between these contexts but not necessarily generalisable to other, very different, contexts. In such cases, the results and explanations are contextually limited as they are not capable of being applied to, or across, a range of different contexts (Brotherton, 1999b).

Comparative research designs may be associated with any of the other types of empirical research designs discussed in this chapter, depending on whether they are of a case or variable-orientated nature. In the next section, we will explore some of these issues as they relate to multiple case study and/or units of analysis designs, where more than one case study may be used so as to make comparisons between the two or more cases or, where there is only one case study, it is subdivided into two or more units of analysis, which are then used to make comparisons within the case itself. Similarly, in observational research, more than one situation chosen for observation may be used to facilitate comparisons between the observations for each. In variable-orientated approaches, too, some experimental research designs are specifically comparative in nature – different experimental and control groups being established to compare the effects of the experimental treatment with that implemented in the control groups. Surveys may also be designed for specific comparative purposes. For example, different samples may be selected to receive the same survey instrument or questionnaire in order that the results from these samples can be directly compared.

## 6.5 Case Study Research

Case study research is seen by some commentators as a design that is most appropriate for initial, exploratory research, often of a qualitative nature. It is a design viewed by many researchers who take a positivistic standpoint as one that is 'completely valueless at worst and markedly inferior to other methodological choices, such as experimentation and large N surveys, at best' (Brotherton, 1999a: 115). On the other hand, 'those researchers with a more phenomenological or interpretivist orientation would argue that case study research, frequently in conjunction with ethnographic and field methods, is at the very least extremely valuable for developing "grounded" theoretical insights through an inductive process and may be seen as a type of research capable of providing valid theoretical generalisations beyond the specific case(s) considered in the study' (Brotherton, 1999a: 115).

In this sense, empirical research designs adopting a case study approach are invariably seen as empirically limited because they are normally (but not exclusively) conducted within a context that is relatively small in scope and may or may not be representative of the wider world it is a part of. This frequently means that attempts to generalise the findings from a piece of case study research to a wider empirical reality are fraught with difficulty because the case context may be atypical of the population as a whole and the volume of data collected is likely to be relatively small, which could preclude the use of statistical extrapolation procedures that are based on the existence of a large amount of data. However, this is not the purpose of case study research, as we will see later in this section.

Case studies are generally seen as valuable for exploring an issue in depth within a specific context, using qualitative data to assist in the development of insights and theory, but not usually as a means of testing existing theory. The research methodology literature in general portrays case studies as suitable for research based on a phenomenological philosophy, using an inductive approach to collect and analyse qualitative data to develop new theory. Although case studies may be useful and appropriate for achieving this, they can also be used in a positivistic, deductive and more quantitative context. For example, it is possible to use a case study to test the applicability of an existing theory to the particular conditions within the case situation – that is, if the theory has been developed as a result of large-scale survey work in the first instance, using large organisations as the sample to verify it, then it may be a worthwhile exercise to carry out a case study of a small organisation to test the extent to which the theory fits this type of organisation. Alternatively, if the organisation selected for the case study was atypical or even unique, then it could be used as the basis for exploring whether the theory is generally applicable to all types of organisation or might require some modification under certain conditions.

The point here is that case study research designs may be more applicable to the type of study you have in mind than the literature might have led you to believe. Given the nature of hospitality and tourism educational programmes, it is quite possible that you have close contact with a particular company, in the form of a work placement or part-time employment, and this could constitute a useful context in which to undertake your research. That said, you need to exercise caution when doing this. Simply seeing a company you have access to as an easy route to obtaining information is not a good enough reason to choose it and a case study approach to collect your data. The empirical design you choose is merely a means to an end and it should always be selected on the basis that it is the most appropriate and feasible way to obtain the data you need to answer your research question(s) and test the hypotheses you have established. Taking what you may see as the line of least resistance can be disastrous, both in terms of being able to justify this choice and in practice when the people in the company who told you that there would be no problem giving you access to the data suddenly leave or decide that it is not now possible!

One reason for choosing a case study design could be that you need to study the particular phenomenon within a situational context because they are interrelated and inseparable – that is, the boundaries between them are not clear. Indeed, this is a key feature of a case situation and one that can be referred to as a 'bounded context', where the phenomenon in question is evident. In short, the premise here is that the phenomenon can only be understood when it is studied in conjunction with the conditions in which it occurs.

This is the opposite of survey research, where specific contextual conditions and variations in these are very much secondary considerations at best because the aim of the survey is to generalise from its results to differing contextual conditions and produce findings that are generally, if not universally, applicable. Hence, while research designs such as experimentation and surveys seek to deliver theoretical and empirical insights that are not determined or limited by the specific conditions existing in any particular context, case studies explicitly recognise that such conditions are an integral part of any explanation.

If a case study design is chosen as the most appropriate design for your research, then the first issue to resolve is the definition of what constitutes the case. In some instances, this may be quite straightforward, but in others it can be more complicated. If it is a particular company or operating unit within a company, the boundaries of the case can be quite clear. If, however, the case is based on particular types of people or events, it can be more difficult to delineate or find these boundaries. For example, if your study involved a case of hotel general managers, airline marketing managers, international sporting events or major festivals, then it would be more difficult to decide which types of these should be included in, or excluded from, the definition or boundaries of the case because there are many of them and they vary considerably.

One thing that can help you to make decisions on what to include and exclude is the notion of the study's 'unit of analysis'. This is the main focus of the study and there may be one or more unit(s) of analysis. Case studies regarded as 'holistic' in nature have a single unit of analysis, whereas those known as 'embedded' have more than one. The other issue here is whether the design is to include a single case or whether it should have more – multiple cases – for comparative purposes.

Yin (1994), one of the leading writers on case study research, puts these two sets of considerations together to produce a typology matrix that generates four types of case study research design (see Figure 6.1).

As Figure 6.1 shows, both single and multiple case study designs can have either a holistic or embedded unit of analysis. Type 1 designs are a single case with a holistic unit of analysis, while Type 2 designs have a single case context but more than one unit of analysis. The primary difference between these two is that the Type 2 design explicitly includes a comparative element by having more than one unit of analysis.

To illustrate the differences between the two types, consider the following example. If we assume that a piece of research is being designed to explore the issue of employee empowerment in a tour operating company, this could be assessed using just one unit of analysis – the company itself. Alternatively, you may wish to explicitly design into this situation a comparison of the views or opinions on empowerment of the managers on the one hand and the employees on the other. This would then give us two embedded (within the context of the one case situation) units of analysis – the managers and the employees – that we would use to make direct comparisons. Therefore, the Type 2 design is used to facilitate 'intra-case' comparisons.

Single cases        Multiple cases

|           | Single cases | Multiple cases |
|-----------|:---:|:---:|
| Holistic  | Type 1 | Type 2 |
| Embedded  | Type 3 | Type 4 |

**Figure 6.1**    The different design options for case studies (Yin, 1994: 39).
Reproduced with the permission of Sage.

The question is, why would we want to complicate matters by having more than one unit of analysis? The answer is because we need to elicit the information that will enable us answer the research question or test the hypothesis. Again, we only design into the empirical research that which we need. This is at least part of the rationale for the design of the research, which is explained in the methodology section or chapter of the research report or dissertation when it is written up.

More specifically, we may choose a single case study design (Type 1 or 2) because:

♦    the case in question is regarded as critical to the research – it has all the conditions necessary to test an established theory
♦    it is an 'ideal' case – for example, the company or person is regarded as the leading or best in relation to the issue being researched
♦    it is a 'unique' case – by definition, it is different from all other possible case situations
♦    it is an 'extreme' case – it is very much not a typical, normal case situation, but one in which there are extreme characteristics relating to the phenomenon, such as a company with profit levels way in excess of others operating in the same field or vice versa
♦    it is a 'revelatory' case – that is, it is new or perhaps was previously inaccessible for some reason, such as a political regime being in place that previously denied access to outsiders.

Types 3 and 4 in Figure 6.1 are multiple case study designs with, respectively, holistic and embedded units of analysis. Both of these types facilitate 'inter-case' comparisons because they are comprised of more than one case situation. However, the Type 4 design enables both intra- and inter-case comparisons to be made because it includes multiple cases and units of analysis. Taking our example above, we could now not only make a number of intra-case comparisons between the employees and managers in each of the cases but also a number of inter-case comparisons between the managers and the employees in the different cases. This, of course, does increase the power of the design in the sense that multiple cases and units of analysis facilitate more comparisons, but, at the same time, it also increases the complexity of the data collection and analysis processes. Again the decision as to whether or not multiple case design is used should be based on what information is required, as explained above. That said, multiple case designs are explicitly comparative in nature, so, where comparison is explicitly built into the research questions or hypotheses, they may be appropriate.

To justify the selection of one of these designs, the principle of replication should be referred to. Having multiple cases is analogous to repeating or replicating experiments under either the same or differing conditions. Where cases are selected on the basis that they conform to the same conditions and, therefore, should produce the same results according to the underlying theory, this is known as 'literal replication' – the conditions are literally repeated in the different cases. Conversely, where cases are selected because they are expected to produce contrasting results, but for predictable reasons, this is known as 'theoretical replication'. To illustrate the latter, if the theory predicts that the profitability of companies is strongly influenced by the level of labour turnover they have – the lower the turnover, the higher the profitability and vice versa – then one way to test the validity of this would be to select companies as cases that had different levels of labour turnover.

## 6.6 Observational Research

Observational research can be undertaken by those having a positivistic philosophy and using a deductive approach – that is, the observation takes place in the laboratory and field (quasi-experiments) – but it is more associated with those who have a phenomenological philosophy and use an inductive approach. Where observation occurs within a relatively highly structured and controlled environment and the data are recorded using formal rating techniques, it would be of the former kind. Where it occurs in more naturalistic (less manipulated and controlled) environments and data are recorded using more open-ended, less formal techniques, then it would correspond to the latter kind of approach.

This type of research is closely associated with what is known as 'ethnography'. Ethnography – from ethno, meaning people, and graphy, meaning description – is concerned with naturalistic enquiry that has the purpose of being able to describe and understand a particular social entity from the point of view of its inhabitants. In this sense it is vital that the researcher is able to develop an empathy with them, to see the situation through their eyes rather than trying to impose the interpretations of outsiders on them. As this perspective contends that it is only possible to understand the reality of a situation by looking at the ways the participants construct and give meaning to that reality for themselves and this can only be achieved by not contaminating the situation by implementing the research process, its proponents claim that this design can produce highly valid results. However, because of the specificity of the situation any conclusions may be difficult to generalise from.

Due to the limitations of time, access and observer skills, observational research may not be a feasible option for you. Although access may or may not be an issue for you, the time required to undertake, record and analyse multiple observations is likely to be a potential problem. Similarly, to be an effective observer, as either a participant or non-participant in the situation, requires quite a range of skills that take time to develop and refine.

Bearing all these things in mind, it is a design that is very appropriate for research attempting to develop an in-depth understanding of a group of interacting people within the context of a particular type of location or setting, who are engaging in their normal activities without any outside manipulation. There are, of course, many situations in the hospitality and tourism industries where such interactions could be studied to develop a better understanding of peoples' perceptions, attitudes, behaviour and so on, but to do this, it is important that you have the necessary time, access and skills which, as indicated above, may not be available. For more guidance on designing and using observational research see Jauncy (1999).

## 6.7 Action Research

Action research – sometimes also referred to as 'action learning' – is a very different form of research design to the others reviewed in this chapter. Whereas surveys and experiments tend to emphasise the independent and distanced role of the researcher, and observation and case studies the non-intervention of the researcher, action research, as the name implies, tends to involve the researcher in implementing some change in order to assess and evaluate its effects and impacts.

Action research can take differing guises (see Lashley, 1999), but it can be seen as a form of live experimentation as, although it is concerned with the making of an active intervention to bring about predicted improvements, the intervention is based on an underlying theory or model. Thus, it is not a 'suck it and see' type of approach, based on guesswork, but one flowing from an analysis and understanding of the situation, which are then used to predict what will happen when the change is introduced. This is very much akin to testing a theory or hypothesis by carrying out an experiment. However, although the principles are similar, the practices are not. In particular, the experimental situation may be regarded as naturalistic rather than artificial and the ability of the researcher to control the environment and the process and be an independent, objective observer of the effects of the change is severely limited. Thus, it raises issues concerning how scientific this from of research is and the ability of the researcher to be certain about cause–effect relationships and mechanisms.

In many instances, action research will not be either the most desirable or feasible design for your research project, but there are circumstances where it could be. One of the key issues would be the extent to which you have access to, and the ability to introduce a change or intervention in, the situation or organisation in question. Without the ability to study the situation and be able to introduce the change and evaluate it, your ability to use action research is zero. As a practising manager well beyond graduation, this may well be a desirable and feasible approach to adopt, but as a student with no such organisational position, you are totally reliant on others to give you this access and authorise the introduction of any change.

Therefore, the only circumstances in which you can consider using action research are if you have this type of relationship with an organisation or an organisational unit. This could be the case if you have been employed on a work placement or have a long-standing, part-time employment relationship with such an organisation. Then, it may be possible to develop a project using action research because you could have the necessary degree of access, familiarity and authorisation to do this. However, you need to be aware that you may not have sufficient time to see it through and/or managers can change their minds about letting you do what you need to do to complete the work. Unless you are absolutely certain that there will not be, often irresolvable, problems further down the line, action research is a high-risk choice.

If, after carefully thinking it through, you do decide to adopt this design, then, following a review of the literature relating to your topic, you would need to collect some initial data on the organisational context where you plan to implement the change. This could be achieved by means of a variety of data collection methods. For example, questionnaires, observation, interviewing, examination of company documents – all could be used to help develop an understanding of the present situation.

At this point, using the insights obtained from the literature and the context, you would then need to put together a conceptual framework to summarise your understanding and develop predictions regarding what the effect(s) of the change will be. From this you will see that this is a typical deductive approach in that the actions you plan to take are based on the underlying theory and designed to test this theory and its predictions. Therefore, once the conceptual aspect has been completed, the planned change can be introduced, the data collected and the actual outcomes evaluated in relation to those predicted.

## SUMMARY

» There are various ways in which to design the empirical research aspect of a research project, none of which is perfect for all types of project.

» This means choices must be made to select the design that is most appropriate for collecting the type of data required to answer the research question and/or test the hypothesis.

» Choosing the appropriate design is vital for validity, reliability and credibility reasons and this needs to be explained/justified in the research report.

» Experimental and survey research designs are likely to be appropriate for quantitative studies, while observational and case study designs are generally appropriate for qualitative studies.

» All empirical research designs can be implemented in differing ways according to the types of data and practical circumstances required and experienced.

» Research designs for quantitative studies often take more time and effort to construct and to get right than those for qualitative studies, but this time to effort ratio is reversed when the data analysis stage is reached. Often it takes considerably more time and effort to analyse qualitative data than it does to analyse quantitative data.

» Replication and comparative research can be useful approaches where previous studies exist and/or explicit comparisons have to be made between units, companies, industries, countries and so on.

## Further Reading

Blaxter, L., Hughes, C. and Tight, M. (1996) *How to Research.* Buckingham: Open University Press. Chapter 3.

Clark, M., Riley, M., Wilkie, E. and Wood, R.C. (1998) *Researching and Writing Dissertations in Hospitality and Tourism.* London: International Thomson Business Press. Chapters 9 and 10.

Denscombe, M. (1998) *The Good Research Guide for Small-scale Research Projects.* Buckingham: Open University Press. Chapters 1–5.

Fink, A. (1995) *How to Design Surveys.* Thousand Oaks, CA: Sage.

Finn, M., Elliot-White, M. and Walton, M. (2000) *Tourism and Leisure Research Methods: Data collection, analysis and interpretation.* Harlow: Pearson Education. Chapters 5 and 6.

Gill, J. and Johnson, P. (1991) *Research Methods for Managers*. London: Paul Chapman Publishing. Chapters 4–10.

Hakim, C. (1994) *Research Design: Strategies and choices in the design of social research*. London: Routledge. Chapters 5–11.

Hantrais, L. and Mangen, S. (1996) 'Method and management of cross-cultural research', in L. Hantrais and S. Mangen (eds), *Cross-national Research Methods in the Social Sciences*. London: Pinter. p. 1–12.

Hussey, J. and Hussey, R. (1997) *Business Research: A practical guide for undergraduate and postgraduate students*. Basingstoke: Macmillan. Chapter 5.

Jankowicz, A.D. (1991) *Business Research Projects for Students*. London: Chapman & Hall. Chapters 9 and 10.

Johns, N. and Lee-Ross, D. (1998) *Research Methods in Service Industry Management*. London: Cassell. Chapters 4 and 6.

May, T. (1993) *Social Research: Issues, methods and process*. Buckingham: Open University Press. Chapters 5, 7 and 9.

Preece, R. (1994) *Starting Research: An introduction to academic research and dissertation writing*. London: Pinter. Chapters 5 and 6.

Saunders, M., Lewis, P. and Thornhill, A. (2003) *Research Methods for Business Students*, 3rd edition. Harlow: Pearson Education. Chapters 4, 8 and 10.

Sekaran, U. (2000) *Research Methods for Business: A skill-building approach*, 3rd edition. New York: John Wiley. Chapters 6 and 7.

Van de Vijer, F. and Leung, K. (1997) *Methods and Data Analysis for Cross-cultural Research*. Thousand Oaks, CA: Sage.

Veal, A.J. (1997) *Research Methods for Leisure and Tourism: A practical guide*. Harlow: Pearson Education. Chapters 7 and 9.

Yin, R.K. (1994) *Case Study Research: Design and methods*, 2nd edition. Thousand Oaks, CA: Sage.

# Chapter

## Collecting the Empirical Data

---

### KEY CONCEPTS AND ISSUES

» *Designing effective questionnaires.*
» *Structured, unstructured and semistructured questionnaires.*
» *Getting the respondent 'onside'.*
» *Types of question and forms of data.*
» *Questions and scales.*
» *Structured, unstructured, focus group and field interviews.*
» *Participant and non-participant observation.*
» *Use of non-standard questions – projective techniques.*

---

## 7.1 Introduction

In the previous chapter we explored the issues and alternatives associated with making the decision as to which overall research design to use in order to structure and organise the collection of the empirical data required for a research project. Once this has been decided, the more detailed decisions regarding how this overall approach and plan is to be put into operation and administered have to be addressed. This means that we have to consider the instruments and procedures we are going to use to collect the data and, once again, there are alternative choices available to us that have to be considered before we can make a decision to adopt one, or possibly more, of these as being the most appropriate for our purposes.

It is to these issues that we now turn our attention and consider the use of questionnaires, interviewing, observation and other, non-standard, approaches such as projective techniques that can be utilised to collect valid and reliable data. As these are each considerable topics in their own right, the approach taken here is one of highlighting and exploring the key principles associated with the alternatives and, within each, the different options available to design and implement their data collection instruments and procedures. In addition, the reasoning behind the choices is given to assist you as you explain and justify the choices you have made in the methodology chapter or section in your research report. Thus, this chapter leads you through the considerations you will have to take into account when making your data collection instrument and process decisions, indicates when and where the alternatives may be more, or less, appropriate and provides discussion and examples of good practice.

## 7.2  Questionnaires and Questions

Questionnaires, of one form or another, are so prevalent in everyday life that I am sure you have seen many different versions of them and the questions they include. However, regardless of the specific format and context, the main purpose of a questionnaire is to provide a vehicle for obtaining accurate information from a respondent, whether the questionnaire itself is very short or long, comprised of questions that are open-ended or closed and implemented by direct or distributed means.

All questionnaires are directive in nature as the questions they contain dictate what is to be asked, though some are more restrictive than others in this respect. They also provide some form of structure in terms of the kinds of responses that are desired and allowed and, in many cases, how these are to be recorded. However, whatever the specific format of a questionnaire, it should never be forgotten that it is only a means to achieving certain desired ends. These, of course are the empirical data requirements of the research question(s), aims or objectives or hypotheses. The questionnaire itself is merely a way of obtaining the data that you require to answer these questions, achieve the aims or objectives or test the hypotheses. Therefore, all the decisions relating to what type of questionnaire to use, what questions to ask and how to implement the process for collecting the data should be made with the aim that they will be the most appropriate and effective ways to achieve the wider purpose. This also needs to be borne in mind when you are constructing a questionnaire, writing the questions and deciding how it will be implemented because the only way you can provide a rationale or justification for the content, structure and implementation choices you make is by clearly indicating that they are consistent with the wider purposes the instrument and processes are designed to achieve.

One of the first issues you need to address when designing a questionnaire is what type of data do you wish to collect? If it is qualitative data – words – the structure and form of the questions will need to be suitable for eliciting this type of response from the respondent. Typically this is likely to lead you towards designing a questionnaire that is not overly structured and has open-ended questions – that is, those where the specific form of the response is not dictated by particular response options that are provided with the question. This may constitute nothing more than a list of interview questions that you wish to put directly to a respondent in a face-to-face situation with, possibly, other 'probes' depending on the responses given as the questionnaire interview progresses. For example, this type of follow-up probing may be brought into play when the respondent says something unexpected that you want to pursue further, something that is not clear so it needs further explanation or something particularly interesting that you would like the respondent to expand on further.

Thus the unstructured, open-ended form of questionnaire allows for a considerable amount of flexibility, in terms of what is asked, what is pursued further and how the data are recorded, and if implemented in a direct manner, it also facilitates the collection and recording of other, non-verbal information, such as body language and so on. This flexibility also enables more in-depth responses to be captured, which are often crucial in the collection of qualitative data. It can also help in situations where you are not sure of the nature and/or breadth of the possible responses that could be given to a question or set of questions. By contrast, questions that elicit closed responses need to meet the criteria we discussed in Chapter 5 – the response options for each question must be both mutually exclusive and collectively exhaustive. To achieve this, the questions invariably have to be quite specific and we will need to know what the possible answers to them could be.

The unstructured, open-ended approach to questionnaire design and implementation is often regarded as being most suitable for relatively small-scale, perhaps exploratory, research studies and/or those where in-depth information is required to generate a 'rich' picture of the issues being investigated. Its inherent flexibility facilitates in-depth enquiry, but this and the nature of the data collected do lead to some potential problems. As the respondents are allowed to provide the responses in their own words and, and to a certain extent, on their own terms, it might be expected that the truthfulness, accuracy or validity of the data would be high. This may be true in the sense that they are not being forced to select a predetermined option as their response, which they would have to do in a more structured, closed form of questionnaire, but for various reasons people do not always give 'truthful' answers. They may over- or understate certain issues. In some cases they may deliberately give false answers to cover up failures or avoid sensitive issues or they may give answers that they believe, but do not know, to be correct. They may express opinion as fact and they may give responses that they think you are looking for or expect rather than the ones that are really correct. In short, it is wise to be somewhat sceptical rather than simply accept responses of this type at face value.

There is also a reliability issue associated with this form of questionnaire. As the questions are not necessarily asked in the same or a standard way for each respondent and the responses are not recorded using a standard format or scale, then the degree of consistency in the questionnaire's design and implementation can be rather low. This is the downside of flexibility as different researchers may implement the same instrument in differing ways, either within the same research project or at a later date if repeated by other researchers, and such inconsistencies may generate inconsistent and unreliable data. In addition, the nature of the data precludes the type of objective, statistical analysis that can be applied to quantitative data. Words have to be interpreted and peoples' interpretations of the same collection of words can vary, leading to differing conclusions. The other aspect to this is that unstructured questionnaires generate a high volume of non-standard data from the words provided by the respondents. This can give rise to problems in terms of not only recording and/or transcribing the data but also in being able to cope with this volume of material when trying to analyse it.

If it is quantitative data that are required, the questions are likely to be much more specific, the options to answer or respond will be prescribed in the questionnaire, it will have a predetermined structure and instructions for the respondent on how to record their responses and progress through the questionnaire, and because of these features the data it collects will be amenable to some form of statistical analysis. This type of questionnaire is frequently referred to as one that is structured, with closed questions that use one of the measurement scales to prescribe the response options available to the respondents. It is a form usually associated with indirect and distributed implementation strategies where, because there is no direct contact between the person asking the questions and those answering them, the instrument and process have to be more prescribed, detailed and standardised.

The structured questionnaire is likely to be the preferred choice in situations where relatively large-scale surveys are being conducted, where the sample is geographically dispersed and can only be accessed by some form of remote communication, such as by mail, electronically or by telephone, and where quantitative data are required. That said, this form is also used for direct interviews such as market research interviews conducted in public spaces, or situations where the sample is self-selecting such as customer comment/feedback questionnaires left in hotel bedrooms, on restaurant tables, or at tourist destinations and attractions and so on. Structured and unstructured questionnaires – usually with predominantly closed or open questions respectively – have different implications for validity and reliability. In general, less structure and more openness in the questions create a less contrived and artificial situation for the collection of data and vice versa. This allows data to be collected in a more naturalistic environment and, hence, validity should be higher, but because it is inherently more flexible in form and application, this can lead to inconsistencies in its implementation that, in turn, will threaten the reliability of the questoinnaire and the process of administering it. The reverse is true for more structured, closed forms. They are much more artificial and constrained, but are applied in a consistent manner so they tend to be regarded as more reliable. Even so, there can be problems regarding validity.

Up to this point, it has been at least implicitly suggested that the choice between designing and using a qualitative and unstructured or quantitative and structured questionnaire is mutually exclusive in nature – that is, if one is chosen then the other cannot be. In reality, this is not the case as questionnaires can, and do, often contain questions that are unstructured *and* structured and designed to collect qualitative *and* quantitative data. This middle route may be described as semistructured or a hybrid, in that it features both open and closed questions to capture both types of data and, in many cases, to address questions not only of a factual nature – the what, when, where, how often and so on – but also those seeking information relating to underlying reasons – the why and how – for peoples' behaviour, attitudes, preferences or opinions. It is quite common for more unstructured, open-ended questions to be used as follow-ups or probes to the structured, closed questions in order to obtain information on the reasons for peoples' responses to the closed questions. For example, if a question asked, 'Which of the following list of holiday destinations would you like to visit the most?' it might be followed up with a request such as, 'Please state the reason(s) for your choice of destination above.'

This can be a very valuable tactic as it can generate data on the reasons certain people prefer certain destinations, in this case, but equally any other form of product, and can be used to elicit the thinking lying behind the attitudes or opinions people have expressed in closed responses. However, it can have negative consequences if it is over-used in a questionnaire. As the respondents have to think about, articulate and physically write responses in these cases, it is more difficult and time-consuming than answering a question where the response options are given and they only have to tick a box. Generally, respondents will not mind answering this type of question on a few occasions, but if they follow many of the questions as they progress through the questionnaire, they may feel that the task is becoming too difficult and time-consuming, become disillusioned and so will then fail to complete and return the questionnaire.

So how do you make the decision to choose one of the alternative forms of questionnaire discussed so far? Unfortunately, as with many decisions that have to be taken when designing and conducting a research project, there are no really hard and fast rules for this. Nevertheless, in general terms, the number of people or organisations to be surveyed, how geographically dispersed they are, the nature of the sample respondents, the type of information you need to collect, how you plan to implement the questionnaire and the data analysis methods you intend to use may all have some bearing on this choice.

Other things being equal, the larger the size of the survey and the more geographically dispersed the sample respondents are, which would imply a distributed implementation, then a structured questionnaire with closed questions is likely to be a suitable choice. Similarly, if the respondents are very busy people, then this format will probabaly be best as it is generally easy and quick to complete. If you need to collect quantitative data and intend to use statistical procedures to analyse it, then once again this format is likely to be best suited to your purposes. If these are not issues for your project, then it may be that a more unstructured, open and qualitative approach to question-naire design could be a better choice.

Whichever format is most appropriate for your needs, there are some basic design and preparation issues to be considered and decisions to be made before the questionnaire can be used to collect the data. As previously mentioned, one key issue is to be clear about is what information the questionnaire is to be used to collect. This is not just an issue of qualitative or quantitative data but also one of why the information is required and the purpose it will serve in the research project. To address this, as mentioned earlier, you need to be clear about the research question(s), aims and objectives and, possibly, the hypotheses to be tested. These will give you the rationale for needing the data, so it is logical to design a questionnaire that contains questions that are capable of helping you to obtain the particular types of information you need to shed some light on them.

Other key issues to consider are how the questionnaire is to be implemented and what the nature of the target respondents in the sample is. If the question-naire is to be implemented directly by yourself, in a face-to-face interview situation, then it will be much less important to include instructions in the questionnaire itself than if either a team of different people were to conduct the interviews or it was going to be implemented at a distance via one of the dis-tributed implementation options discussed earlier. Similarly, the format or style of the questionnaire will differ – even though the questions may be written in the same way – when different distribution strategies are used.

If on the one hand you are undertaking a direct interview with a respondent, then your ability to talk your interviewee through the questionnaire as the interview progresses is straightforward. On the other hand, if you are imple-menting the questionnaire by telephone, then the 'talk through' that you can give in a face-to-face situation needs to be written into the questionnaire as a form of script because you cannot see the interviewee and you cannot show him or her the questionnaire and questions you wish to ask. Similarly, when you send a questionnaire by mail, fax or electronic means to a respondent, you need to write 'instructions' into the questionnaire to tell the respondents what you wish them to do and how they should answer the questions. The important thing to do when you are not physically present to articulate the questions and show or explain how you wish the respondents to respond is to include this ele-ment of the implementation process in the questionnaire. How this is done will differ depending on whether you have some or no interactive contact with the respondent. The principle here is one of being able to control the implementa-tion process in such a way that it is as consistent as possible across all the respondents which, in turn, helps to avoid or reduce the possibility of error.

In terms of considering the nature of the respondents and how this might affect the way you design the questionnaire and write the questions, you need to try and put yourself in their position as the recipients of the questionnaire. If they are busy managers who have other, more important, priorities to attend to before they can even think about spending time completing your question- naire, then the way you design your questionnaire should reflect this. The implication here is that you need to try and ensure that it is as easy and quick as possible to complete – otherwise, they may simply decide that they cannot afford to spend the time necessary to complete it, which could dramatically reduce the response rate you are able to achieve. Interestingly, this does not automatically mean that you should attempt to keep the questionnaire as short as possible in terms of the number of questions and/or pages.

It is not the overall length of the questionnaire or the number of questions per se that can make it quicker or longer, easier or harder to complete. A ques- tionnaire might be quite long in terms of the number of questions and pages it covers, but relatively quick and easy to complete and vice versa. What is more critical than its physical length or the number of questions is the nature of the questions. In general terms, closed questions are quicker and easier to answer than open ones because the responses are included in the questionnaire and the respondents do not have to think about how they should word this answers – all they have to do is tick a box, circle a number and so on. Hence, a longer ques- tionnaire with a lot of closed questions may be quicker and easier to complete than a shorter one containing mainly open questions.

This is not to say that you should therefore choose closed rather than open questions per se. What you choose will depend on the type of data you wish to obtain, so opting for closed questions simply because they are quicker and eas- ier to complete would be like the proverbial tail wagging the dog! Nevertheless, some questions can be asked in either closed or open forms without there being any detriment to the resulting data. Where this is the case, it would be sensible to choose the former rather than the latter form. For example, you could ask a question about the respondents' gender in an open form, such as 'Please state your gender below' and the respondents would have to write male or female. Alternatively, you could provide these two responses with boxes alongside and ask, 'Please indicate your gender below by ticking the appropriate box.' This involves slightly more effort on your part, but it makes life easier for the respon- dents. This may also have a positive effect on respondents because they may be more interested in helping you if you show, in the way that the questionnaire is constructed, that you have considered their needs by making it as easy as pos- sible for them to cooperate in completing the questionnaire.

Regardless of whether your target respondents are busy people or not, you are asking them to do you a favour. Generally, there will be no benefit to them in giv- ing up their time and taking the trouble to think about and answer the questions, so why should they bother? A poorly designed questionnaire that does not con- sider that the respondents may not be particularly interested in your project and its questions is likely to result in a lower than expected, or hoped for, response rate. Thus, in addition to attempts to make the questionnaire as easy and quick to complete as possible, it is important to try and generate some interest, enthusiasm and desire on the part of the respondents to assist you by completing the questionnaire. You would be wise to try and motivate them in some way.

This can be achieved by giving careful consideration to the questionnaire's introduction. The introduction is your opportunity to not only inform the respondents of the nature and purpose of the questionnaire, but also to try and sell the exercise to them in such a way that their interest is generated and they become motivated to engage more enthusiastically in the exercise.

If this is successful, then it is likely to improve the response rate because more questionnaires will be completed and returned. Exhibit 7.1 shows an introductory statement from a postal questionnaire that was cold-mailed to the companies in the sample I used in a research project (Brotherton, 2004a) and that generated a response rate of 38.5 per cent. This is a figure considerably in excess of that normally associated with this questionnaire implementation strategy. Of course, an alternative would be to include this text within a covering, or explanatory, letter sent with the questionnaire, but this may not be as effective because it is a separate piece of paper that could become detached from the questionnaire or not read at all. Furthermore, you may wish, or need, to put other important information in the introductory statement to explain or clarify certain terms used in the questionnaire that could be open to differing interpretations on the part of the respondents, as is the case in Exhibit 7.2. Exhibit 7.2 is from the same project as Exhibit 7.1 and was included as it was important to try and ensure, as far as was reasonably possible, that the people completing the questionnaire all had the same understanding of what a particular term meant in the context of that questionnaire.

---

### Exhibit 7.1    Framing the Questionnaire's Introduction

#### Introduction

The primary aim of the research this questionnaire is being used for is to identify the critical success factors (CSFs) within UK Hotels PLC and to undertake a comparative analysis of these CSFs to determine the extent to which generic CSFs may be identified for this sector of the hospitality industry. This questionnaire will be the main data collection instrument for this survey. As you will see the questionnaire is divided into two sections as follows: hotel information and departmental CSFs. The responses provided in the first section will be used to structure the responses in section 2 for classificatory and comparative analysis purposes. Those in section 2 will comprise the substantive data for this research study.

I appreciate that you are a busy professional with little free time to engage in an exercise of this nature and that this will certainly not be one of your main priorities, but I sincerely hope that you can find the time to complete and return this questionnaire because without your cooperation it will be impossible to achieve the aim of this project.

Therefore, can I thank you in anticipation of your cooperation and ask that the completed questionnaire be returned to me in the enclosed reply-paid envelope by the date given at the end of the questionnaire. ***Please note***: **The information you provide on this questionnaire will be treated in the strictest confidence and will only be used for academic research. Should the results obtained from this questionnaire be published in an academic paper they will not be attributed to any individual. Neither will the results be released to any third party for commercial gain.**

---

### *Exhibit 7.2    Defining Terms that Could be Interpreted in Different Ways*

Before completing this questionnaire it is important that all respondents have the same understanding of the terms used in order that consistent results are obtained. Therefore, I would be obliged if you could take a couple of minutes to read the definition of *critical success factors* given below before responding to the questions.

**Critical success factors** (CSFs) are defined as: *the limited number of factors that have ensured successful performance.* They are not objectives, but the factors critical to successfully meeting business objectives. In short, CSFs are a means to an end.

---

The same principle, of trying to get the respondents on side, can also be addressed via the style, appearance, layout and structure of the questionnaire by ensuring the following.

- It is easy to understand – it has clear questions and directions.
- It is easy to complete – it has closed rather than open questions where appropriate, with simple response recording techniques that are sequenced from easier to harder, less to more sensitive/personal, and general to more specific.
- It generates sufficient interest to keep respondents going to the finish – achieved by having a suitable introduction and a variety of question formats.
- It is structured using appropriate sections.

All these things can help to improve the chances of the questionnaire being completed and returned.

Much of this is really common sense, yet it often seems to be forgotten when questionnaires are designed. Put yourself in the recipients' shoes and think – if you received a questionnaire that was poorly designed and laid out, with unclear questions sequenced in no apparent order, without any subdivisions, with either no or few useful directions to help you understand how to answer the questions, requiring you to write long answers, how likely is it that you would feel motivated to complete that questionnaire? The answer to this is self-evident – highly unlikely. Similarly, if you are going to take the time and trouble to do someone else a free favour by completing a questionnaire, you might feel happier about doing so if the person who sent it to you thanked you for doing so. A statement to this effect can obviously be included at the end of the questionnaire, but it may also be useful to insert such a statement at the end of the introduction or after it, thanking people in advance or in anticipation of them completing the questionnaire. Finally, the inclusion of a reply-paid envelope may also help to improve the response rate because this again shows you recognise the return of the completed questionnaire incurs a cost and that you do not expect the respondent to bear this.

To make life easier for yourself, once the completed questionnaires have been returned, you may also want to consider 'precoding' the closed question response options by entering coding numbers on the questionnaire. This is not always necessary, such as where your questions use a predetermined scale of say 1 to 5 as the numbers to enter into the data analysis software already exist, but, where the questions do not use such a scale, then there is the issue of converting categories or responses into numbers. For example, if you include the gender question mentioned above, respondents are going to indicate whether they are male or female by either writing this or ticking the appropriate box, but entering numbers into data analysis software is easier, quicker and can facilitate other calculations. So, for example, you may choose to code the response of 'male' as the number 1, and that of female as 2.

One thing you should note about this coding is that it is not a good idea to use zeros as a code number because these will contaminate any calculations you may wish to perform on the data. For example, if you wanted to calculate averages or percentages, then zeros would distort the calculations. If you do not want to include code numbers on the questionnaire itself, you can still precode the responses by having either a coding sheet that contains the code numbers to be used when the data is entered at a later date or by putting these on to a master, coding copy of the questionnaire that you use to enter the data from the completed questionnaires.

By now you should have a good idea of the issues to be considered when compiling and structuring a questionnaire, but we have not yet discussed key issues associated with formulating and writing the questions that are going to form the substantive content of the questionnaire. The term 'questions' is a little misleading, however. Although you may have items that are worded as questions in your questionnaire, you may also have items that are worded as statements. Indeed, it is quite possible to ask essentially the same thing by wording it as either a question or a statement. Individual questionnaires may clearly differ in terms of the specific questions or statements that are included in them because they have different contexts and purposes. That said, questionnaires tend to contain basic types of questions or statements designed to obtain information on the respondents' characteristics, behaviour or perceptions and attitudes.

Questions designed to obtain information on the respondents' characteristics are used to classify or group respondents with the same characteristic. For example, if the respondents are individuals, as opposed to people responding on behalf of an organisation, then you may wish to know their gender, age, occupation, income level, marital status, where they live or work and so on. There are two main reasons for collecting this type of information. One is to help you describe the characteristics of the repondents in your sample. This is often important if you wish to claim that the realised sample is representative of the population as a whole. Second, you may want to compare the responses given to other types of question on the basis of differences in your respondents. For example, you may want to examine whether the behaviour or views of male and female, younger or older, richer or poorer, married or single respondents are the same or different. Exhibit 7.3 shows a set of questions taken from a recent study (Brotherton, 2005) that were designed to obtain this type of information.

---

### Exhibit 7.3  Questions Designed to Obtain 'Categorical' Data from Individuals

**Q6**  What is your gender?                    Male ❑          Female ❑

**Q7**  Have you stayed in this hotel before?   Yes ❑           No ❑

                                               *(Go to Q8)*     *(Go to Q9)*

**Q8**  Approximately how many times?      _____

**Q9**  What is your stay here for?            Business ❑      Leisure ❑

**Q10**  Which of the following best describes your ethnic origin?

White European          ❑          Black Afro-Caribbean   ❑

Asian Indian            ❑          Oriental               ❑

**Q11**  Which of the following age groups do you belong to?

18–24 ❑     25–34 ❑     35 44 ❑

45–54 ❑     55–64 ❑     65+ ❑

**Q12**  How would you describe your occupation?

Managerial/professional      ❑          Clerical/administrative      ❑

Skilled manual               ❑          Unskilled manual             ❑

                                                          *(Cont'd)*

---

**Q13** Finally, could you tell me what level of education best describes you?

| | | | |
|---|---|---|---|
| GCSE (or equivalent) | ❑ | GCE A level (or equivalent) | ❑ |
| Higher National Diploma/ Certificate | ❑ | Bachelor's degree | ❑ |
| Master's degree | ❑ | Doctorate | ❑ |

---

In the case of a questionnaire addressing representatives of organisations, you may ask similar types of questions, but the content of these will clearly be different. You may typically want to know about the size of the organisation, where it is located, what brand it belongs to, what standard or quality it is (for a hotel, what star rating it is, for example) and other criteria that might be useful when analysing similarities or differences between the organisations in the sample in their responses to other questions . Exhibit 7.4 provides examples of these types of classificatory questions, used to gather the data for the Brotherton (2004b) study.

---

## Exhibit 7.4    Questions Designed to Obtain 'Categorical' Data on Companies

**1  Your hotel's brand**

| | | | | | |
|---|---|---|---|---|---|
| Travelodge | ❑ | Premier Travel Inn | ❑ | Holiday Inn Express | ❑ |
| Campanile | ❑ | Comfort Inn | ❑ | Premier Lodge | ❑ |
| Lodge Inns | ❑ | IBIS | ❑ | | |

**2  Your hotel's name:**

**3  Your position/title:**

**4  The hotel's location**

| | | | | | |
|---|---|---|---|---|---|
| Motorway | ❑ | A road | ❑ | Airport | ❑ |
| City centre | ❑ | Town suburb | ❑ | Rural | ❑ |

**5  Number of bedrooms in the hotel**

| | | | | | |
|---|---|---|---|---|---|
| Fewer than 20 | ❑ | 21–30 | ❑ | 31–40 | ❑ |
| 41–50 | ❑ | 51–60 | ❑ | Over 60 | ❑ |

**6  Room price:**        £_____

---

---

**7  Average annual room occupancy for the hotel:** _____ %

**8  Number of staff employed in the hotel:**

Full-time _____                    Part-time _____

**9  Approximate breakdown of annual business**

Business guests _____%                    Non-business guests _____%

---

Behavioural questions are designed to collect information on, not surprisingly, the behaviour of the respondents – what they do, when they do these things, how often they do them, where, in what ways and so on. In the case of an organisation, these may be the types of products and/or services they provide, the standard(s) of them, when and where they are available, how much they cost and so on. Behavioural questions, then, collect factual information on what individuals or organisations do and, possibly, what they own. Typically, in a hospitality or tourism context, you might be interested to know which hotels, destinations or attractions people visit, when they tend to do this, how often or frequently, whether they do this alone or with friends or family, how far they travel to make such visits, how much they spend and so on.

Perceptual or attitudinal questions do not focus on the actual behaviour of individuals or organisations but on how they think of, view or rate particular things. This might be the image they hold of something, their preferences and/or intentions, an explanation of why they make particular choices or their opinions on specific issues. Such questions are widely used to gather information on the extent to which people agree or disagree with certain statements or issues, how important or unimportant the items are to them, how they compare a range of items against one another using criteria given to them and so on. Although many perceptual and attitudinal factors may influence the present and/or future behavioural patterns of individuals and organisations – and thereby will provide information on the reasons for their actual or intended behaviour – these perceptions and attitudes are also formed from their previous behavioural experiences and, as such, can be used to elicit opinions and judgements on these experiences.

Although, in an unstructured questionnaire, these three types of questions may be asked in an open-ended format, they are more associated with closed formats using a scale to record the responses. From Chapter 5, you will recall that there are four basic types of measurement scale: nominal, ordinal, interval and ratio. Classification questions tend to use nominal and possibly ratio-type scales because all that is required of these questions is that they obtain information to enable you to place the respondents into certain groups or categories based on their characteristics. In Exhibit 7.4, questions 1, 4 and 5 are examples of closed, single response, nominal scale questions; 6 and 7 are single response, ratio scale questions; 8 is a multiple response, ratio scale question; and 9 is a multiple response, nominal scale question.

Behavioural and attitudinal questions may be formulated using either nominal or ratio scales, but ordinal and/or interval scales are more frequently used for these questions because they facilitate the collection of more detailed or fine-grained information on the issue(s) in question. For example, it is possible to ask whether a respondent agrees or disagrees with a statement or regards something as important or not, but these dichotomous, nominal scale questions only collect what is known as bipolar information on the issue. This simply means that a response to the extremes of agreement or disagreement, importance or unimportance, good or bad, expensive or cheap and so on can be obtained, but nothing will be known about the gradations between these extremes.

With questions formulated in this way, you may be able to identify the black and white of the issues, but not any of the shades of grey between the extremes – in the jargon, your measurement scale will lack precision. Also, because you are forcing the respondents to choose an extreme positive or negative position in order to make a response, this raises issues of validity. Simply put, the respondents may not hold such extreme views and would wish to give a response that is slightly positive or negative, but they are not able to because the scale forces them to record one that is either totally positive or negative. Thus, the data may not be valid or true reflections of peoples' views, beliefs and so on on the issue(s).

Questions using an ordinal scale ask respondents to place items in order within a given range using a criterion given in the question. For example, 'From the list of ten items below that may influence your satisfaction with the visit to this museum, please place them in order in terms of which would have the greatest influence on your satisfaction to the least by entering a single and different number from 1 (most) to 10 (least) against each one.' The important feature of this type of question is that a reason or criterion is given for respondents to make their choices. This provides a basis for the respondents to make relative comparisons between the items. Such criteria could be wide ranging, as the context and content of this type of question can be equally broad. However, criteria such as cost or price, quality, availability, frequency of purchase or visit, desirability, value for money, attractiveness and so on may typically be used.

It is questions using an interval scale that tend to have lots of variations on the specific scale type or form. You will know many of these from your own experiences of seeing and completing questionnaires in your everyday life, though you may not know the more technical terms for them that are used in research methodology jargon.

One of the most common forms of interval scale used in questionnaires is known as the Likert scale. Devised by Rensis Likert in the early part of the twentieth century, the Likert scale uses statements to which respondents indicate the extent of their agreement or disagreement. Likert scale questions – or, more accurately, statements – can be written in positive or negative forms regarding the relationship with the variable being investigated. This simply means that the implications of agreement and disagreement are reversed.

Exhibit 7.5 shows an example of this. Here the same statement is written in positive and negative forms. Any 'agree' response to the first version would indicate a positive relationship between the independent variable 'loyalty cards' and the dependent variable 'repeat business'. In the case of the second version, this type or relationship would be signified by a 'disagree' response. Therefore, where negatively worded statements are associated with positive independent–dependent variable relationships, the scale scores have to be reversed.

---

### Exhibit 7.5    Positively and Negatively Worded Likert Scale Statements

|  | Strongly agree | Agree | Neither agree nor disagree | Disagree | Strongly disagree |
|---|---|---|---|---|---|
| **Version 1** Loyalty cards help to increase repeat business in hotels. | 1 | 2 | 3 | 4 | 5 |
| **Version 2** Loyalty cards do not help to increase repeat business in hotels. | 1 | 2 | 3 | 4 | 5 |

---

This may sound complicated, but it is quite simple in practice. If respondents indicate that they strongly disagree with the statement in Exhibit 7.5 that loyalty cards do not help to increase repeat business in hotels, then, logically, they are expressing the opinion that they strongly agree they do have this effect. In Version 1 of the statement, a strong agreement would score 1 on the 1–5 scale, but, in Version 2, effectively the same response would score 5 because of the reversed statement. Without converting the response to Version 2 from a score of 5 to 1, effectively the same opinion would be recorded as positive in the first instance and negative in the second. Clearly that would be nonsense.

Varying the polarity of statements in a set of Likert scale items can be useful because it can help to keep the respondent alert, but be careful here as too much changing from positive to negative wordings can be confusing and irritating.

However, used judiciously, it can form a type of cross-checking mechanism. In our example, including both versions of the statement in a set of items could help check the consistency of the responses as we would expect both forms of the statement to elicit a consistent underlying response. However, where this tactic is employed, it is not a good idea to place the two forms of the statement adjacent to each other because this could annoy the respondents.

Another common form of interval scale used in contemporary question-naires is known as the itemised rating scale. Again, you are likely to be familiar with this. It is commonly used to obtain responses within a bipolar range that varies between very positive and very negative. Rather than asking respondents if they are satisfied with an experience or if something is important to them, which invites a simple yes or no answer, this scale explores the intermediate positions between these opposites. Therefore, using this example, an itemised rating scale would ask respondents to indicate the 'extent' to which they are sat-isfied or the item is important. So, for example, the question might be, 'To what extent have you been satisfied with your visit to this theme park today?' and the response options would be given on a sliding scale of 'Extremely, Very, Fairly, Not very, Not at all'. Alternatively, and using the same response options, a ques-tion might ask organisational respondents to indicate the importance of a sys-tematic quality assurance system for customer satisfaction.

Itemised rating scales are really quite straightforward, but there are some issues to be resolved when constructing and using them. One of these is whether to use a balanced or unbalanced scale. If you think about it, this is a simple matter. There are only three possible categories of response – positive, neutral or negative. A balanced scale will have at least one of each, but, more typically, will have at least one neutral option and two or three positive and neg-ative options in the form of five or seven-point scales. The neutral response option is only ever a single point in the scale, as it is not possible to differenti-ate between two or more points of indifference between the positive and nega-tive reactions, but it is possible to have more positive or negative points. This would increase the precision of the scale, but as the number of points increases, respondents may find it difficult to produce such finely differentiated responses. In reality, most researchers find that either a five- or seven-point scale is sufficient. The other problem that arises if you increase the number of points in the scale is the difficulty of finding suitably worded descriptions for each point that are sufficiently different from each other to warrant their inclu-sion. For example, to differentiate between 'extremely' and 'very' is reasonably simple, but to try and find suitably differentiated descriptors for another two or three points between these two would be more problematic.

An unbalanced scale will not have a neutral option but will have equal numbers of positive and negative points. These are therefore also known as even-numbered scales, whereas balanced scales are odd numbered. An unbalanced scale creates what is known as a forced choice for respondents. In other words they are forced to make a positive or negative response as there is no intermediate option. In the literature, the jury is out over whether a balanced or unbalanced scale is more appropriate. Some commentators argue that everyone has an opinion one way or the other and therefore the neutral option is essentially a cop-out. Others argue that an unbalanced scale denies respondents the opportunity to express a legitimate response where they have no strong opinion in either direction or wish to indicate indifference, so this raises issues of validity. My personal view on this issue is that it is preferable to use a balanced, odd-numbered scale because this avoids the forced choice issue and potential validity criticisms.

What are known as semantic differential scales are also widely used in research questionnaires. The term semantic differential simply means different meanings. In some respects, it is a similar idea to the Likert and itemised rating scales because it facilitates a response between bipolar opposites, such as fast and slow, bright and dark, modern and old-fashioned, hot and cold, expensive and cheap. Although it is used to obtain data on single items or issues, in common with the other types, it is particularly useful for collecting comparative data. For example, if you wanted to compare the characteristics of different hotels, restaurants, theme parks, museums, destination resorts or countries, brands of a product and so on, then a semantic differential scale with a set of suitable bipolar opposites relating to the context could be used to compare quite a range of such entities.

Whatever type of scale is used to provide the response options for the question or statement, it is important to remember that there should be a match between how these are worded. This may sound obvious, but in my experience, it is not always recognised. For example, if you are using a Likert scale, which invites respondents to agree or disagree with statements, then these should not be written as questions. Alternatively, if you are using an itemised rating scale – from extremely to not at all – then you need to ask them a question. In addition, when writing the questions or statements, there are innumerable pitfalls that, if not recognised and addressed, can have significant implications for the clarity and/or validity of the questions. These are highlighted, with illustrative examples, in Exhibit 7.6.

---

### Exhibit 7.6    *Writing Questions – Potential Problems to Avoid*

- Only ask *one* question at a time – avoid what are known as double-barrelled questions. For example, a question that asks, 'Have you visited this hotel before and were you satisfied with it? Yes ☐ No ☐' is asking two questions in one. The respondent may have visited the hotel previously but was not satisfied with it, so would want to answer 'yes' to one part but 'no' to the other. Splitting the question into two separate ones could easily solve this problem.

*(Cont'd)*

- Questions should not 'lead' a respondent to give a particular response. This introduces bias into the question. For example, a question that asks 'Do you believe that airlines in general should reduce the price of flight tickets?' is likely to attract either a 100 per cent 'yes' response or something very close to it because most people would like to travel more cheaply. It would be in their interests to say yes rather than no!
- Using partial or incomplete lists of response options is also to be avoided as this partiality may mean that the choices respondents wish to make are not there. For example, a question that asks, 'Which of the following destinations would be your preferred choice for your main annual holiday? Mediterranean □ USA □ Caribbean □' would be very limited. The remedy for this is to provide a much wider listing of possible destinations or to include a catch-all category that respondents could use to indicate an alternative preference, such as 'Another destination □ (please specify)_____'.
- Forcing respondents to take an extreme position, when they may not wish to do so, by asking a question in a 'loaded' manner should also be resisted. For example, a statement such as, 'Trade unions will always reduce labour flexibility in the workplace', inviting agreement or disagreement, is likely to polarise responses, especially if only agree or disagree options are given, as the word 'always' loads this question. Respondents who believe that trade unions may sometimes have this effect, but not always, would have to disagree, even though they believe trade unions may have this effect on some occasions.
- Questions that are said to be recall-dependent – that is, they rely too much on people's memory – are likely to be problematic because, if they cannot remember the real answer, they are likely to guess to provide a response. In this situation, it will be impossible for you to distinguish between accurate answers and those based on guesswork! Therefore, it is advisable to only ask questions relating to contemporary issues, behaviour and so on or the immediate past. Unfortunately, the term 'immediate past' can be a rather moveable proposition, but some commonsense judgement has to be applied, depending on the context. For example, it may be quite justifiable to ask a person where they have travelled to on holiday for the last two, three or possibly five years, but to ask them more detailed questions on what they did on these trips would be more difficult for them remember.
- Bear in mind that not all your respondents will have the same sophisticated language skills as you or will be familiar with the jargon related to the topic, so try to avoid using complicated language and jargon. For example, let's consider the question, 'Would you regard the olfactory nature of the food in this restaurant as inviting or not? Yes □ No □'. The term 'olfactory' may not be understood by some, perhaps many, of the respondents. This would cast doubt on the validity of the responses because if people do not understand the question, they cannot answer it properly. It would be preferable to ask, 'Was the aroma of the food inviting?' as this is a term understood by all.

- Direct questions should be exactly that – they should not be phrased in vague or ambiguous terms. Thus, to ask, 'Would it be likely that you might consider making a visit to a museum within the next year? Yes ☐ No ☐', confronts respondents with a number of issues to resolve in their minds before they are able to given an answer. Essentially, what is being asked here is, how likely is it that they will even consider making a visit to any museum, anywhere, in the next 12 months? This is not easy to give a considered answer to because there are so many imponderables, so many conditional factors that make a definitive answer difficult to arrive at.

- In terms of making questions clear and unambiguous it is a good idea to avoid using double or triple negatives in the wording. For example, a question such as, 'Would you never even consider visiting this destination at any time in the future?' would be a poor one. It would be better to ask, 'Would you consider visiting this destination in the future?' because this would elicit the same information – yes or no – but it is stated in positive and much clearer terms than the first question.

- Hypothetical questions invite hypothetical answers and, as such, are highly suspect in terms of the validity of the data provided in the responses. For example, a question that asks respondents to assess the likelihood of something hypothetical happening, or how they might react to a hypothetical situation, invites speculation and it is extremely difficult, if not impossible, to discern the basis on which such speculative responses are arrived at by respondents.

- The use of emotive and/or sensitive words in a question is likely to generate either emotive responses, or no responses at all, because respondents may be annoyed that you are asking such questions. For example, asking respondents to give their exact income or age may be resented. Similarly, highly personal questions about people's private thoughts or behaviour or asking companies to answer commercially sensitive questions are likely to remain unanswered on the basis that they are unnecessarily intrusive.

- Asking questions that require respondents to make calculations before they can answer is fraught with problems because it is invariably impossible to tell whether the calculations they have made are accurate or not and peoples' abilities to employ such skills are highly variable. Therefore, the accuracy or validity of such responses is likely to be very suspect. For example, a question that asks, 'What proportion of your annual income would you spend on your main holiday?' would be problematic as it is likely respondents would guess the answer rather than take the trouble to actually calculate this accurately. Also, unless another question asks what respondents' annual income is, which would be problematic as it is sensitive, personal information, it would be pointless anyway because, without knowing what the annual income is, you cannot determine the actual value of the proportion indicated.

Finally, in terms of the form or type of question to be used, it is worth noting that there are 'standard' and 'non-standard' forms of question. The former is really quite self-explanatory. Standard questions are of the type you will be familiar with from questionnaires you will have generally come into contact with. They are comprised of a direct question or statement that is formulated in words and will have a response option or options formulated in either a similar manner or by utilising some form of graphic(s). Non-standard questions tend to use a different type of stimuli for respondents to react to. This form of questioning is discussed further in Section 7.5, Projective Techniques, later in this chapter, but the non-standard approach may mean the use of stimuli, such as pictures or photographs, cartoons, advertisements, company logos and so on, or more indirect forms of questioning, where purposely vague stimuli are used to provoke respondents into revealing their more subconscious perceptions, feelings, associations and so on.

With these more indirect forms of questioning, it is always vital to ask respondents why they have chosen a particular response. Without doing this, it is impossible to know what connotations the responses have for them. Furthermore, this type of follow-up question may also help to reveal which aspects of the stimulus have been particularly instrumental in helping to form or influence the respondents' perceptions or opinions. For example, if pictures of different tourist destinations were used in a questionnaire and respondents were asked to indicate what type of animal they associated with each one, they may respond with a wide variety of animals, from normal domestic dogs and cats to more exotic species. Without asking them why they have chosen those animals, you would not know what they meant to them in that context and, therefore, what their real reactions to the stimuli were.

Once you have completed your draft questionnaire, you need to evaluate it. This is sometimes referred to as questionnaire piloting or pre-implementation testing. The purpose of this is to identify any potential deficiencies, omissions, errors and so on in the questionnaire and eliminate them before it is used to collect actual data.

There are various ways in which this can be achieved, but the most appropriate is usually regarded as being a pilot test conducted on the same types of people who are going to be the actual respondents. The reason for doing this is fairly obvious. If this small-scale test indicates that there are no problems, then it is highly likely using it on a larger scale with similar people will generate a similar reaction and vice versa. The respondents in the pilot test are asked to complete the questionnaire as though it was a real exercise, but are also asked to indicate any difficulties they encountered – were the questions and response options clear and unambiguous, were the instructions/directions clear and helpful, were any questions worded in a leading or loaded manner, were any of the questions double-barrelled (with two questions in one), were any questions worded in an offensive or insensitive way and so on.

Although using respondents for the pilot who are the same type of people as those you plan to give the actual questionnaire to later is ideal, it may not always be practicable in the context of a student research project. This is because it can take some time and involve additional costs, particularly if the survey's sample is geographically dispersed, which may not be an option or too expensive. Therefore, a more limited form of testing may need to take place, using for example, academic tutors, family members, friends, fellow students or others who are readily available and have the time to help you. Though this may not be the ideal or perfect way to test your questionnaire, it is better than doing nothing at all and it is often surprising when other independent and uninvolved people see something that you have not picked up on because you are so involved in and close to the work.

However you conduct your questionnaire evaluation, this, along with any amendments you make and why you are doing so, should be recorded in the methodology chapter or section of your project report or dissertation because it helps to show that a process has been gone through to try and ensure that the data collection instrument (the questionnaire) is as free from error as possible and, therefore, that the data it has collected should be considered as credible.

## 7.3 Interviewing

Research interviews can take a variety of forms and can be conducted in a number of ways. An interview may be highly structured, controlled and specific stimulus-response affair conducted within a formal interviewer-interviewee situation, or may be much more flexible, open-ended, discursive and more like a non-directive, two-way conversation. It may take place face to face or via some form of technology, such as the telephone, video-conferencing, or webcam, that still facilitates real-time interaction between the parties. These interviews can be conducted on a one-to-one basis or in a group environment. Further, as we will see later in this chapter, they may be utilised as one approach to collecting data within field or observational research projects and to facilitate the implementation of non-standard techniques, such as projective techniques.

Whatever the specific form and method of implementation, the basic purpose of an interview remains the same – to obtain the required information from the respondent or repondents. Thus, the interview method shares the same characteristics as other types of data collection, in that it is a means to an end, with the end being defined by the information required to answer the research question(s), achieve the aim or objectives and/or test the hypotheses. In this sense, the primary reference point for determining what should be asked, in what form and how the interview should be conducted is derived from these overall purposes.

That said, we might still ask, why should interviewing be chosen as the preferred form of data collection rather than the other alternatives available? Unfortunately this is not a simple question to answer as there can be many factors affecting such a decision. However, interviewing is generally regarded as a useful approach where qualitative data are required and more in-depth exploration is necessary. Although interviewing can be, and is, used in formal questionnaire-based survey research, where respondents are interviewed on a face-to-face basis with a structured questionnaire, it is perhaps more commonly associated with a more open, less structured instrument and process, within which dialogue between the interviewer and interviewee is guided by the interview questions, but is also allowed to flow around these in a more iterative and interactive manner.

Indeed, one of the advantages of interviewing when compared to other more structured and deterministic methods of data collection is sometimes seen to be the degree of flexibility that exists while the process of collecting the data is taking place. Of course, this varies according to the type of interview and how it is conducted, but regardless of this, as there is real-time contact between the two parties, the opportunity will arise for interaction and, therefore, deviations from a standard script to take place as a consequence of the responses given. This, of course, is not possible at all in the case of a distributed survey questionnaire, where the content and process have to be standardised and contained within the data collection instrument itself, and is often more limited in, say, telephone interviewing, where the recording of responses is frequently more standardised than in face-to-face situations.

On the other hand, as interviewing does tend to attract such idiosyncratic implementation, this very flexibility can be seen as a potential problem. Because it is not standardised, each interview is something of a unique event, due to the varying dynamics that are created between the interviewer and interviewees. This is a feature that is likely to be even more problematic when there are a number of different interviewers, but even where there is only one, the fact remains that the way an interview unfolds and, hence, what happens in it, will vary according to the nature of the relationship established between the interviewer and successive interviewees. It is axiomatic that the different personalities and behavioural characteristics encountered within a set of seemingly similar interviewees will generate different dynamics and relationships in the interview situation, thereby making them different from one another. Therefore, although the flexibility inherent in interviewing can help to explore and probe issues more thoroughly, it can, because of this, make comparing data from different interviews problematic.

In general terms, interviewing is frequently viewed as a desirable method of data collection where in-depth data are required. Where the purpose is not simply to obtain data relating to questions concerned with what, where, when or how frequently but also explanations of the why and how of the issue, interviewing is a method that, relatively easily, facilitates this type of investigation. As explanations of the why or how of some action or behaviour tend to be more idiosyncratic and complex than descriptions of the actions or behaviours themselves, it is not easy to devise standardised questions to elicit this information. Even if it were, the nature of the responses is that they are likely to be conditional, contingent and rather long.

Group interviewing – also known as focus groups (FGs) – is an interviewing method used where it is important to capture the interactions between the group members and see how these affect the overall response. Though FGs are generally regarded as a non-directed form of interviewing, as the group discussion and interactions flow more freely than in a traditional, scripted, one-to-one interview, they do have a particular focus, hence the name! The focus could be almost anything, but typically, FGs have been used to gauge customers' or employees' feelings about and reactions to new developments, policies, products, advertising messages and identified problems. Whatever its specific nature, this focus provides the basic parameter used to guide the group discussions, though this may also be supplemented with other stimuli to aid the discussion in general and/or provide a vehicle to steer it towards certain desired aspects of the overall purpose.

FGs, typically, are comprised of six to 12 'appropriate' members with a group leader or facilitator to oversee the process. What makes for an 'appropriate' member is difficult to define, but, in order to generate discussion, there is a need to invite or select a range of different members who have some interest in the issues to be discussed. A focus group comprised of very similar people (a homogeneous composition) would not reflect a sufficient variety of views, opinions and reactions and the ensuing discussion may turn out to be limited and rather sterile. On the other hand, a group comprised of people who were all very different (a heterogeneous composition) with nothing at all in common may result in disagreement for disagreement's sake. Thus, a composition that lies somewhere between these extremes, with a suitable balance of 'appropriate' members, is preferable.

As FGs are small and, usually, the members are not selected at random, they are not regarded as representative samples and, therefore, the ability to generalise from their results to the wider population is problematic at best and, realistically, inadvisable. In addition to the characteristics of the sample, the fact that the environment for the focus group may be regarded as artificial, that there is often a high degree of subjectivity in the process itself its management and in the interpretation of the results, plus that the results can be strongly influenced by the groups' leaders, makes valid generalisations impossible.

As a consequence of these attributes, FGs are often viewed as an interviewing method more suitable for the exploratory and/or initial testing and evaluation stages of a research project than the main empirical data collection phase. Given the nature of the FG environment and process, it is particularly suitable for identifying the issues or aspects of a particular phenomena that are important to companies, customers, employees and so on that can then be used to develop more structured data collection instruments or test the validity of such instruments prior to their implementation. That said, because FGs can help to establish insights into underlying thinking and reasoning, they can be used alongside other data collection methods to add this type of information to that which is more descriptive.

# 7.4 Observation

If you are an undergraduate undertaking a research project, then data collection using observational methods is likely to be a choice precluded by time and, possibly, access, considerations. If you are a postgraduate student, these may not be such significant issues. That said, if you are interested in this approach to data collection, the chapter written on observational research by Jauncey (1999) and the two books by Leidner (1993) and Watson (1997), containing details of observational approaches to different issues within McDonald's in the USA and East Asia, would be useful places to start.

Although observational methods of data collection can include laboratory or field experimentation, where the research environment is highly structured, they are more commonly associated with what is often referred to as field research which takes place in naturalistic settings. In these contexts, observation may be of a participant or non-participant nature. Both contain the same potential problem of contamination that can generate validity issues. In short, the presence of an outsider observing behaviour, whether participating or not, can influence or distort normal patterns of behaviour and, hence, give rise to questions regarding the validity of what is being observed.

Such changes in behaviour can occur for a variety of reasons. Those being observed may regard the observer as a potential threat, a type of spy, and may seek to hide behaviour that might be perceived as damaging to them if revealed. Alternatively, they may see the observer as an ally who can be used to serve their purposes to some extent and so over emphasise certain behaviour, such as being more positive than usual or seeking to use the observer as an unwitting agent to further their desire for improvements in the workplace, distorting normality for their own ends. If disturbances to the normal set of conditions in a situation do occur, this is said to reduce the ecological validity of the data being collected, as the presence of the observer has effectively contaminated the true situation.

The reliability of observational data is also an issue. Reliability can be assessed on both an internal and external basis. Internal reliability, or consistency, is concerned with the plausibility and coherence of the picture that is revealed via observation. External reliability is more of a verification process, in that the observations are cross-checked with other sources of data or other researchers to confirm, or otherwise, that this new evidence is consistent with the observational data. As observational data do not solely consist of recording observations as a result of watching, looking, listening, taking notes or making recordings but also include some degree of interaction, in the form of informal conversations or interviews with the people being observed, the credibility of the people and what they say is an issue. As noted earlier, people can, for a variety of reasons, seek to mislead an outsider by means of evasion, misinformation, deception or straightforward lies and these can be individually or group-based, depending on whether the agenda is individual or collective in nature.

However, before any observational data can be collected, a situation has to be identified and selected and the entry negotiated. Neuman (1994) suggests that there are three key factors to be taken into consideration when selecting a site – richness of data, unfamiliarity and suitability. Not all sites having the same situational setting hold the same potential for richness of interactions, variety and diversity and, therefore, there should be some initial screening of possible sites so that it is possible to select the one with the greatest potential. Other things being equal, selecting a site that is unfamiliar to you is seen to be preferable to one that is more familiar as your observations are less likely to be contaminated with your preconceived ideas. Site suitability is an issue concerned with more than the empirical/theoretical richness it offers. It is also a practical, if not pragmatic, issue. Its proximity, accessibility and potential barriers, such as legal or political restrictions, may be considerations, as indeed may be the ethical restrictions on field research invoked by your institution.

Another key issue is how to secure permission to enter the site. This may also affect the final selection of a site, in the sense that selecting an 'ideal' site that is also one where access cannot be secured is obviously a non-starter. Thus, it may be necessary to identify a shortlist of suitable sites and make the final choice on a more practical basis – considering ones where access can be negotiated. Without an agreement to enter and have appropriate access to those you wish to observe, a site is useless, no matter what its potential richness may be. In negotiating entry to a site, it is important to plan a strategy to secure this before initiating the negotiations. It is also important to recognise that some degree of flexibility and bargaining may be involved in securing such an agreement.

What is equally important is the need to be as honest and comprehensive as possible when explaining what you want access to and how you intend to behave within the situation. Often organisations are suspicious about giving relatively unknown outsiders access to their premises and employees because they can do harm, albeit perhaps unintentionally, to the established condition. Outsiders can be a disruptive influence and do more harm than good, from the organisation's perspective. Similarly, attempting to secure access by deliberately understating the breadth and extent of what you will really require and the time you will need to demand of insiders for interviewing is likely to be disastrous because, when the real extent of these requirements becomes known later, they may well be denied, leaving you with a major problem.

Given a successfully negotiated entry to a site, issues of how you behave and interact within the situation then arise. Observational data collection, unlike surveys or other techniques where the researcher and respondents never actually meet, occurs within a context where you, the observer, are physically present on more than one occasion with the people being observed. In short, you become at least a quasi-member of the situation, with all the implications that has. To collect good-quality observational data, it is important to develop an empathetic understanding of the situation – that is, to be able to see it through the eyes of the insiders – but, at the same time, it is likely you will not be regarded as a fully paid-up member of the group(s) in the situation and, therefore, will be something of an outsider at best. Overlaying this is the paradoxical need to retain the more detached view of an outsider in order not to develop an insular and possibly biased stance and the need to decide what ethical position should be taken in terms of revealing the real purpose(s) of the research. All these aspects raise issues of striking the correct balance between being the detached observer and 'going native', truthfulness versus deception, respecting confidentiality and the desire to disclose information and how to leave the situation without causing any damage when the project ends.

As observational research is contextually contingent – that is, the physical context and what happens within that environment are inseparable – observational data have to include both aspects. The behaviour to be observed occurs within a context and, therefore, the observation of the nature and characteristics of that context are vital elements of the observational data because these will have some impact on the behaviour that occurs within this context. Similarly, the organisational nature of the context also has to be observed. At one level this may be stipulated and defined in company documentation – in an organisational chart indicating responsibilities and relationships between people – but a formal statement of how the situation is structured and seen to operate may not accord with how it actually works in practice.

In terms of people and their actions, the observer should not only record who is present and what they say and do but also what is not said or done, and by whom, as this can reveal valuable information. In addition, non-verbal behaviour, such as body language, can add insights because what people say and do or how they react to others does not always accord with their body language. Also, all situations tend to be idiosyncratic in some respects and one of these is invariably the use of a particular language or jargon specific to the situation. This specialised language is known as the 'argot' or *lingua franca* of the insider and needs to be interpreted by the observer in terms of what these specialised terms mean in the context of the situation and how they may be translated for the outside world.

The recording of observations normally involves taking notes and constructing maps and diagrams, though these may be supplemented in some cases by audio and/or video recordings. During an observational session, it is usually not possible to take detailed and comprehensive notes because events are unfolding in real time. Therefore, the notes are usually jotted as short memory triggers, sometimes in the researchers' own forms of shorthand, to be used as the basis for writing up the more detailed observational notes after the observational session and it is these that provide an exact, as possible, recording of the session. Maps and diagrams sketched during observation sessions can be useful aids for compiling the observational records as they can add physical, spatial and social, or interaction, dimensions to the records.

Once the descriptive, observational notes for each session have been completed, the raw material for initial analysis and interpretation will be available and further notes can be added. For example, it may be possible to begin to infer wider, more generalised meanings from specific observational records and possibly analyse these in relation to existing theory. In turn, this may suggest further types of observation that would be useful and/or questions that should be asked in future sessions.

As the collection, recording and analysis of observational data are inevitably affected by subjective influences, it is also important to make 'personal' notes for each session. These record the observer's personal states and feelings, as they could have some influence on the observation. For example, if the observer was relaxed or stressed, bored or interested, in a good mood or a bad one could clearly affect what was perceived and how it was perceived during an observational session.

In observational data collection, field interviews are usually juxtaposed with actual observations. These are somewhat different from survey-type interviews as they are less structured, more informal, flexible and closer to a two-way conversation than a closed question and answer session. Interviewing people in the situation helps to both supplement the observational data and may be iterative with it in the sense that observations may suggest issues to be explored during interview sessions, while responses given in interviews may help to guide future observations. In a similar way, the two might be used to verify or crosscheck conclusions being reached for either type of data.

Field interviews are likely to be repeated over time with the same people, but as time progresses the purpose may change, from seeking further background, descriptive information in the beginning, to helping develop a basic understanding, to conversations more concerned with structural and process issues as the researcher's knowledge and understanding of the situation evolve and he or she seeks to analyse issues in more detail and depth.

## 7.5 Projective Techniques

Projective techniques (PTs) – sometimes also known as 'enabling techniques' – are used to collect qualitative data and, essentially, are an indirect form of questioning that asks respondents to interpret the stimuli they are being presented with. In this sense, they are very different from the normal, standard, direct kinds of questions discussed earlier in the context of questionnaires and questions.

In the case of PTs, many of the rules and the dos and don'ts that apply to standard questions do not apply to them. For example, one of the key premises of PTs is that if respondents are presented with a vague stimulus, then they will have to reveal more of their subconscious thinking to be able to articulate an interpretative response. Thus, PTs are often seen as a mechanism for accessing the private worlds of individuals to reveal their innermost thoughts.

PTs can be used for descriptive or diagnostic purposes and especially when direct questioning may be regarded as inappropriate, such as in sensitive situations where there may be significant barriers inhibiting open communication. Where respondents may be reluctant to reveal what they really feel because of embarrassment or sensitivity or where the truth may conflict with their rationalised self-image, PTs can be used as an indirect and less threatening or confrontational vehicle to facilitate the revelation of their true feelings and so on. Similarly, many forms of direct questioning, almost by definition, reveal the true purpose of a question to respondents. This can result in them formulating and articulating the response that they feel the questioner wants to receive rather than necessarily the one they truly believe in.

PTs generate a very unstructured form of response because what is important in the process is the freedom given to individuals to respond in their own words. The ambiguous nature of the stimuli used as a vehicle to elicit these responses is important as the more ambiguous it is, the more the respondents have to draw on their experience and inner thoughts to project these on to the stimuli in order to be able to provide an interpretation and, hence, the more they must reveal about the nature of these 'hidden' thoughts in the process. This means that PTs are designed to explore the issue(s) in some depth, to access peoples' underlying reactions, perceptions and interpretations of the stimuli, revealing what the objects or images really mean to them.

Widely used in clinical psychology for some considerable time, PTs have also been used in marketing and advertising research to obtain peoples' reactions to new products, advertising images and so on. However, there is no particular reason not to use these techniques to explore a wide range of other issues in the hospitality and tourism fields.

PTs in general are very useful where direct questioning may be problematic, such as where there may be some reluctance or resistance on the part of respondents to respond to potentially sensitive or embarrassing questions and more in-depth information is sought concerning how people really think about the issues in question. They are often thought to be particularly useful in the exploratory stages of a research project because of their ability to surface issues and aspects of the phenomena under investigation that may not have been previously considered. However, the down side is that the interpretative nature of the process and data analysis can require considerable ability on the part of the researcher and the nature of the sample used will almost certainly preclude the ability to generalise from the results.

The literature suggests that there are five main types of PT procedures:

♦ associative
♦ completion
♦ construction
♦ expressive
♦ choice-ordering.

Associative procedures seek to elicit the respondents' associations with the stimuli they are presented with. This may be as simple as word association, where, in its traditional format, respondents react (either orally or in writing) to a rapidly presented series of words with the word(s) they associate with the stimulus words. Alternatively, respondents may be given a single word and invited to record the word(s) they associate with it (see Brotherton, 2005, for an example of this in a hospitality context). The associative stimulus may also be a picture or other type of image, such as a photograph of a tourist destination, a company's logo, or an object, as is the case in new product development, when alternative prototypes of the product are presented to respondents to discover what their associative feelings are or for them to project a personality on to the object in question. In the latter case, respondents are asked to imagine the object as a type of person and describe the personality characteristics of that person.

Associative procedures may also utilise metaphors as a vehicle to surface peoples' feelings about a particular situation or experience. Metaphors are used in everyday conversation as associative phrases to help interpret and explain relatively unfamiliar situations by transferring knowledge from a relatively familiar situation or domain. For example, we might describe certain type of hotel as 'bed factories' or some forms of transport as 'cattle wagons'. In doing so, we are associating certain characteristics of mass production or crowded forms of animal transportation with other contexts to indicate the nature of the hotel or form of transport we are talking about. However, the metaphor itself, whether given to the respondents to use as an association with the context or elicited from them in their response, can be useless on its own without an explanation being provided by the respondents as to why they chose it. For example, Brotherton (2005) illustrates this in a study that used certain metaphors as vehicles for respondents in hotels to describe their feelings about the physical and service aspects of hospitality they received as guests in the hotels included in the study. The hotel guests were asked to describe their individual experience of the service they had received in the hotel as if it were an animal. This alone would have been quite useless information without the follow-up questions that asked them to give their reasons for choosing those animals, because it is the reasons for making the associative choice that reveal the thinking or criteria they used to make this choice.

Completion procedures are another form of PT where the stimuli are a little more extensive. Sentence or story completion is a popular form of this type of procedure. Respondents are given the beginning of a sentence or story and then asked to complete it. They freely project their inner feelings, assumptions and perhaps prejudices on to the vehicle, which acts as a form of third party. In other words, the responses given by the respondents are not seen by them as being directly attributable to them as they are simply responding to a situation that is presented. However, the only way they can make such a response is to project their feelings on to the stimulus to complete it and, hence, it acts as a type of neutral vehicle for surfacing this information.

Again, objects, or quasi-objects, can also be used in completion procedures. For example, respondents could be presented with a list of brand names and be asked to group them together into related categories, then explain their reasoning for the groupings that emerge. This could be used to discover how consumers segment a market for a particular type of hospitality or tourism product, what they see to be related and unrelated or differentiated brands in the marketplace. It could also be used for different types of tourist destinations or attractions.

Construction procedures tend to require more complex and controlled intellectual input from respondents than the procedures described above because they have to construct a response to a limited stimulus. Once again, these procedures use a third person format that enables respondents to record their thoughts, feelings and so on without having to do so directly. These techniques all allow respondents to present their own feelings, but to do so via a neutral third party.

These encompass:

♦ third person questions, such as, 'What would a businessman think of hotel brand X?'
♦ 'thought bubbles', where a picture or cartoon of a situation is presented and respondents have to record the feelings or thoughts of the person or people in the thought bubble(s) in the image
♦ story construction, where a scenario is presented and respondents are asked to describe the characters and how they feel about the situation they are in
♦ persona construction, where certain characteristics of a person, object or quasi-object are given and respondents have to describe the personality of the stimuli type – for example, 'Here is the corporate logo of British Airways. Describe the company's personality' or 'Here is a list of the holiday destinations this person has visited. What is his personality?'

Expressive procedures, such as role-playing or 'give us a clue', can be used to obtain a response without the need for an oral or written question and answer framework. In role-playing, respondents might be asked to play the role of a particular product, brand, type of manager or destination and express the persona of this to an audience. For example, 'Speak to the audience as though you were Disneyland'. In 'give us a clue', respondents may be asked to enact the staff of a particular type of company or brand or perhaps the users of a particular type of product, with the other respondents being invited to guess its real identity. These procedures are designed to illuminate how people view the target stimuli and surface their perceptions, preconceived ideas, prejudices, stereotypes and so on.

Finally, choice-ordering procedures are used to elicit information regarding the priorities and preferences of people. Typically, respondents are presented with a list of stimuli items and asked to group and rank them according to the criteria given to them and explain the reasoning behind the final outcome. For example, given a list of airlines, respondents may be asked to group or rank these in terms of cost, quality, reliability, safety, destination coverage and so on.

## SUMMARY

» Any data collection instrument and procedure is merely a means to an end, but to achieve this end effectively, it must be designed and implemented in a credible manner.

» The aim of data collection in general is to obtain sufficient valid and reliable data to be able to answer the research questions and/or test the hypotheses.

» Highly structured questionnaires, with closed questions, are best suited to collecting quantitative data, whereas interviewing, observation and projective techniques are more appropriate for collecting qualitative data.

» The validity of data is often thought to be greater when more open-ended, naturalistic forms of data collection are used and vice versa, but the reliability of data is invariably low in these cases. It can be much higher where more predetermined, but artificial, forms are used – that is, highly structured questionnaires.

» The nature and location – particularly the level of dispersion – of the target respondents may influence the choice of data collection instrument and procedures, due to pragmatic considerations.

» Respondents or informants do not always provide true or valid data, as they may distort their responses for various reasons. This factor needs to be recognised and dealt with, as far as is possible, in the design of the instruments and processes.

## Further Reading

Blaxter, L., Hughes, C. and Tight, M. (1996) *How to Research*. Buckingham: Open University Press. Chapter 6.

Bourque, L.B. and Fielder, E.P. (1995) *How to Conduct Self-administered and Mail Surveys*. Thousand Oaks, CA: Sage.

Clark, M., Riley, M., Wilkie, E. and Wood, R.C. (1998) *Researching and Writing Dissertations in Hospitality and Tourism*. London: International Thomson Business Press. Chapters 9–13.

Denscombe, M. (1998) *The Good Research Guide for Small-scale Social Research Projects*. Buckingham: Open University Press. Chapters 6–8.

Fink, A. (1995) *How to Ask Survey Questions*. Thousand Oaks, CA: Sage.

Finn, M., Elliot-White, M. and Walton, M. (2000) *Tourism and Leisure Research Methods: Data collection, analysis and interpretation*. Harlow: Pearson Education. Chapters 5 and 6.

Flick, U. (2002) *An Introduction to Qualitative Research*, 2nd edition. Thousand Oaks, CA: Sage. Chapters 8–13.

Frey, J.H. and Oishi, S.M. (1995) *How to Conduct Interviews by Telephone and in Person*. Thousand Oaks, CA: Sage.

Gill, J. and Johnson, P. (1991) *Research Methods for Managers*. London: Paul Chapman. Chapters 6–8.

Hague, P. (1993a) *Interviewing*. London: Kogan Page.

Hague, P. (1993b) *Questionnaire Design*. London: Kogan Page.

Hussey, J. and Hussey, R. (1997) *Business Research: A practical guide for undergraduate and postgraduate students*. Basingstoke: Macmillan. Chapter 6.

Jankowicz, A.D. (1991) *Business Research Projects for Students*. London: Chapman & Hall. Chapters 11–13.

Johns, N. and Lee-Ross, D. (1998) *Research Methods in Service Industry Management*. London: Cassell. Chapters 4 and 6.

Lucas, R. (1999) 'Survey research', in B. Brotherton (ed.), *The Handbook of Contemporary Hospitality Management Research*. Chichester: John Wiley. pp. 77–96.

Preece, R. (1994) *Starting Research: An introduction to academic research and dissertation writing*. London: Pinter. Chapter 5.

Saunders, M., Lewis, P. and Thornhill, A. (2003) *Research Methods for Business Students*, 3rd edition. Harlow: Pearson Education. Chapters 8, 9 and 10.

Sekaran, U. (2000) *Research Methods for Business: A skill-building approach*, 3rd edition. New York: John Wiley. Chapters 9 and 10.

Sharp, J.A. and Howard, K. (1996) *The Management of a Student Research Project*, 2nd edition. Aldershot: Gower. Chapter 6.

Veal, A.J. (1997) *Research Methods for Leisure and Tourism: A practical guide*, 2nd edition. Harlow: Pearson Education. Chapters 7–11.

Wilkinson, S. (2004) 'Focus group research', in D. Silverman (ed.), *Qualitative Research: Theory, method and practice*, 2nd edition. London: Sage. pp. 177–199.

# Chapter

## Sampling

> **KEY CONCEPTS AND ISSUES**
>
> » *The nature and importance of sampling and why it is necessary.*
> » *Representativeness and generalisation.*
> » *The population, population elements and population parameters.*
> » *The sample frame, subjects, selection, respondents and statistics.*
> » *Sample size, composition, response rates and errors.*
> » *Confidence levels.*
> » *Probability-based, random sampling strategies and techniques for quantitative studies.*
> » *Non-probability-based strategies and techniques for qualitative studies.*

## 8.1 Introduction

In the two previous chapters we considered the decisions involved in selecting the overall research design for the project and the methods, instruments and procedures required to put this design into practice. Having considered how to structure and operationalise the data collection process, the next issue to confront is the one discussed in this chapter – who are we going to select as the people or organisations to provide the information we need and why? This means that we have to explore sampling.

Sampling and, in particular, sampling theory and the statistical basis of much of this is something that tends to confuse many students because they can get lost in the mathematical equations and other jargon associated with the subject and lose sight of the key principles that underlie sampling decisions. Therefore, this chapter largely takes a non-mathematical and non-statistical approach to explaining what sampling is and the techniques that can be used to select samples. This does not mean that the mathematical and statistical basis of sampling and sampling theory is ignored, but, rather, that it is explained in a manner that, hopefully, is more readily understandable to the non-mathematician. If you decide that you require a more technical discussion of these issues, Hemmington's (1999) chapter on sampling would be a good choice.

So, here we will consider the nature of sampling and its importance, the relationship between a sample and the population it is obtained from, what would be required for you to be able to generalise from the results of the sample back to the larger population, how the response rate from the sample can be responsible for error and why the expected response rate needs to be taken into account when deciding what the size of sample should be. We will also explore the main sampling strategies and techniques associated with quantitative and qualitative studies, as well as the implications that the size and composition of the sample may have for future decisions concerning the statistical techniques that can be used to analyse the data obtained from those samples.

## 8.2 What is Sampling and Why is It Important?

Sampling, or taking a sample, is really very straightforward and simple – certainly in terms of its basic rationale and principles. Essentially, a sample is a smaller version of the whole it is obtained from that reflects the same characteristics as those of the whole. For example, if you were ill and the doctor wanted to take a blood sample for analysis to try and make a diagnosis, the smaller amount of blood in that sample would be identical to the remainder of the blood in your body. Similarly, if you were asked, in a supermarket, to try a sample of a food item or a drink, then, again, the sample would be a smaller, but identical, version of the full portion or bottle. In each of these cases, the analysis or tasting of the sample would be used to make inferences about the larger entity it was derived from. So, if you liked the sample of food or drink, then you might reasonably infer that you would like that food or drink because the larger entity would have the same characteristics as the sample you tasted. Similarly, if the doctor found a particular abnormality in the blood sample, then he or she might reasonably infer that this would be present in your blood as a whole. However, to make inferences beyond this point may not be justifiable. For example, if your food sample was a particular type of cheese and you liked it, then it would be reasonable to infer that you would like that type of cheese but not that you would then like all types of cheese.

From this we can see that there is an important relationship between the whole the sample is taken from and the sample itself. The whole is known as the 'population' and it is the relationship between this and the sample that is critical for making valid inferences from the sample results to the wider population. Ideally, the sample must be as identical as possible to the population it has been obtained from, in terms of its composition and characteristics, for it to be regarded as sufficiently 'representative' to be able to make valid inferences from. On the other hand, if the sample is not representative, then it will be biased in one way or another and so inferences made on the basis of that sample are likely to be wrong. For example, if the population contained 70 per cent males and 30 per cent females and the sample taken from it contained 50 per cent males and females, then the results from the analysis of the sample would be biased in the sense that they would under-represent males and over-represent females in terms of the proportions of these genders found in the real population.

This issue of the sample being representative is particularly significant where statistical inferences are to be made, but may be less so in qualitative studies, where the aim is not to generalise results from a sample to the wider population it is drawn from. Sampling in small-scale qualitative studies, such as case studies and observational research, is invariably undertaken for different purposes and in different ways, for both theoretical and practical reasons, to that employed for larger more quantitative work, as we will see later in this chapter. However, in quantitative work, the desire to use a sample to make valid and reliable generalisations about a population is a central purpose of this kind of research, so it is important to understand the issues in order to be able to do this successfully.

Why do we have to have a sample? Why not simply collect information from the population as a whole? The answer is invariably practical in nature, but, conceptually, this is an issue of population heterogeneity or, put another way, because most populations are not comprised of identical (homogeneous) members, they embody at least some degree of variety. If all members of the population were homogeneous or identical, then, logically, a sample of one would be sufficient because the results from this could be generalised to everyone else in the population. Thus, as we shall see later, the amount of heterogeneity or variation in the population has an implication for the size of sample required. Other things being equal, the greater this is, the greater the need to increase the size of the sample to reflect the extent of variability in the population.

A population, in research terms, is not necessarily simply comprised of people. Populations may be comprised of particular types of companies, products or brands, destinations, events, processes and so on. 'Population' in this context is a term used to denote a collection of related elements, all of which share some characteristics relevant to the study. This means that the first issue that needs to be addressed is that of defining the population – not only in terms of the type(s) of elements that should be included in it but also its boundaries or parameters. For example, it would be easy to define a population as four-star hotels, but would this mean all the four-star hotels in the world, in Europe, in the UK, in a region of the UK or within a particular UK city? Would it mean all four-star hotels regardless of the type of ownership – independently or corporately owned – and those of any size, from fewer than ten bedrooms to those with over 1000?

Defining the population should, in fact, be a relatively simple matter, as long as the parameters of the research have been articulated in the original research question(s) and/or aims or objectives. For example, if the study was specified as one investigating business guest satisfaction in four-star corporate hotels in London, the population, at least in principle, is already defined.

This also highlights the issue of geographical dispersion. In our example above, it may not be necessary to sample because, if there are only 200 four-star corporate hotels in London, it could well be quite feasible to send question-naires to them all. On the other hand, if our population had instead been defined in terms of this type of hotel in the UK as a whole or on a wider basis than that, both the increased numbers of four-star hotels that would be included in the definition and their greater geographical dispersion may well dictate that a sample is needed. In this instance, the greater size and dispersion would make access to the population elements much more expensive and time-consuming and, therefore, perhaps not practicable or feasible in relation to the resources and time constraints for the work. This is also a feature of a great deal of commercial research, where budgets are limited and results are required as quickly and as cost-effectively as possible.

Once the population has been defined, taking these matters into consideration, then it is possible to begin thinking about what size of sample should be selected and how to do this. These are issues that we shall address shortly. However, before we do so, it may be helpful for you to become familiar with some of the sampling terminology or jargon. All the elements contained within your chosen population are known as the 'sample frame', from which the actual sample can be drawn or selected. Those selected to form part of the sample become known as 'sample subjects' and the actual people who respond to the questions put to them are the 'sample respondents'. The data or values generated from the respondents' responses are known as the 'sample statistics' and the corresponding values in the population are referred to as the 'population parameters'.

How large does a sample have, or need, to be? In my experience, this has invariably been a question that has confused and perplexed students because, for whatever reason, the size of the sample tends to be seen as being directly related to how representative it will be. That is, they tend to think that as the sample gets larger, then it will automatically become more representative. This, is a fallacy as it depends also on how the sample has been selected.

As indicated earlier, the amount of variation in the population is much more important in this respect. Variation can be measured by using the standard deviation, and the greater the variability in the population, the higher the value of the standard deviation. Hence, a more variable population will tend to indi-cate that a larger sample size will be required to ensure that the breadth of that variation is reflected in the sample.

Similarly, the sample size required may be influenced by the degree of preci-sion desired – that is, the extent to which the sample statistics can be regarded to be a true reflection of the population parameters. However, to increase precision significantly, the sample size would need to be increased quite considerably, which may not be feasible. Indeed, it is claimed that, to double the level of precision, the size of sample may need to be quadrupled.

As precision is concerned with the relationship between the sample statistics and the population parameters, the size of the sample and how it is selected are potential sources of variance between these two. This is known as 'sampling error'. A sample selected on a random basis is likely to have less potential for bias and, therefore, error than one selected using an alternative technique. Similarly, the larger the size of the sample, the less is the likelihood that alternative samples drawn from the same population would produce different sample statistics or estimates of the population parameters. For example, a sample of ten drawn from a population of 100 would be quite small and subject to significant error because nine other alternative samples of 10 could be drawn from the same population. On the other hand, if the sample size was 50, only four other samples of the same size could have been drawn. This should illustrate that, as the sample size increases, the potential for sampling error declines.

The implication of this would appear to be that a high proportion of the population should be included in the sample to minimise error. Although this is true, there are obvious practical difficulties with such a view, especially when the population is very large. It has been found that to increase precision and reduce error by increasing sample size is an exercise subject to diminishing returns – that is, as the sample size is increased, the effect this has on reducing error and increasing precision decreases, as indicated above. Indeed, many commercial research organisations, seeking to generalise their survey results from things such as national opinion or political polls, may typically use a sample in the 2000–3000 range to predict the population parameters for a population of tens of millions.

What is more important than the proportion of the population contained in the sample is its absolute size and how it is selected. *The Economist* (1997) suggested that a minimum 'realised' sample size of 30 is required for statistical analysis. This is a useful rule of thumb, but you need to remember that this is the final, realised sample available for analysis, not the original sample size – an issue discussed below. Another useful rule of thumb is that the larger the sample and the smaller the standard deviation, or variability, in the sample, the lower the level of sampling error is likely to be.

A more practical issue is the relationship between the initial and realised sample. This is essentially determined by the response rate and has an inverse relationship with initial sample size determination. If the expected response rate is low, then it may be necessary to increase the size of the initial sample to secure a viable realised sample and vice versa. For example, to obtain a final, realised sample of 50 where the expected response rate is 50 per cent, an initial sample of only 100 would be required, but if the response rate was expected to be only 20 per cent, then to secure a realised sample of 50, the initial sample would have to be 250.

Another issue is the degree of subsample analysis that you may wish to undertake when the data are available. If you wish to explore similarities or differences between subgroups or categories, each of these will need to be large enough to facilitate such analysis. To obtain sufficient numbers of respondents within each of these subgroups, it may be necessary to increase the original sample size. For example, if you wanted to compare the frequency with which different types of people visited an art gallery, based on the age category they belonged to, this may involve five or six separate categories. With a total realised sample of 30, and assuming the respondents were equally distributed across the age categories, this would only give you five or six cases in each category. However, if the realised sample was twice as large, using the same assumption, each category would then have ten to 12 cases.

Once you have the sample data and begin the analysis process, it is a relatively simple matter to assess the degree of confidence – that is, the likelihood that the sample statistics are accurate in relation to the population parameters – by computing the 'confidence interval'. As we shall explore in Chapter 9, using a data analysis package such as SPSS, it is straightforward to set the confidence interval for the statistical test to be used. Given the assumption of normally distributed data – that is, the symmetrical, bell-shaped curve – 95 per cent of the cases in such a distribution will lie within two standard deviations above and below the mean, its centre. The same applies to the distribution of sample means, so it is possible to say the same of the sample means or, in other words, that 95 times out of 100 the sample mean will be within this range. In effect, we are saying here that we can be 95 per cent confident that the sample statistics are a true reflection of the population parameters.

## 8.3 Quantitative Data Sampling

Sampling in quantitative studies is known as probability-based sampling. In this approach, each population element has a known, non-zero and, usually equal, chance of being selected for inclusion in the sample. A process of selecting the elements for the sample in a random manner ensures that this is the case and biased selection cannot occur because, by definition, randomness cannot be predicted or controlled. Unsurprisingly, this is commonly referred to as random sampling and is used where generalisation from the results for a sample back to the population as a whole is critical and it is intended for statistical techniques to be applied to analyse the sample data. The generation of an appropriate list of random numbers can be easily achieved using the random number generator function in Excel. How to do this is specified in Exhibit 8.1.

---

### Exhibit 8.1    Using Excel to Generate a Set of Random Numbers

1   Open a new worksheet, go to the Tools menu and select 'Data Analysis'.
2   Select 'Random Number Generation', click on 'OK' and this will open a dialogue box so that you can set the requirements.
3   For the 'Number of variables', enter '1'. This will provide a list of random numbers in one column of the spreadsheet.
4   In the 'Number of Random' option, enter the number of random numbers you need. For example, if you want to select a sample of 50 from a sampling frame of 300, then enter '50' here.
5   In the 'Distribution' option, select uniform.
6   In the 'Between' option, enter the lowest and highest values between which you want the random selection to be made. So, in our example above, this would have been between 1 and 300.
7   Click on the 'OK' button and you should have a list of 50 random numbers in the column on your spreadsheet.
8   You may want to tidy up the output as it will be displayed to a number of decimal places, unless you have previously specified the cell output to be different to this. To do this, go to the Format menu and select 'Cells' to open the cell formatting options box. In the 'Number' option, simply change the output to one with no decimal places and you will get whole numbers in the column.

---

The main probability-based sampling strategies are known as:

♦   simple random
♦   systematic random
♦   stratified random
♦   cluster.

Each of these will now be discussed in turn.

## 8.3.1  *Simple random sampling*

This is a relatively straightforward procedure, but it does demand that the sampling frame is known and each item in the frame is numbered or coded. Each item has an equal chance of being, or not being, selected and that chance cannot be influenced by the sample selector as it is made on a random basis. Random number tables can be used for this, but using Excel as described above is a quick and easy way to generate a set of random numbers for this purpose as it can be tailored to the size of the sampling frame and the size of sample to be selected from this.

## 8.3.2 *Systematic random sampling*

This is conducted by selecting the items for inclusion in the sample at systematic or regular intervals by means of the sampling frame, using a randomised starting point. For example, to select a sample of 30 restaurants from a sampling frame containing 270, the sampling interval would have to be $270/30 = 9$. If the random number selected to start the process was 4, then the 4th, 13th, 22nd, 31st ... would be selected until the total of 30 had been reached. Ideally, the items in the sampling frame should organised randomly before selection takes place, to avoid the problem of 'periodicity'. This happens because the items in the sampling frame are likely to be ordered in some way, so a systematic selection may result in some types being over- or under-represented, even though the selection proceeds from a random point. To avoid this, it is necessary to mix, shuffle or randomise the list comprising the sampling frame before selection takes place.

## 8.3.3 *Stratified random sampling*

This technique assumes some prior knowledge of the population that can be used to separate it into distinct, mutually exclusive groups or strata. This may be on the basis of age, location, gender, occupation and so on or, in the case or organisations, size, location, brand, quality and other such aspects. This may be done where it is hypothesised that a particular characteristic could constitute a source of variance. So, if it was proposed that men and women would have significantly different opinions on certain issues, then it would be important to ensure that the correct proportions of each gender were included in the sample. So, for example, if it was known that the population was comprised of 60 per cent males and 40 per cent females, it would be important to ensure that these groups were proportionately represented in the sample by selecting 1.5 more male subjects than female in order to explore the 'between-group' variations.

## 8.3.4 *Cluster sampling*

Geographic area cluster sampling can be used to alleviate costly and time-consuming access to a sample where it is very geographically dispersed, which is possible when using any of the sampling techniques discussed above. It is most suitable where the clusters contain the same variability as the population and where they are relatively homogeneous. If there proved to be a high degree of between-cluster variability, then a much larger number of clusters would need to be included in the sample. The sampling frame is comprised of the list of clusters rather than individual cases. From this, a number of clusters are selected on a random basis and data are collected from every case contained in the clusters selected.

The random selection of clusters effectively makes this form of sampling probability-based, but the nature of cluster sampling is likely to generate a sample that is inherently less representative than one selected using the stratified random procedure. More recently multistage cluster sampling has been advocated as a way to minimise such an eventuality. This approach is essentially a repeated form of cluster sampling within which, at successive stages, subgroups within each cluster are selected as further samples. This is akin to an 'ever-decreasing circles' approach to sampling as the sample focus moves to ever smaller subgroups within the clusters.

## 8.4 Qualitative Data Sampling

Sampling designs and strategies to collect qualitative data are known as non-probability-based sampling, although they can also be used to collect quantitative data where statistical extrapolation (generalisation) is not a primary concern. It may be that your research aim and objectives do not require generalisation from sample estimates to the population these are from, but an in-depth case study relating to the issues under investigation. Similarly, if your study is being pursued via an inductive approach, then it is highly likely that you will not be able to identify a population as such and sensibly apply a probability-based approach to selecting a sample. Indeed, if you are working within the confines of a relatively small and limited empirical situation, then it is probable that the people within it will not be equally valuable to you in terms of collecting the data required. For example, there may be just a few people (often called key informants) who hold the information you require in general and there may be only single individuals who hold specific types of information.

Often in such situations you may be feeling your way into the issues as you go along and so the sampling strategy and selection of subjects proceeds as you gain more knowledge and understanding of them. Such an approach is frequently known as 'grounded theory' because the evolution of the empirical data collection strategies and techniques and the development of theoretical understanding take place in conjunction with each other. In short, as data are collected, this helps to generate theory grounded in the empirical reality and, in turn, the emerging theory helps to inform the data collection process as it begins to indicate what information would be required to develop the theory further.

### 8.4.1 *Convenience sampling*

This is the simplest form of non-probability-based sampling. It is, as the name implies, a way of selecting a sample that is convenient – that is, available at the time and place of your choice. This may be as straightforward as using your student peers as a sample because they are conveniently available to collect the data from. Alternatively, it might constitute stopping people in the street and asking for their cooperation or approaching visitors at a tourist destination or attraction and asking them if they would complete a questionnaire or be interviewed.

Given that your ability to determine or control the selection of the sample is extremely limited under these circumstances, as it is essentially dependent on peoples' goodwill, the likelihood of the sample being representative of the population is extremely low, so you should be very circumspect about trying to make generalisations based on such a 'self-selecting' sample. Though the data you collect via this form of sampling may be valid, the nature of the sample makes it unreliable for generalisation purposes. Despite this, many hospitality and tourism organisations use a 'self-selecting' procedure to obtain feedback information from their customers by, for example, leaving questionnaires in guest bedrooms, on restaurant tables and so on. They then, erroneously, extrapolate the results from these to make claims about the percentage of their customers who are happy or satisfied. This alone would be suspect enough, but they then also may use this information to make business decisions!

## 8.4.2 *Purposive sampling*

This can be used to select sample subjects on the basis of some important characteristic(s) they possess. For example, as referred to earlier, a person may be regarded as a 'key informant' because of the position they hold. Alternatively, particular types of operation, destination or event may be regarded as 'key' because they possess the relevant characteristics. What is regarded as 'key' may vary. It may be that an extreme or atypical case is desired, such as studying the brand or market leader to help understand why other competitors are less successful. On the other hand, selecting a typical case may be viewed as a way to generate a more representative view.

In some situations, who should be included in the sample as key informants is quite obvious from the outset, but in others this may not be the case. Where it is not and assistance is required to identify potentially valuable sample subjects, it is possible to employ either the 'snowball' or 'expert choice' approaches. These are essentially referral mechanisms whereby, in the former, initial sample subjects are asked to recommend others who could provide the information required and, in the latter, experts are asked to recommend potential subjects who have the desired characteristics. Both of these approaches can be helpful, but they have the disadvantage that sample selection can become rather haphazard and dependent on the subjective opinions of the people making the recommendations.

## 8.4.3 *Quota sampling*

This is a quasi-representative sampling strategy. Although the sample subjects are not selected randomly, so the sample is less representative than probability-based strategies, it is closer to these strategies than other forms of non-probability-based sampling. Proportionate quotas for subjects to be included in the sample are devised so that the proportions are the same in the sample as they are in the population. Thus, if the population was comprised of 50 per cent males and females, then the sample would need to include equal quotas of the two genders. In the case of organisations, the sample should include the same proportions of larger and smaller companies, however defined, that exist in the population as a whole. This makes selection relatively easy, but has the disadvantage that the influence of the selector or researcher over exactly which people or companies are selected can introduce bias.

Although quota sampling is a form of stratified sampling, the sample selection is not made randomly, so cannot be as representative. That said, it is a quicker and cheaper form of sampling, within which control over the sample is quite high, and it has a reasonable degree of representativeness. The down side is that it can be a difficult strategy to employ where the characteristics that are used to determine the quotas or proportions are numerous. For example, to sample proportionate numbers on the basis of gender, three occupation types and three age ranges (2 x 3 x 3) would create 18 categories of subjects to select. If a category such as a previous or new guest or visitor were added, then the number of categories would double to 36!

## SUMMARY

» Samples are necessary where populations exhibit heterogeneity and/or they are geographically dispersed.

» To be able to make reliable generalisations from the sample data back to the population as a whole the characteristics and proportions within the sample must be sufficiently representative of those in the population.

» The size of sample that needs to be selected depends on the degree of variability or homogeneity in the population. Where there is quite a bit of variety, the sample needs to be large to reflect and cope with this variability.

» The size of sample selected and, perhaps more importantly, that realised, will have implications for the type of data analysis techniques that can be used to analyse the sample data.

» Sampling in quantitative studies is probability-based and random in nature. It uses established statistical formulae and techniques to address the key sampling questions.

» Sampling in qualitative studies is not based on statistical probability theory and is more flexible and emergent in nature. This does not mean that the data collected will be less valid – it may even have greater validity – but it does limit the extent to which it is possible to generalise from the results.

# Further Reading

Clark, M., Riley, M., Wilkie, E. and Wood, R.C. (1998) *Researching and Writing Dissertations in Hospitality and Tourism*. London: International Thomson Business Press. Chapter 8.

Denscombe, M. (1998) *The Good Research Guide for Small-scale Social Research Projects*. Buckingham: Open University Press. Chapter 1.

Fink, A. (1995) *How to Sample in Surveys*. Thousand Oaks, CA: Sage.

Finn, M., Elliot-White, M. and Walton, M. (2000) *Tourism and Leisure Research Methods: Data collection, analysis and interpretation*. Harlow: Pearson Education. Chapter 7.

Flick, U. (2002) *An Introduction to Qualitative Research*, 2nd edition. Thousand Oaks, CA: Sage. Chapter 7.

Hussey, J. and Hussey, R. (1997) *Business research: A practical guide for undergraduate and postgraduate students*. Basingstoke: Macmillan. Chapter 6.

Jankowicz, A.D. (1991) *Business Research Projects for Students*. London: Chapman & Hall. Chapter 9.

Saunders, M., Lewis, P. and Thornhill, A. (2003) *Research Methods for Business Students*, 3rd edition. Harlow: Pearson Education. Chapter 6.

Sekaran, U. (2000) *Research Methods for Business: A skill-building approach*, 3rd edition. New York: John Wiley. Chapter 11.

Veal, A.J. (1997) *Research Methods for Leisure and Tourism: A practical guide*, 2nd edition. Harlow: Pearson Education. Chapter 12.

# Chapter

## Analysing Quantitative Data

---

### KEY CONCEPTS AND ISSUES

» *Tidying up and entering your raw data into SPSS.*
» *Getting a feel for your data using descriptive statistics – frequencies, distributions, measure of dispersion and central tendency.*
» *Establishing the reliability of your measurement scales.*
» *Analysing associations and differences between two variables – cross-tabulation, correlation, regression and statistical significance.*
» *Inferential statistics and hypothesis testing – parametric and non-parametric tests.*
» *Data reduction techniques – developing a more parsimonious solution using factor analysis.*

---

## 9.1 Introduction

Having progressed through the prior stages of the research process, you now have your reward in the form of all the quantitative data from your completed questionnaires and, hopefully, these are of sufficient quantity and quality for you to begin analysing what they are telling you. However, after the initial euphoria you may have felt as you received all this data and knowing that your earlier design and implementation decisions have now been validated, you may be asking yourself what you can do with all this. Obtaining the data is one thing, but now you have to analyse and interpret these and that involves statistics!!

Fear not, you do not need to have a detailed understanding of the mathematical and statistical formulae that underlie the type of quantitative data analysis you may wish to do. Of course, such an understanding is useful, but, what is more important in this context is a knowledge of the types of statistical techniques and procedures that you can use to conduct this analysis, what these can be used for and how to set these up and interpret the results. It is the purpose of this chapter to explain, in straightforward language, all these aspects of quantitative data analysis so that you can utilise software such as SPSS to do all the hard work of calculating the results for you and be confident in interpreting and using the results.

## 9.2 General Issues

When all the data are available for processing and analysis, the first task is to tidy, clean up or edit the raw data. This is necessary because all the questions on a questionnaire may not have been answered, so there will be missing responses, and/or perhaps respondents have recorded their responses to some questions in an unclear or inappropriate manner. Where there are missing responses, because not all the respondents have chosen to answer all the questions, there are a number of options available. These may be simply ignored, if you are prepared to accept a lower response rate to the question(s) concerned. If the number of non-responses is low, this is probably the easiest way to deal with them. Alternatively, where there is a higher non-response rate, you may wish to enter a 'proxy' response. This could be based on the mid-point value in the case of an interval scale or the mean value of all the responses to the question. In cases where the recording of the response is unclear or not in the form asked for, then you have to make a judgement as to whether it is possible to edit these responses to make the response clear and/or appropriate or to ignore them if it is not, effectively treating them as non-responses.

If the questionnaire has not been precoded, then you will need to code the questions, both in terms of the variables they address and the values of the responses to them that are to be entered into the data analysis software. This is a relatively simple procedure because all you are trying to do here is to ensure that each question or variable is differentiated from the others and that the numbers to be entered relating to the response options are logical and mutually exclusive. For example, in the case of a question asking for a respondent's gender, where the response will be either male or female, it would be sensible to give the variable a title of 'Gender' and code the two responses as male = 1 and female = 2. In general, it is not a good idea to use zero as a code number because, if you wish to calculate average values at a later date, these will be distorted, for obvious reasons, if zeros are included in such a calculation. If the responses to a question are organised using an interval scale, perhaps from 1 to 5, then the coding is quite simple as the numbers 1 to 5 can be used for the five response descriptors employed in the question.

If a question has used an ordinal scale, for respondents to rank items using the criterion given in the question, it may be necessary to regard each of the items as a separate variable in order to record the rankings given to them by all the respondents. For example, a question asking respondents to indicate the most to least important influences on their degree of satisfaction with a visit to a restaurant might include items such as the portion size, speed of service, ambience, cost of the meal and friendliness of the staff. Each of these could be ranked as 1, 2, 3, 4, or 5. By treating each one as a separate variable, any of these ranking numbers can be recorded against each one for later analysis. Where a ratio scale has been used, this will have generated ungrouped, or raw, data that, at least theoretically, could range from zero to infinity. Probably the best way to deal with this type of data is to simply enter these in their raw form, then, following an initial evaluation of its distribution and range, to order or recode these on the basis of sensible groupings. The SPSS data analysis software procedure for recoding data using new variables is shown in Exhibit 9.1

---

### Exhibit 9.1    *Using SPSS to Recode Data*

1   Go to the Transform menu, select 'Recode', then select 'Into Different Variables' (see the note below) to open this dialogue box.
2   Select the variable you wish to recode from the list and move it into the 'Numeric Variable > Output Variable' box. Then type the name for the new variable into the 'Output Variable/Name' box. Click on 'Change' and it will be inserted in the 'Numeric Variable > Output Variable' box.
3   Now you need to tell SPSS how to change the values of the original variable to the new one. To do this, click on the 'Old and New Values' button to open this dialogue box. There you have options to change single values or ranges of values from the original to the new variable (see the example below). Whichever option you choose, you need to enter the new value in the 'New Value' box and then click on the 'Add' button to add it to the new values list in the adjacent window.
4   When you have entered all the old for new values, click on the 'Continue' button to return to the main dialogue box, then click on 'OK'. A new variable with the name you have given it will then appear in the datasheet in the Data View window.

*Note*: It is possible to recode a variable without creating a new variable by using the 'Into Same Variable' option *but* this will mean that you will lose your original data, as it will be changed into the new format.

*Example*: If you have a range of raw, or ungrouped, data values and wish to recode them into categories, then you will need to specify the ranges to be included in each new category. So, you might inform SPSS that the old values up to 20 should

*(Cont'd)*

be the first category by checking the 'Range (Lowest Through)' option and entering 20 in that box. This will place all the values up to and including 20 into the first new category you specify. For the highest category, you follow essentially the same procedure, but use the 'Range (Through Highest)' option, entering the lowest value of this category. So, if you want this category to be from 70 upwards, enter '70' in the box. For intermediate categories between the lowest and highest, you need to use the 'Range (Through)' boxes to enter the lowest and highest values for the category.

Once the data have been coded, the next task is to set up the data analysis package so that it can be entered. Perhaps the most commonly used package, widely available in most institutions, is SPSS. The first stage in using SPSS is to set up, or configure, the 'data sheet'. The SPSS data sheet is similar to an Excel spreadsheet, in that it is a blank matrix of columns and rows into which the data are entered. However, before this is done, the columns, which constitute the variables, have to be named or numbered according to the codes they have been given on the questionnaire. You can simply give each column a variable number (Var1, Var2, Var3 and so on) or else a more descriptive name (Gender, Age, Occupation and so on, for example). Whichever option is chosen will make no difference to later analyses of the data, but it may have implications for ease of use. By this I mean that using descriptors rather than numbers for the variables is likely to make life easier later when analysis output is produced because the output will bear the variable name. Thus, something headed 'Gender' will be easier to recognise than something headed 'Var1'.

The SPSS data sheet, in versions 10.5 onwards, has two views that can be selected from the opening screen. The opening view will be the data view, as this is the data sheet that the data are entered into. To name or configure the variables (each column in the data sheet), you need to select the variable view by clicking on the tab at the bottom of the screen. This screen provides various options for you to not only name each variable but also specify the type of data to be entered, descriptors relating to the code numbers to be entered, how missing responses should be treated and so on. In the variable view, each row is a separate variable and the columns contain the options for formatting the data to be entered for each one. Exhibit 9.2 details what these options are.

### Exhibit 9.2 Using SPSS to Format Variables for Data Entry

1 In the first column – Name – type the name you wish to give the variable. This is limited to eight characters or fewer, but you will have the option later to provide a longer name or description for the variable (see 3 below).

2   In the second column – Type – you need to specify whether the type of data is of a numeric or string form – that is, numbers or words. The default for this is numeric. To change it to a particular type of numeric value, a string format or specify the format of the numeric value, click on the grey button to the right of the word 'Numeric'. This opens the 'Variable Type' box, which contains these options. Assuming that you do not wish to specify a particular type, all you may wish to change are the default numbers of 8 and 2 in the 'Width' and 'Decimal Places' boxes. If you have data with more than eight digits, then you may wish to adjust this value. Similarly, if all your data are comprised of whole numbers, then you might want to set the 'Decimal Places' number to zero. If you make changes to any of the default values, then these will appear in the third (Width) and fourth (Decimal Places) columns once you have clicked on 'OK' and returned to the 'Variable View' window.

3   In the fifth column – Label – you have the opportunity to enter a longer description for each variable, which can be useful when you produce some output. For example, the variable name might be 'Occ', for 'occupation'. Here, the complete word can be entered as a fuller description to facilitate identification of the variable when output statistics are produced. To do this, simply click on the cell and type in the longer name.

4   The sixth column – Values – gives you the opportunity to enter value labels, or descriptors, for the categories or scale intervals in your data. For example, in the case of the variable 'Gender' there will be categorical values for males and females. You may have decided to code these as 1 for males and 2 for females, but, unless you tell SPSS what the 1s and 2s mean, it will not know. Similarly, in the case of a scale, say a five-point Likert scale, you will be entering numbers between 1 and 5, but, again, SPSS will not know what these relate to unless it is told. Clicking on the right-hand side of the 'Values' cell will open the 'Value Label' box. In it you can enter the value and its corresponding label. So, from the example above, if you type '1' in the 'Value' box and then 'Male' in the 'Value Label' box, then click on 'add', this will appear in the 'Summary' box below as '1 = Male'. You then simply repeat this procedure for the remaining items until you have labelled them all, then click on 'OK' to return to the 'Variable View' window. There you will see that these values are displayed in the relevant 'Values' cell.

5   The seventh column – Missing – enables you to specify how SPSS should deal with any missing values in the data. Unless you wish to provide a specific instruction to deal with missing values in a particular way, this can be ignored.

6   The eighth column – Columns – is used to set the width of the columns in the data sheet. The default for this is eight characters wide and this is usually sufficient. So, unless you have long numeric or string data, it is best to leave this as it is.

7   The ninth column – Align – sets the alignment of the data in the cells of the data sheet. The default setting is 'Right' and, once again, there is little to be gained by changing this, unless you have particular reasons for doing so.

*(Cont'd)*

8   The final column – Measure – enables you to specify the type of data relating to the variable. The default setting for this is 'Scale', which is for interval or ratio data, but this can be changed to 'Nominal' or 'Ordinal' if your data for the variable are one of these types. To make the change, simply click on the right-hand side of the cell and select the appropriate option.

*Shortcuts*: Once you have set up all the attributes for a variable, it is possible to save time and effort in setting up others that have either all or some of the attributes. If other variables have all the same attributes except the name and label, then you can copy and paste them to save entering all the same information again for each one. Where you want to copy and paste all the variable's attributes, you can do this as follows. In the variable view, click on the row number of the variable you wish to copy the attributes from. This should highlight the whole row. Then press 'Control-C' to copy the information and click on the empty row you want to use for the new variable. Now press 'Control-V' to paste the information in. All you will have to change is the variable name and its label. Where you only want to copy and paste the attributes from one or two cells, then you can simply select the cell(s) concerned, copy their contents, select the cell(s) you want to put this information into and paste it in.

When all the variables and their formats have been specified, a return to the data view will show that each column now has a distinctive number or descriptor relating to the variable concerned. The detail relating to the formatting of the data entries for each will not be shown, but the software will have been informed what this is from the options chosen in the variable view. You are now ready to start entering your data on the basis that each column is a variable and each row is a case – effectively one completed questionnaire. Therefore, the first row will have all the responses recorded from the first questionnaire, the second row those from the second questionnaire and so on. Either before or as you enter the data from each completed questionnaire it is a good idea to simply number each questionnaire so that, at a later date, if you need to identify which data row has been entered from which questionnaire, this is easy to do. You may need to do this if, later, you find that errors have been made typing in the data. If you have previously decided to ignore any missing responses, then you simply do not enter anything in the cells relating to these on the data sheet as SPSS will recognise empty cells as missing values.

With all the data entered, the next task is to check that these have been entered correctly and the data sheet does not contain errors as a result of typing mistakes. This can be done by carefully reviewing the data sheet entries on screen or by printing out the sheet and proofreading it. Either of these actions should help you to identify rogue entries and correct them before any analysis is undertaken. When you are sure that the data are 'clean' – correct – then you are ready to begin using the software to analyse these.

In the following sections of this chapter we will consider various options for producing basic, descriptive, bivariate (associations or differences between two variables), inferential and data reduction statistics from your data, but first, it may be helpful for you to be aware of the split files and select cases options available within SPSS. When you are using any of the statistical techniques that follow, you may wish to perform or set these up to deal with particular cases meeting certain conditions and/or for the calculation to be repeated for separate categories or groups relating to a particular variable. For example, you may wish to test to see if the responses given by males and females are both statistically significant or whether one set is and another is not. Similarly, you may wish to pick out certain cases from your total data set to perform a particular analysis on those that meet certain conditions. For example, you may wish to analyse all the coastal resort destinations but not the other types of destination. To do the former, you would need to use the split file option, and for the latter, the select cases option. The SPSS procedures for using these options are outlined in Exhibit 9.3.

---

### Exhibit 9.3    Using SPSS to Split Files or Select Cases

#### Splitting files

Splitting files enables you to repeat an analysis for all the categories or groups within a variable.

1   In the data view go to the Data menu and select the 'Split File' option.
2   In the 'Split File' dialogue box, your list of variables will be displayed in the left-hand window. Select which one(s) you wish to use to split the file and move these to the window headed 'Groups Based On'.
3   From the three options above this box, if you click on 'Compare Groups', this will produce the groups' results together, or, if you click on 'Organise Output by Groups', the results for each group will be presented separately and successively.
4   Click on 'OK' to return to the data view window.

#### Selecting cases

Where you wish to select particular values for your variable or categories rather than repeating the same analysis for all the variable's categories, then this option will enable you to do exactly that.

1   Go to the Data menu and click on the 'Select Cases' option.
2   In the 'Select Cases' dialogue box, there are various options to specify the basis on which the cases should be selected, but perhaps the most commonly used one is the 'If' option. Selecting this opens the 'If' dialogue box for you to specify the conditions to be used to select the cases.

*(Cont'd)*

3 To inform SPSS which variable the cases are to be selected from, highlight this in the left-hand window and press the button to move it into the window at the top of the 'If' dialogue box. Now you have to specify the condition or value of the variable to be used to select the cases. This can be done using the keypad or 'Functions' options below the window. For example, if you only want the analysis to apply to the category of male respondents and this has previously been coded as 1, from the variable 'Gender', then you need to set the window as 'gender=1'. It is also possible to set the condition to include more than one category for selecting the cases using the 'And' or 'Or' operators.

4 Once the condition has been set, click on 'Continue' to return to the 'Select Cases' dialogue box, then click 'OK' to return to the data view window.

*Note*: When you return from the 'Split File' or 'Select Cases' boxes, you will see that changes have occurred to the organisation of your data in the data sheet and, in the bar at the bottom of the screen, either the words 'Split File on' or 'Filter on' will be displayed, respectively.

These changes are not permanent, but once you have completed the analysis for the split file or selected cases you need to turn off the function, otherwise any further analyses will only be conducted on this basis. To turn off the split file and return the data sheet to a normal format, go to the Data menu, select 'Split File', click on the first option – 'Analyse all cases, do not create groups' – and click on 'OK'. To turn off select cases, go to the Data menu, choose 'Select Cases', click on the 'All Cases' option, then Click on 'OK'. You can tell when these options are switched on or off by looking at the display in the status bar at the bottom of the data view window.

## 9.3 Descriptive Statistics

The first stage in quantitative data analysis is to produce some relatively simple output to get an initial feel for the data. This is likely to address questions such as do the data provide the type of picture expected, do they contain possible relationships that weren't expected, do they indicate a fairly normal distribution or are they skewed in a particular direction, what do they tell me about the characteristics of the sample?

So, how do you set about doing this? Essentially, you need to produce some statistics or output that summarises or describes the characteristics of your data. Perhaps the easiest way to achieve this is to use SPSS to produce some frequency distributions for your data and, if appropriate, some measures of central tendency and dispersion. The procedure you need to follow to do this is contained in Exhibit 9.4.

---

### Exhibit 9.4    *Using SPSS to Obtain Frequency Distributions/Tables*

1   Go to the Analyze menu, select 'Descriptive Statistics', then 'Frequencies'.
2   In the 'Frequencies' dialogue box, select the name(s) or number(s) you have given to the variable(s) you wish to see the frequencies for and press the arrow key to place these in the 'Variables' window.
3   If you then click on 'OK', without changing the other options available, SPSS will do the calculations and display these as tables in an 'Output' window that you can save as a separate file using the 'Save As' command.

---

Simply by looking at the relative proportions, or distribution, of the values across any nominal categories in a frequency table, you will get a feel for whether they are even or uneven and, in the case of tables containing interval or ratio data, whether they are fairly evenly dispersed or skewed towards one extreme or the other. An alternative way to do this is to produce some charts (see Exhibit 9.5).

---

### Exhibit 9.5    *Using SPSS to Produce Charts and Graphs*

1   In SPSS you can do this quite easily by going to the Graphs menu and selecting the type of chart you wish to produce. There you will be given the options to produce bar or pie charts, histograms, line graphs and other types of chart.
2   Selecting one of these will open the appropriate dialogue box for you to specify the variable to be charted or graphed and the format for this.
3   You can also produce bar and pie charts and histograms at the same time as when you request frequencies from within the 'Frequencies' dialogue box. Having selected the variable(s) you wish to chart, click on the 'Charts' button, select the desired type in the options box this opens, click on 'Continue' to return to the 'Frequencies' box and click on 'OK' to activate the process.

---

However, as useful as frequency distributions and charts and graphs may be for getting an idea as to what your data are indicating, there is often value in trying to summarise the key characteristics in a more parsimonious manner (discussed in section 1.3.9). Working out the 'average' value in the data, providing an indication of their variability or spread and the nature of their distribution, is often helpful. This requires you to consider the measures of location, or the central tendency, dispersion and skewness. There are three commonly used measures of central tendency: the mode, median and mean. The modal value is simply the one that occurs most frequently in a data set and is the simplest measure of central tendency. This can be used for all types of data, from nominal to ratio, but it is rarely used for data above nominal level. It can be misleading if the modal value is extreme and it is possible to have more than one modal value in a set of data – that is, when the same frequency is evident for different values.

By contrast, the median is not influenced by extreme values and there can only be one median value. This is because the median is the middle value within a set of data. The median can be used for ordinal data upwards.

The third measure of central tendency is known as the mean. Most people would generally refer to this as the average as it is calculated by taking the sum of the values in the data set and then dividing it by the number of values in the set. The mean can only be used for interval or ratio data and its advantage lies in the fact that all the data in the set are used to calculate it. However, extreme values can 'pull' the mean value towards one end of the distribution or the other, providing a somewhat distorted picture. Therefore, the amount of skew in the data set influences the mean value. If the data are very skewed, in either direction, this will tend to pull the mean value up or down. This is particularly true where there is a limited amount of data in the set, but far less true when there is a large amount. In view of this, it may be advisable, with a very skewed data set, to consider using the median value as a more appropriate measure of central tendency for the data.

To obtain an indication of the variability within the data set, you can examine the range and dispersion of the data. The range is a very simple and crude statistic, it is the difference between the smallest and largest value in the data set. As the range can be distorted by a single extreme value in the set, it may provide a misleading picture of the distribution of the data.

This problem can be avoided by using the interquartile range instead of the simple range, but this cannot be used with nominal data. If you have ordinal data however, the interquartile range can be used and it is really quite a straightforward concept. A quartile is a quarter, thus the data set is divided up into four equal parts, two each side of the middle value (the median) in the set. This means that 50 per cent of the data is above the median and 50 per cent below it. By taking the two central quarters, the interquartile range provides an indication of the range of data falling between the second quarter and the third quarter in the set or, in other words, the 50 per cent of the data clustered immediately above and below the median. Although the interquartile range avoids the distortion caused by extreme values, it only uses half of the data in the set and this may give a misleading picture of the degree of clustering in the set.

The standard deviation statistic, for interval or ratio data, eliminates this partiality problem because it is calculated using all the values in the data set, which are compared with the mean. However, it is possible that extreme values can distort it. That said, the standard deviation is a widely used statistic for representing a measure of dispersion within a data set. Generally, the smaller the standard deviation, the more clustered the values are around the mean and vice versa. However, you need to remember that the actual value of the standard deviation statistic is related to the value of the mean, which, in turn, is related to the range of the data set.

This may sound complicated, but it is really quite simple. Taking two hypothetical examples, if you had a data range of 5 because the question asked used a five-point scale and the mean was 3, you would not expect a large standard deviation value. If the standard deviation value for this data were to be 1, then it would mean that approximately just over two thirds of your data would be clustered within the range of 2 to 4 – that, the value of one standard deviation above and below the mean of 3. On the other hand, if your data ranged between 1 and 100 and the mean was 50, you might expect the value of one standard deviation above and below this to be greater than 1. So, if the value was 10, you would say that one standard deviation above and below the mean indicated that just over two thirds of the data would be clustered between 40 and 60. In turn, two standard deviations above or below the mean would account for around 95 per cent of all the data, three standard deviations almost 100 per cent (actually 99.7 per cent).

Therefore, in the range of 1 to 100 used in the example above, the value of two standard deviations would be 20, as the value of one was 10, so 95 per cent of the data would lie between the values of 30 and 70. The values for the mean and standard deviation used in these examples would suggest that the distribution of these values is symmetrical or, in the jargon, approximates to a 'normal distribution', where the mean lies in the centre of the distribution with 50 per cent of the data above it and 50 per cent below it.

One way to determine whether or not the distribution is normal in shape is to examine the values for the mode, median and mean. If these are the same, it indicates that the distribution is symmetrical and normal in shape. Where the mean is higher or lower than the median, then the distribution will be skewed in a positive or negative direction and it will be asymmetrical in shape. The procedure used to obtain these measures of central tendency, dispersion and skewness in SPSS is outlined in Exhibit 9.6.

---

### Exhibit 9.6    *Using SPSS to Obtain Measures of Central Tendency, Dispersion and Skewness*

1   Go to the Analyze menu, select 'Descriptive Statistics', then 'Descriptives'.
2   In the 'Descriptives' dialogue box, you then need to place the variables you wish to have these measures calculated for into the 'Variables' box.
3   Click on the 'Options' button, select the statistics you require, then click on 'Continue' to return to the 'Descriptives' box.
4   Click on 'OK' and the results will then appear in an 'Output' window.

*Note*: The interpretation of these results should be straightforward, but if you have selected 'Skewness' and/or 'Kurtosis' to get a feel for the shape of the data distribution,

*(Cont'd)*

these may not be so familiar. Skewness provides an indication of how symmetrical the distribution is and kurtosis how peaked or flat it is. If the distribution is normal, both of these will have a value of zero. A positive skewness value would indicate a clustering of data to the left of the distribution, while a negative value would be the reverse of this. Kurtosis values that are positive indicate the distribution is peaked and those that are negative indicate a flatter distribution.

These types of exploratory data analysis will give you some idea about what your data can tell you and may help to indicate whether or not they are suitable for further statistical analysis. They can also form the basis for presenting a descriptive picture of your data where this might be required in the report or thesis. This could be useful for providing the reader with a background picture or context of the scope and scale of the situation you have been investigating that can then be used to relate other analytical results to. Also, you may wish to use some of the univariate (single variable) data relating to your respondents' characteristics to indicate the representativeness, if that is possible, of your sample. Exhibit 9.7 contains a piece of text taken from a paper written by myself (Brotherton, 2004) that indicates how this might be approached.

## Exhibit 9.7    Expressing Sample Representativeness

The size of the realised sample (n = 239) was very encouraging in terms of providing a representative data set from the budget hotel sector. Not unsurprisingly, it was dominated by the two leading brands Premier Travel Inn and Travelodge. Though this did skew the sample in favour of these brands, this nevertheless reflects the population distribution of budget hotel brands in the UK. The sample was also dominated by budget hotels, in motorway and A (trunk road) road locations, with these accounting for almost two-thirds of the respondent hotels. However, this again reflects the nature of the population distribution for budget hotel locations. Interestingly the more recent growth locations of suburban and city centre sites also feature quite strongly, accounting for nearly a further 30 per cent of the sample. The size distribution shows the 31–40 bedroom range to be the largest single category, followed by the over 60 bedroom group. Cumulatively these two size categories account for 74 per cent of the total. If the 41–50 category were to be added to these, this would account for some 90 per cent of the total. Once again, this is strongly representative of the budget hotel population distribution by size. Other categorical data also indicates that the sample is very representative of the breadth of budget hotel operations, as this is comprised of a considerable range of responses in relation to average room occupancy, number of full-part-time staff and the business mix. Given all of these characteristics it is reasonable to claim that the sample as a whole is highly representative of branded budget hotel operations in the UK.

*Source:* Brotherton, 2004: 949–50

One other issue that you may also wish to address at this stage is the reliability, or otherwise, of the scale(s) you have used to collect the data. There are a number of different aspects to the issue of reliability, but perhaps the main one is the internal consistency of the set of scale items used – that is, whether or not they are all measuring the same construct. There are a number of ways to assess reliability, but perhaps the most common statistic is known as Cronbach's alpha coefficient. The SPSS procedure to obtain this is outlined in Exhibit 9.8.

Essentially, the calculation lying behind this overall statistic is one of inter-item correlations in a two-dimensional matrix or, in other words, all the items in the scale are correlated with each other and an overall value (the alpha coefficient) is produced to summarise all these relationships. Given that a perfect, positive correlation between two, or a set of, items would be 1, it follows that the closer to 1 the alpha value is, the better the correlation is between the set of items and vice versa. It is generally accepted that the alpha value should be at least .7, preferably higher. A value in the .8 or .9 range would be regarded as indicative of adequate to very satisfactory scale reliability.

---

### Exhibit 9.8    Using SPSS to Calculate Split-half Reliability

1   Go to the Analyze menu, select 'Scale' and then 'Reliability Analysis'.
2   Select all the variables that are included in the set or scale and move these into the 'Items' box.
3   Select 'Alpha' in the 'Models' section of the box.
4   Click on the 'Statistics' button and select 'Item, Scale and Scale If Item Deleted' in the 'Descriptives For' section. Click on 'Continue' to return to the 'Reliability Analysis' box.
5   Click on 'OK' and the results will appear in an 'Output' window.

*Note*: This can produce a lot of data, especially if there are many items included in the scale, but the key results to examine are as follows. First, at the end of the output, there will be a figure for the alpha value. This is the Cronbach's alpha coefficient and it indicates the internal consistency or coherence of the set of items. It is the sum of all the correlations between the items and, the closer it is to 1 (remember, a correlation coefficient of 1 indicates a perfect correlation), the greater the relatedness or consistency of the set of items. It is generally accepted that, for the scale to be considered reliable, the alpha value should be at least .7, with higher values moving towards 1 indicating greater reliability. If the alpha value is less than .7, then you may be able to improve it by removing items that have a low correlation with others in the set. The column headed 'Alpha if Item Deleted' will indicate what the alpha value would be if an item was deleted from the scale. If, when doing this for any of the items, it shows that the overall alpha value would be higher than .7 if it were to be removed, then you may wish to consider doing this. You can also examine such a column even if the alpha is .7 or

*(Cont'd)*

greater to see if it could be improved by removing any of the items. However, you need to be careful because you may find that removal of one or more items only improves the alpha value by a very small amount, which may not be a price you are prepared to pay to gain a small increase in reliability.

## 9.4 Bivariate Analysis

In the section above, we examined some of the issues associated with producing basic descriptive statistics for individual variables to get an initial feel for the data, but you are likely to want to ask questions concerning whether there are differences between, say, the behaviour or opinions of males and females, larger and smaller companies, public- and private-sector organisations and so on. Similarly, you may wish to explore if there are connections or associations between two or more of your variables – that is, to what extent the frequency of visits to an art gallery, for example, is associated with the price of admission. This leads us into what in known as bivariate (two variables) analysis.

In everyday life, we might ask the question, is there a connection between peoples' incomes and the number of holidays they take each year? What we are really asking here is, does the level of income affect or influence the number of holidays people take? Lying behind this may be the unstated assumption that, the greater the income, the more holidays they are likely to take, simply because they have the economic means to do so. In research terms, we might have expressed this as a hypothesis that postulated an association between income levels and frequency of holidays purchased in the form 'People with higher incomes will go on holiday more frequently than those with lower incomes' or, alternatively, 'There is no relationship between peoples' incomes and the frequency with which they go on holiday'. This type of data is likely to be nominal in nature – that is, it will be the result of a question in the questionnaire that simply asked respondents to tick a box to indicate their annual income levels and another question that asked them to tick the appropriate box to indicate how many holidays they take in a year.

To establish whether or not an association exists between income levels and the frequency with which people go on holiday using this type of data, a cross-tabulation procedure can be used. We have already hypothesised what the dependent and independent variables are in this case – the former is the frequency of holidays and the latter the level of income. If we now put the values for these two variables into the columns and rows of a table, we can begin to see if the frequency of holidays does vary with income level. However, a table with actual values across, say, five income groupings and five holiday frequency categories may be difficult to interpret. Also, because the number of responses within each of the two sets of groupings may be very unequal, viewing a table with the frequency values displayed may give a misleading picture.

To avoid this problem, it is a good idea to format the cross-tabulation output in percentages rather than actual values. This makes interpretation easier, but the type of percentage formatting you use depends on where you have placed the dependent and independent variables. If the columns have been designated for the dependent variable and the rows for the independent variable, then the percentage values in each cell should be set for the rows and vice versa because it is the effect of the variation in the independent variable on the dependent variable that you are interested in. This will enable you to make comparisons down the table for holiday frequency categories to identify whether or not there are large differences between the rows, which are the levels of income. It is the size of the differences between these percentages that indicates the strength of any association between the two variables. The closer this gets to the maximum (100 per cent difference), the greater the association and vice versa. As a basic rule of thumb, 100 per cent difference can be regarded as a perfect association and 0 per cent difference as no, or zero, association, while something in the region of 50 per cent difference indicates a moderate association (Finn et al., 2000). The SPSS procedure for cross-tabulation analysis is shown in Exhibit 9.9.

---

### Exhibit 9.9    Using SPSS to Produce Cross-tabulation Results

1   Go to the Analyze menu, select 'Descriptive Statistics', then 'Crosstabs' to open this dialogue box.
2   There, you need to select the dependent and independent variables from the list of variables in the box on the left. This is done by specifying which variables are to be used for the rows and which for columns of the table. You can choose to enter the dependent variables in either the rows or the columns, but it may be preferable to enter the independent variables in the rows and the dependent variables in the columns. This is done by simply selecting the appropriate variable from the list and pressing the relevant arrow key to place it in either the 'Rows' or 'Columns' boxes.
3   Once you have completed this task, click on the 'Cells' button and check the 'Row' and 'Total' boxes in the 'Percentages' section to ensure that the percentages are calculated by rows – the independent variables. If you have decided to place the independent variables in the columns of the table, then, of course, you need to check the 'Columns' box.
4   Click on 'Continue', then, when the display has returned to the 'Crosstabs' dialogue box, click on 'OK' and the results will appear in an 'Output' window.

---

It is also possible to use the 'Crosstabs' option in SPSS to produce more summarised statistics relating to the degree to which the covariance of the two variables is related, or correlated. These statistics are correlation coefficients and measure the strength of the statistical association between the two variables.

The phi coefficient is one such statistic used for two-by-two tables – that is, where both the independent and dependent variables have two categories each. Its value will range from zero to +1 and the interpretation of the value is the same as the percentage difference referred to earlier, so the closer it is to zero the weaker the association, and the closer it is to +1 the stronger the association.

In situations where the table is larger than two-by-two categories, then Cramer's V coefficient can be used. Once again, the value of Cramer's V will vary between zero and +1 and its interpretation is the same as that specified for the phi coefficient.

Both of these correlation coefficients are suitable for nominal and/or ordinal data.

Where association is being explored for variables comprised of interval or ratio data, producing a scatter graph or diagram is often a useful first step in being able to visualise whether or not the two variables might be associated. This should indicate whether or not the distribution of the data points on the graph is clustered together in some way or scattered with no discernable pattern. The procedure used to produce a scatter graph in SPSS is shown in Exhibit 9.10.

---

### Exhibit 9.10    Using SPSS to Produce Scatter Graphs

1  Go to the Graphs menu and select 'Scatter'. In the dialogue box, ensure that 'Simple' is highlighted and click on the 'Define' button.
2  From the list of variables displayed, select the one you wish to be the independent variable and add this to the x-axis box, then do the same for the dependent variable, adding this to the y-axis box.
3  If you wish to add titles and labels to the graph, you can do this using the 'Titles' button. Click on 'OK' to activate the calculation and open the output window containing the scatter graph.

---

If a perfect correlation exists between the two sets of data, then all the points would sit in a straight line on the graph. However, as a correlation can be positive or negative (which indicates an inverse relationship between the two variables) the slope of this line can differ accordingly. Given that the independent variable is always placed on the x (horizontal) axis of the graph and the dependent on the y (vertical) axis, in the case of a perfectly positive relationship, the line would slope upwards from left to right at an angle of 45 degrees, indicating that a given change in the value of the independent variable would be associated with the same change in the value of the dependent variable. For example, a 10 per cent increase in the number of bed spaces available at a destination would be accompanied by a 10 per cent increase in the number of overnight stays at that destination and vice versa. This is also known as a 'unitary' relationship, as the unit of change for both variables is the same in either direction – a 10 per cent increase/decrease in the independent variable is accompanied by a 10 per cent increase/decrease in the dependent one. Where the association is perfectly negative, the line will slope downwards from left to right, indicating an inverse relationship. For example, a 10 per cent increase in the price of airline tickets would be associated with a 10 per cent reduction in the number of airline passengers and vice versa.

However, in many cases the association will not be perfectly positive – with a correlation coefficient of +1 – or perfectly negative – with a value of –1. Indeed, where no association exists between the two, the coefficient will have a value of zero. To interpret the intermediate values, a useful rule of thumb is that a value of either +0.5 or –0.5 indicates, respectively, a moderately strong positive or negative association. Therefore, values between plus or minus 0.5 and zero indicate a weak positive or negative association, with this becoming weaker the closer the value gets to zero in each case. The same logic applies to intermediate values lying between plus or minus 0.5 and plus or minus one, except here, as the value moves closer to these extremes, it indicates a stronger association. For example, a correlation coefficient of 0.6 would not indicate a very strong association, but one of 0.8 would. Producing correlation coefficients to assess possible association between variables in SPSS is quite straightforward (see Exhibit 9.11).

---

### Exhibit 9.11    Using SPSS to Produce Correlation Coefficients

1   Go to the Analyze menu, select 'Correlate' and then 'Bivariate' (for two variables).
2   In the dialogue box, select the two variables to correlate, add these to the 'Variables' box, then select the appropriate correlation calculation – either Pearson's or Spearman's – in the 'Correlation Coefficients' section (see the note below). Also at this point select the '2 Tail' box, unless you have good reasons to support the view that the correlation will take a specific direction, in which case you can choose the '1 Tail' option.
3   Next, click on the 'Options' button and, in the window that opens, select 'Exclude Cases Pairwise' under 'Missing Values'. If you wish to include the means and standard deviations in the output, then you can also select those there.
4   Click on 'Continue' and then 'OK' when you return to the previous window to produce the results in an 'Output' window.

*Note*: If all of your data are of the interval or ratio kind, then the preferred choice of correlation coefficient should be Pearson's product moment correlation coefficient. However, this does assume that the data for both variables are normally distributed. If they are not, or any of your data are ordinal or ranked, then choose the Spearman's rank correlation coefficient. Both methods produce the same type of output, but they may not produce the same value for the coefficient!

The matrix produced in the output will indicate the correlation coefficient between the two variables and something known as a *p* value. We will look at this in the next section of this chapter, but essentially it indicates the probability that the result (correlation coefficient) may have occurred by chance rather than being a true reflection of the association between the two variables. If the *p* value is small, then this indicates a small probability that the result has occurred due to chance and so it is statistically significant. Generally, a value of 0.05 is used as the decision point for this. It indicates that we can be confident that, 95 times out of 100, the same result would be obtained or, in other words, that we can state a confidence level of 95 per cent for the result. However, the accepted practice is to be a little more circumspect than this and to demand a *p* value of less than 0.05 before regarding the result as being statistically significant.

One thing that you need to be careful about here when examining the implications of a correlation coefficient and the *p* value for it is that the two statistics are not related – they express different things. This means a very weak correlation coefficient of, say, 0.22 with a *p* value of less than 0.05, which is statistically significant. As the two are unrelated, the latter does not improve the former. Therefore, in this case, all you could say is that the degree of association between the two variables is weak, with a correlation coefficient of 0.22, and you could be 95 per cent confident that this weak association is applicable to the population from which the sample was taken.

Where only categorical data are available to investigate any possible association between two variables, the chi-square test for independence can be used to test for this. It compares the frequencies of cases in the categories of one categorical variable with those in another with the values that might be expected if the two sets of data were totally independent. The test calculates the probability that the data could have occurred by chance and, therefore, whether there is a statistically significant association between the variables or not – that is, whether the relevant statistic is less than 0.05 or not. The SPSS procedure to obtain the chi-square statistic is outlined in Exhibit 9.12.

---

### Exhibit 9.12     Using SPPS to Obtain the Chi-square Test for Independence

1   Go to the Analyze menu, then 'Descriptive Statistics' and select 'Crosstabs'.
2   In the 'Crosstabs' dialogue box, select and move your variables into the 'Rows' and 'Columns' boxes.
3   Next, click on the 'Statistics' button, select 'chi-square' and then click on 'Continue' to return to the 'Crosstabs' dialogue box.

> 4   Now, click on the 'Cells' button and, in the 'Counts' box, click on the 'Observed' and 'Expected' options. In the 'Percentage' section, click on 'Column, Row and Total'. Click on 'Continue' and then 'OK' after returning to the 'Crosstabs' dialogue box.
>
> 5   The results will now appear in an 'Output' window.

If you have kept alert as you have been reading the material in this section, then you will have noticed that, in the discussion on correlation, the term 'association' will have always been used to refer to any possible connection between two variables. This has been deliberate because a correlational association is not the same as a cause–effect relationship, or causation. In other words, even though we may be able to establish that there is a *statistical* association between two variables, it does not prove that a change in one is the cause of a change in the other. All we can say, with certainty, is that they covary and the strength of this covariant relationship is stronger or weaker. Of course, we may have made assumptions about the cause–effect nature of the identified relationship and this may have been specified further in the research hypotheses, but correlation alone does not provide proof of the existence of such a relationship and it does not tell us the size of the impact that one variable has on the other. This can be determined by means of regression analysis.

This type of analysis is something that often seems daunting to students not well versed in statistical methods, but it is not necessary to have a detailed understanding of the underlying theory and computation required to generate a regression value to actually produce a result. What is more important is the interpretation of what the regression value means. In short, a regression line is one that best fits the distribution of data on a scatter graph, which is why it is often referred to as the 'line of best fit'. As we saw earlier, it is unlikely that a scatter graph will have a distribution of data points that are perfectly correlated – that is, all on a straight line – but they may be distributed in a pattern suggesting a relationship between the two variables that can be identified by establishing the strength of the correlation coefficient. Thus, regression analysis is an extension of correlation. Where correlation analysis produces a coefficient of association (the r value), regression takes this one stage further by calculating the square of r (the $r^2$ value) to produce a line that best fits the distribution of data points.

Logically, the closer the data points are to lying in a straight line on a scatter graph, the more accurate the regression analysis can be, as the values it estimates to produce the line will be closer to the true values represented by the data points. If you think of this as a type of averaging, then the regression line represents an average path through the data points. Now, remember our earlier consideration of the mean and how this could be affected by extreme values. A similar issue arises here in that, if there are some of what are called residual outliers – values lying some distance away from most of the others on the graph – then the average that is calculated, the regression line, is a good indication of the true values near to this line but a poorer one of those lying much further away from it. Thus, the greater the number of outliers and the further they are away from the line, the less robust that regression value is. See Exhibit 9.13 for the steps you need to take to produce a regression value using SPSS.

---

### Exhibit 9.13    Using SPSS to Produce Simple (Two Variable) Regression Analysis

1  Go to the Analyze menu, select 'Regression' and then 'Linear'.
2  In the 'Linear Regression' dialogue box, select and move the independent and dependent variables into the respective boxes.
3  Before clicking on 'OK' to produce the regression results, it is possible to request other statistics by pressing the 'Statistics' button. In the box this opens, a range of options is available, but unless you are very familiar with regression analysis, it may be advisable to select only 'Estimates', 'Model Fit' and 'Descriptives'. You may also wish to select 'Casewise Diagnostics' and set the 'Outliers' value to 3 standard deviations in the 'Residuals' section (see the note below).

*Note*: The 'Casewise Diagnostics' option allows you to identify whether or not there are any very large residuals or outliers that could be eliminated from the analysis to improve its reliability.

---

The output this produces may appear to be complex and confusing at first glance, but you do not need to consider all the values SPSS produces. The key statistics are the multiple R and R square figures. The former indicates the correlation between the variables and the latter the regression value. We saw earlier in our discussion of correlation that the closer the correlation coefficient value is to $-1$ or $+1$, the stronger the negative or positive association is between the two variables, and the same logic applies here, except that the regression value, or coefficient, will have a value between zero and $+1$. Therefore, the closer to $+1$ the regression coefficient, or R square figure, is, the closer the 'fit' of the regression statistic. For example, if the correlation coefficient, the multiple R value, is 0.85 and the regression coefficient, the R square value, is 0.75, this tells you that there is a strong, positive correlation between the two variables and 75 per cent of the variance in the dependent variable can be accounted for by the independent variable. Conversely, if the multiple R value is 0.3 and the R square value is 0.2, then you have to conclude that there is an extremely weak correlation between the variables and only 20 per cent of the variation in the dependent variable could be explained by the independent variable or, in other words, the vast majority (80 per cent) of any change in the dependent variable is being caused by something else. Again, the SPSS output for regression analysis will provide an indication of the statistical significance of the result and this should be interpreted in the same way as discussed earlier.

## 9.5 Inferential Statistics

The very term 'inferential statistics' may be offputting if you do not understand what it means. It often appears to be complicated and so may not be considered. However, making or drawing inferences from statistics is really quite a simple concept.

Inferential statistics are concerned with how confident you can be about making valid inferences about the population from your sample data. Logically, the greater the degree of error in the sample data, the less confident you can feel about generalising from the results to the population as a whole. Alternatively, think of it as trying to answer the question 'How likely is it that I can apply the sample statistics to the population?' What inferential statistics do is provide you with an objective basis for making such a claim, as opposed to one based on pure speculation.

The inferential statistical tests available for this purpose are varied, as we shall see, but essentially they are all designed to determine the degree of statistical significance of the results obtained by using statistical procedures. What does this mean? As mentioned briefly in the previous section, the idea is to determine the extent to which the results could have been due to chance – that is, some form of error – or the likelihood that they are a true reflection of the population from which the sample was obtained. In terms of testing a hypothesis, a statistically significant result indicates that you can be confident about making a decision to accept or reject the hypothesis and have the evidence to support that decision.

Earlier on it was stated that the cut-off point for deciding whether a result can be regarded as statistically significant or not is if the relevant statistic has a value of less than 0.05 (the 95 per cent confidence level). It is also the case that higher confidence levels can be claimed for or may be evident in the statistic. The other $p$ values commonly used for this are 0.01 and 0.001. These indicate the higher confidence levels, of 99 per cent and 99.9 per cent respectively. Therefore, if the statistical significance of the result was 0.002, you could state that this is a significant result at the 99 per cent confidence level, but not at the 99.9 per cent level as the value of 0.002 is not less than the value of 0.001, which is used for that confidence level.

As we saw in Chapter 5, the accepted convention in research is to operate from an assumption that there is no association or difference between the variables specified in the negative, or null, form of the hypothesis and, if this can be disproved or rejected, then the positive, or alternative, form of the same hypothesis, which states that there will be an association or difference, is accepted.

Another way to think about this is to use the analogy of a legal trial. The assumption is that the accused is innocent until proven guilty on the basis of the evidence presented and this is very similar to the process of accepting and rejecting hypotheses. In the trial situation, either sufficient evidence is presented to reject the defendant's innocence and, hence, accept the opposite condition of guilty or the evidence supports the innocence of the person concerned. In short, there are only two outcomes, and if one is accepted the other must be rejected.

When testing a hypothesis, there are two general types of tests that can be conducted. These are known as directional or non-directional and one-tailed or two-tailed tests respectively. They are really quite straightforward as the difference between the two, which will decide for you what test you will use, is embodied in the hypothesis you wish to test. For example, a non-directional hypothesis might state that the respondents will not indicate that the price of a holiday is extremely important or unimportant in influencing their decision to book it. In other words, they will effectively be indifferent to the price. To test this it would be necessary to use a two-tailed test because you would want to know whether the pattern of responses to the question asked indicated that they did regard it as important or unimportant to be able to reject the hypothesis. If, however, the hypothesis stated that the respondents will not indicate that the price of a holiday is extremely important in influencing their decision to book it, then a one-tailed test could be used as only one side of the frequency distribution needs to be explored to establish whether the data support the hypothesis or not.

In choosing the type of statistical test to use in order to assess association or difference, the type of data you have on the variables concerned is a major influence. Inferential statistics fall into two basic types, known as parametric and non-parametric. Parametric tests can only be used on interval or ratio data, but there are non-parametric equivalents available for nominal and ordinal data (see Table 9.1). Parametric tests are based on the assumptions that the sample data has been derived from a population with a normal distribution, and if there is more than one sample, they each have the same variance. Non-parametric tests are not constrained by these assumptions, but both types do assume that the sample data have been obtained from a probability-based sampling procedure.

As there are many parametric and non-parametric tests available, it is not possible to discuss all of them here, but details on those not included here, and how to use them in SPSS, can be found in the excellent books by Kinnear and Gray (2000) and Pallant (2001). One widely used parametric test is the student t-test and versions of this are available for independent samples, paired samples and just one

**Table 9.1**    Parametric and non-parametric tests for confirmatory analysis

| Parametric (P) and non-parametric (NP) tests | Type of data | Purpose |
| --- | --- | --- |
| Confidence intervals (P) | Normally distributed univariate | Estimating from samples |
| Pearson's product moment correlation coefficient (P) | Bivariate (interval or ratio data) | Measuring association and exploring relationships |
| Spearman's rank order correlation coefficient (NP) | Bivariate (at least ordinal data) | Measuring association and exploring relationships |
| Independent samples t-tests (P) *(NP equivalent is the Mann-Whitney U test)* | Bivariate (at least interval data for the dependent variables) | Measuring difference and comparing independent groups |
| Paired samples t-test (P) *(NP equivalent is the Wilcoxon signed-rank test)* | Bivariate (at least interval data for the dependent variables) | Measuring difference and comparing the same subjects on more than one occasion |
| One sample t-test (P) | Bivariate (at least interval data) | Measuring difference and comparing the sample subjects to a test value |
| Chi-square test for independence (NP) | Bivariate (nominal data) | Measuring difference and comparing groups |
| Chi-square test for goodness of fit (NP) | Bivariate (nominal data) | Measuring difference and comparing groups |

sample. The independent samples test would be used where two different and independent samples, say males and females, were asked the same questions separately and you wished to establish whether or not there was a statistically significant degree of difference between them. Where, for example, the same sample of people were asked the same questions before and after some intervention or 'treatment' or asked different questions in an attempt to measure the same variable, then these samples would be paired or related and the paired t-test would be appropriate. The procedure to access these tests in SPSS is outlined in Exhibit 9.14.

---

### Exhibit 9.14    *Using SPSS to Conduct Student T-tests*

#### Independent samples t-tests

These tests are used to compare the mean score, from a continuous variable, with two separate groups of sample subjects.

1   Go to the Analyze menu and click on 'Compare Means', then select 'Independent samples t-test'.
2   In the dialogue box that opens, select the dependent variable – the continuous variable – from the list of variables in the box on the left and click on the button to move this into the 'Test Variable(s)' box.

*(Cont'd)*

3   Next, select the independent variable from the list and click on the button to move this into the 'Grouping Variable' box.
4   Then click on 'Define Groups' to enter the numbers used to code each group in the data file. For example, if the variable were 'Gender' and 1 = males and 2 = females, then you would enter 1 in the 'Group 1' box and 2 in the 'Group 2' box. Click on 'Continue'.
5   Back in the main dialogue box, you will now see the two group numbers in brackets after the name of the variable in the 'Grouping Variable' box – in our example, 'Gender(1 2)'. Click on 'OK' to produce the results.

Note: In the output for this test, you need to examine the significance (sig.) figure for Levene's test for equality of variances first. This examines whether or the variation in scores across the two groups is the same. If the sig. figure for this is greater than 0.05, which indicates no significant difference, then the 'Equal Variances Assumed' results can be used. If it is less than 0.05, then this assumption is not valid and the 'Equal Variances Not Assumed' results should be used. In both cases, the 'Sig. Two-Tailed' column is the one you are interested in as the result there shows whether there is a significant difference ($p < 0.05$) between the groups or not ($p > 0.05$).

### Paired samples t-tests

These tests are used where you have two samples from the same respondents – that is, when you have collected data from them on two separate occasions or under different conditions.

1   Go to the Analyze menu, click on 'Compare Means' and then 'Paired Samples t-test'.
2   Click on the two variables you wish to use for the analysis in the left-hand box and these will appear, highlighted, in the 'Current Selections' area under the variables list box. Click on the button to place these into the 'Paired Variables' box on the right, then click on 'OK' to produce the results.

Note: The table entitled 'Paired Samples Test' is the one you are interested in. In the final column of this, labelled 'Sig. (Two-tailed)', you have the $p$ values to indicate whether the test has found any statistically significant differences between the two variables ($p < 0.05$) or not ($p > 0.05$). To establish the nature of this difference, examine the 'Mean' scores for the two variables in the 'Paired Samples Statistics' table.

### One sample t-tests

These are used to test the confidence interval for the mean of a single population. Here, as there is only one sample and one mean, we do not have other sample means to make comparisons with, but this is dealt with by establishing a test value to represent another mean.

1   Go to the Analyze menu, click on 'Compare Means' and then 'One Sample t-test'.
2   In the dialogue box that opens, select from the list of variables in the box on the left the variable you wish to use for the test and click on the button to move this into the 'Test Variable(s)' box.
3   In the 'Test Value' box, enter the figure to be used as the comparator for your variable's mean. For example, if the variable had scores based on a 1–5 scale, the null hypothesis could be rejected if this was very close to the 'indifference' point in this scale of 3. Therefore, in this case, to establish if the data indicate that you can reject the null hypothesis, you set the 'Test Value' to 3 so that the mean of the variable is compared to it to establish whether it is significantly different or not.
4   Click on 'OK' to produce the results.

*Note:* The most important figure in these results is the sig. two-tailed figure in the one sample test table. If it is $> 0.05$, then the difference between the variable's mean and the test value is not statistically significant and the null hypothesis cannot be rejected and vice versa.

In situations where only one sample exists, the one sample t-test would be used. This operates slightly differently from the independent or paired sample tests because, in this case, there is only one mean value from the single sample. In the other t-tests, there are two means – one from each of the samples – for the test to compare in order to establish if there is any statistically significant difference between the two, but this is obviously not the case where there is only one sample. Therefore, the one sample t-test uses what is called a 'test value' to compare the mean from the sample with. This test value should be set at the midpoint value in the scale used. The reason for this is that, if you have a five-point scale, then two of these points will lie at the negative end of the scale or distribution, two will lie at the positive end and the midpoint then becomes the null or indifferent point in the scale. If this sounds complicated, consider the following example and it should become clearer.

If a question such as 'How important is the cleanliness of the hotel in determining guest satisfaction?' had been asked using a five-point scale (ranging from 1 = Extremely unimportant, 2 = Unimportant, 3 = Not really important or unimportant, 4 = Important and 5 = Extremely important), then if all or a large majority of the respondents indicated a value of 3, they would effectively be saying that cleanliness had no real relationship with guest satisfaction. Now, consider the null hypothesis that this question was designed to collect the data to test. It may well have been something like, 'There will be no relationship between cleanliness and hotel guest satisfaction', or alternatively, 'The respondents will not indicate cleanliness to be either very important or very unimportant as a factor influencing guest satisfaction. For either of these to be accepted, the pattern of responses would have to cluster strongly around the value of 3 on the scale. Thus, the midpoint of the scale effectively embodies a mean test value that will support acceptance of the null hypothesis.

Therefore, logically, if the actual mean from your sample data lies some distance from this midpoint test value, it is likely that the t-test, in comparing these two means, will find that this difference is large enough to be regarded as statistically significant and produce a $p$ value that is less than 0.05. So, for example, if your sample data mean for the above question is 4.5 indicating an average response between 'Important' and 'Extremely important', then you might reasonably expect that, when this is compared with the test value of 3, it will be found to be a statistically significant difference or result.

To further illustrate this, consider the data in Table 9.2. These show a selection of the summarised one sample t-test results for a piece of research that I conducted (see Brotherton, 2004) using questions based on a five-point scale similar to the one referred to above, which were designed to identify the factors budget hotel operators regarded as being most critical to their success. As you can see from the table, most of the actual sample means lie in the 4–5 range of the 1–5 scale and, therefore, not surprisingly, the t-test results indicated that most of these were statistically significant. Interestingly ,you can see that the two factors not found to be statistically significant by the t-test have mean values very close to 3 and are less clustered than the others – that is, their standard deviations (SDs) are larger.

A non-parametric alternative to t-tests is the chi-square test. This assumes that the data have been collected using a random sampling procedure and that they are in numerical form – frequencies as opposed to percentages – but not that the data are of interval or ratio status. This means that it can be used on nominal data where the categories are mutually exclusive and where one respondent cannot be counted in more than one category. Earlier, we saw that the chi-square test for independence can be used to establish whether or not two categorical variables are associated with each other. Here, we are concerned with the chi-square tes being used to determine whether or not there are statistically significant differences between two or more categorical variables or between two or more samples.

This is known as the chi-square test for one sample data or the test for goodness of fit. This test compares the actual set of frequencies in your data with an expected distribution, which is usually defined by the data analysis software on the basis that each category in the set would have the same, minimum number of cases. The SPSS procedure for using this test is described in Exhibit 9.15. The output it produces is fairly straightforward to interpret. There is a table with the actual and expected frequencies for the categories and one headed 'Test Statistics', which contains the chi-square statistic, the degrees of freedom (df) associated with this and the statistical significance of the result (Asymp. Sig.). The key figure here is the latter and you are looking for this to have a value of less than 0.005 for it to be statistically significant.

**Table 9.2**    Summarised one-sample t-test results

| Critical success factors | Mean | SD |
|---|---|---|
| 1  Central sales/reservation system | 4.13 | .82 |
| 2  Convenient locations | 4.43 | .65 |
| 3  Standardised hotel design | 3.81 | .90 |
| 4  Size of hotel network | 3.92 | .90 |
| 5  Geographic coverage of hotel network | 4.09 | .81 |
| 6  Consistent accommodation standards | 4.76 | .43 |
| 7  Consistent service standards | 4.75 | .50 |
| 8  Good-value restaurants | 4.03 | .81 |
| 9  Value for money accommodation | 4.68 | .57 |
| 10  Recognition of returning guests | 4.43 | .69 |
| 11  Warmth of guest welcome | 4.71 | .52 |
| 12  Operational flexibility/responsiveness | 4.05 | .75 |
| 13  Corporate contracts | 3.12 | 1.2 |
| 14  Smoking and non-smoking rooms | 4.14 | .85 |
| 15  Design/look of guest bedrooms | 3.99 | .79 |
| 16  Size of guest bedrooms | 3.77 | .83 |
| 17  Guest bedrooms' comfort level | 4.33 | .69 |
| 18  Responsiveness to customers' demands | 4.42 | .64 |
| 19  Customer loyalty/repeat business | 4.56 | .60 |
| 20  Disciplined operational controls | 4.13 | .76 |
| 21  Speed of guest service | 4.35 | .69 |
| 22  Efficiency of guest service | 4.50 | .60 |
| 23  Choice of room type for guests | 3.71 | .92 |
| 24  Guest security | 4.46 | .71 |
| 25  Low guest bedroom prices | 3.79 | .95 |
| 26  Limited service level | 3.07 | 1.0 |
| 27  Hygiene and cleanliness | 4.86 | .37 |
| 28  Quality audits | 4.23 | .87 |
| 29  Staff empowerment | 3.91 | .88 |
| 30  Strong brand differentiation | 4.08 | .90 |
| 31  Customer surveys/feedback | 4.08 | .92 |
| 32  Staff training | 4.74 | .47 |
| 33  Added-value facilities in guest rooms | 3.55 | 1.0 |
| 34  Staff recruitment and selection | 4.27 | .72 |
| 35  Standard pricing policy | 4.11 | .88 |
| 36  Quality standards | 4.73 | .56 |

*Note:*  All the CSFs are significant, In a positive direction, at the $p < 0.001$ level, except factors 13 (Corporate contracts) and 26 (Limited service level), which are not significant.

*Source:*  Brotherton, 2004: 952. Reproduced with permission of Emerald Publications.

---

## *Exhibit 9.15     Using SPSS For the Chi-square Goodness of Fit Test*

1   Go to Analyze, Non-Parametric Tests and select 'chi-square'.
2   In the 'chi-square' dialogue box, place the variable you wish to use for the test in the 'Test Variable List' box and make sure that the 'Get From Data' option is ticked in the 'Expected Range' settings and the 'All Categories Equal' option is ticked in the 'Expected Values' settings.
3   Click on 'OK' and the results will appear in an 'Output' window.

# 9.6 Data Reduction Techniques

Data reduction techniques are somewhat different from those discussed thus far in this chapter, but are useful when you wish to seek a more parsimonious solution (see section 1.3.9) from a large range of explanatory variables or respondents. Cluster analysis is one of these techniques and it seeks to identify groups or clusters of related respondents based on the responses they have given to the questions. This can be a powerful analysis, but is often complex to interpret and somewhat controversial. Cluster analysis will not be dealt with here, but, if you wish to explore it further, a useful discussion is provided by Ryan (1995).

The other technique is perhaps the one you are more likely to use. It concentrates on grouping variables together to produce a solution that concentrates on the variables explaining the greatest amount of variance and is often referred to as 'factor analysis'. One of the most commonly used techniques in this category is known as principal components analysis (PCA). PCA uses an underlying model to divide the set of variables into separate 'components' or groupings. Each of these explains a certain proportion of the variance, with the first explaining the most and successive ones less. Therefore, the first component contains the variables that explain the highest percentage of the variance, making them the most important, explanatory ones.

PCA can produce a small number of components – say three or four – but may produce a much larger number – possibly eight, nine or more – as it uses all the variables in the original set to explain all the variance. However, the explanatory power of the later components will be much less than that of the first or second, which gives rise to the issue of how many components should be used. This can be determined by using the eigenvalue produced in the PCA output statistics. The eigenvalue is an index of the amount of variance the component accounts for in the original set of variables and it is generally agreed that retaining the components having an eigenvalue of greater than one is sensible.

However, before conducting a PCA, it is important to assess the quality or suitability of your data for this type of analysis. The two tests generally accepted to be indicative of this are known as the Bartlett's test of sphericity (BTS) and the Kaiser-Meyer-Olkin (KMO) test of sampling adequacy. These may sound complicated, but they are really quite simple to set up and interpret. The procedure for conducting these in SPSS is outlined in Exhibit 9.16.

---

### Exhibit 9.16    Using SPSS to Assess Data Suitability for Principal Components Analysis

1   Go to the Analyze menu, select 'Data Reduction' and then 'Factor' to open the 'Factor analysis' dialogue box.
2   Select the variables that you intend to use for the analysis and move these into the 'Variables' window in the dialogue box.

3  Click on the 'Descriptives' button, then, in the 'Correlation Matrix' section, click on the 'KMO and Bartlett's test of sphericity' option.
4  Click on 'Continue' to return to the main 'Factor Analysis' dialogue box and then click on 'OK'.
5  The results will appear in an 'Output' window.

What you are looking for in the output from these tests is as follows. In the BTS, for the significance level to be less than 0.005, and in the KMO test, for the KMO value to be close to 1. Pallant (2001) suggests that a minimum KMO value of 0.6 is required to justify undertaking PCA, while Ryan (1995: 256) provides a useful categorisation of KMO values as follows:

KMO > 0.9          'Marvellous'        KMO in the 0.8s     'Meritorious'

KMO in the 0.7s     'Middling'          KMO in the 0.6s     'Mediocre'

KMO in the 0.5s     'Miserable'         KMO < 0.5           'Unacceptable'

If you have successful results for the BTS and KMO tests, then conducting a PCA can be justified. To do this in SPSS, follow the instructions in Exhibit 9.17. PCA produces quite a lot of output data, even when you have not selected more of the additional options, which can be quite confusing at first glance. The 'Correlation Matrix' simply indicates the correlation coefficients for the combinations of items and the 'Total Variance Explained' table contains the eigenvalues referred to above, from which you can decide how many components should be retained, as explained previously. The 'Communalities' table contains information, in the 'Extraction' column, on the proportion of the variance that is accounted for by each of the variables. The 'Component Matrix' indicates which component the variables have been initially allocated to before 'rotation' has taken place. Finally, the 'Rotated Component Matrix' shows the allocations of the variables to each component after rotation.

### Exhibit 9.17    Using SPSS to Conduct a Principal Components Analysis

1  Go to the Analyze menu, select 'Data Reduction' and then 'Factor' to open the 'Factor analysis' dialogue box.
2  Select the variables you wish to use for the analysis and move these into the 'Variables' window in the dialogue box.
3  Click on the 'Descriptives' button and then select the 'Coefficients' and 'Reproduced' options in the 'Correlation Matrix' section. These will produce the correlation matrix and communalities in the output. Click on 'Continue'.

*(Cont'd)*

4   Now you are back to the main 'Factor Analysis' dialogue box. Click on the 'Extraction' button. In this box, make sure that, in the 'Methods' section, 'Principal Components' is selected, in the 'Analyze' section select 'Correlation Matrix', in the 'Extract' section ensure the 'Eigenvalue over' option is ticked and set it to '1', then click on 'Continue'.

5   Next, click on the 'Rotation' button, and in the box that opens click on the 'Varimax' option in the 'Methods' section, or the 'Rotated Solution' in the 'Display' section and then on 'Continue'.

6   Now, click on the 'Options' button and select the 'Exclude Cases Pairwise' in the 'Missing Values' section. In the section called 'Coefficient Display Format' click on 'Sorted by Size', and in the box for 'Suppress Absolute Values Less Than' enter the figure '.3' and click on 'Continue' (see the note below).

7   Click on 'OK' to produce the results in an 'Output' window.

*Note*: Setting a value of .3 here will make the output easier to interpret because this will mean that any variables not meeting this minimum criterion for 'loading' will not be displayed. It is also logical because that is the value below which you would probably not consider conducting PCA when you inspect the correlation coefficients in the correlation matrix table. However, you can set this to a higher level, such as .4 or .5, if you wish, but this may exclude some variables that possibly should be included in the solution.

Rotation does not change the component solution produced in PCA, but makes the interpretation of this solution easier because the figures in each component column in this table indicate the 'loading', or strength, of membership of the variables for each component. As any variable may 'load' on to more than one component in this table, what you need to look for is the highest loading value for each variable to decide which component it should be allocated to. For example, if the variable 'Price' has loading figures of 0.2 for component one, 0.6 for component two and 0.8 for component three in the rotated component matrix table, then it should be allocated to component three.

Although PCA will usually produce a solution for you, it will not always produce the solution you may have been expecting, and sometimes it produces a set of components that doesn't make sense as it may allocate seemingly unrelated variables to a particular component. The other issue here, of course, is that although PCA will group the variables together to create the components, it will not tell you what these components are or what they mean. In short, it will not give you descriptive headings for the components and this is where you have to interpret what each of the components is. In other words, you have to examine the variables that comprise the components and decide whether or not these are sensible groupings and what they should be called.

For example, in a piece of research that I conducted to establish the most critical factors for successful budget hotel operations in the UK (see Brotherton, 2004), the original 34 possible variables in the questionnaire were reduced by the data analysis, including use of PCA, to the five most critical, which were allocated to two components or categories. One of these had the variables 'Convenient location' and 'Central reservation systems' and it was decided that both of these were essentially concerned with making the hotels easy to access for the customer or guest. Hence, these were combined to form the component labelled 'Accessibility'. The other had the variables 'Consistent accommodation standards', 'Value-for-money accommodation' and 'Hygiene and cleanliness'. These three were interpreted as being aspects of how well the hotels performed their basic operational purpose and so formed the category named 'Performance'. Therefore, at the end of this research exercise, it was concluded that the two most critical components or dimensions influencing the success of budget hotel operations were how accessible they were and how well they performed and these, in turn, were determined by the five variables.

## SUMMARY

» Data invariably need to be cleaned up before they are entered into an analysis package.
» Once they have been entered, the first task is to produce some basic, descriptive statistics to get a feel for the its characteristics – in the form of frequencies, graphs, charts, measures of dispersion and central tendency – and, perhaps, some indication of the reliability of any scales used.
» Following this, to explore the extent to which variables may be associated and/or if there are any differences between some subaspects of your sample, the use of appropriate bivariate analyses, such as cross-tabulation, correlation, regression, and establishing if any associations or differences can be regarded as valid (statistically significant) or have merely occurred due to chance, and therefore cannot be regarded as significant, is an important task.
» Inferential statistics are used to indicate how confident you can be when making inferences about the population as a whole from your sample statistics.
» The use of student t-tests or chi-square can help to establish whether your sample results are statistically significant or not and if the null hypothesis can be rejected.
» Data analysis techniques, such as factor analysis, can help to reveal underlying categories in your data and provide a more parsimonious solution.

## Further Reading

Blaxter, L., Hughes, C. and Tight, M. (1996) *How to Research*. Buckingham: Open University Press. Chapter 7.

Bryman, A. and Cramer, D. (1994) *Quantitative Data Analysis for Social Scientists*, revised edition. London: Routledge.

Clark, M., Riley, M., Wilkie, E. and Wood, R.C. (1998) *Researching and Writing Dissertations in Hospitality and Tourism*. London: International Thomson Business Press. Chapters 14–18.

Denscombe, M (1998) *The Good Research Guide for Small-scale Research Projects*. Buckingham: Open University Press. Chapter 10.

Fink, A. (1995) *How to Analyze Survey Data*. Thousand Oaks, CA: Sage.

Finn, M., Elliot-White, M. and Walton, M. (2000) *Tourism and Leisure Research Methods: Data collection, analysis and interpretation*. Harlow: Pearson Education. Chapters 9–11.

Hussey, J. and Hussey, R. (1997) *Business Research: A practical guide for undergraduate and postgraduate students*. Basingstoke: Macmillan. Chapter 7.

Johns, N. and Lee-Ross, D. (1998) *Research Methods in Service Industry Management*. London: Cassell. Chapter 5.

Preece, R. (1994) *Starting Research: An introduction to academic research and dissertation writing*. London: Pinter. Chapter 7.

Saunders, M., Lewis, P. and Thornhill, A. (2003) *Research Methods for Business Students*, 3rd edition. Harlow: Pearson Education. Chapter 11.

Sekaran, U. (2000) *Research Methods for Business: A skill-building approach*, 3rd edition. New York: John Wiley. Chapter 12.

Sharp, J.A. and Howard, K. (1996) *The Management of a Student Research Project*, 2nd edition. Aldershot: Gower. Chapter 5.

Veal, A.J. (1997) *Research Methods for Leisure and Tourism: A practical guide*. Harlow: Pearson Education. Chapters 13 and 14.

Van de Vijer, F. and Leung, K. (1997) *Methods and Data Analysis for Cross-cultural Research*. Thousand Oaks, CA: Sage. Chapters 4 and 5.

# Chapter 10

## Analysing Qualitative Data

---

### KEY CONCEPTS AND ISSUES

» *Are the qualitative data quantifiable or not?*
» *Have they been collected deductively or inductively?*
» *Unitising, coding and categorising the data.*
» *Content analysis and semiotics.*
» *Computer-assisted analysis.*
» *Dealing with objectivity, validity and reliability issues in qualitative data analysis.*

---

## 10.1 Introduction

In general, analysing qualitative data tends to be more challenging than analysing quantitative data. This is largely because the latter benefits from established techniques and procedures that can be applied in standard ways to the data. That said, there are reasonably well-established techniques for analysing qualitative data that can be used as a basis or framework and will help to guide and structure the analytical process. However, the main problem with analysing qualitative data is the inherent variability of them. Not only are the types of qualitative data potentially more variable than numeric data – it can be text, pictures and so on – but the form these types take is also highly variable. This means that the analysis of qualitative data has to be much more flexible and interpretative in nature than is the case for numeric data.

Given the breadth and diversity of qualitative data and the types of analysis that can be employed to interpret these, it is not possible to cover all of this ground in this chapter. Therefore, here we shall concentrate on issues concerned with the type of qualitative data you possess, how they have been collected and for what purpose. We will also consider the basic principles and processes used in this type of analysis, along with two techniques – content analysis and semiotics – that are often used to analyse deductively obtained data. Finally, in common with quantitative data analysis, there is a need to address validity and reliability issues to ensure that the analysis and consequent interpretative results are seen to be credible.

## 10.2 What Kind of Qualitative Data do You Have?

On the one hand it may seem a rather silly question to ask, but on the other, it is relevant to the type and nature of analysis you may wish, or are able, to apply to the data. At a simple level, qualitative data may be comprised of words or text, still or moving visual images, such as photographs or video material, or other observational recordings, such as maps, diagrams and so on. Regardless of the form, these may have been collected inductively or deductively – that is, with either no pre-existing conceptual framework or to test such a framework. This, of course, has implications for the purpose of the data – whether they are to build a theory or test it – and for how the analysis is organised and proceeds.

Where the data have been collected inductively for theory-building purposes, they are likely to be far more voluminous, wide-ranging and disparate than data collected deductively to test specific hypotheses. In addition, some qualitative data may be quantifiable, in the sense that they can be enumerated, usually in the form of frequencies and percentages. However, you may ask, 'Why would I want to convert qualitative data into some quantified format?' The short answer to this is that it may help you to identify patterns within the data that, in turn, may begin to indicate the existence of categories or dimensions in the data as a whole.

An example of this is provided by Brotherton (2005) where, within the context of a comparative case study research project conducted in two hotels to identify how hotel guests thought about or perceived the concept and experience of hospitality, textual data were converted into frequencies. The result of one part of this process is shown in Table 10.1.

Here, the data relate to the question, 'What word or words do you associate with hospitality?' Given the relative frequencies of the occurrence of the words proffered by the respondents, the analysis of these frequencies clearly indicated that the overwhelming majority were concerned with some behavioural aspect of hospitality, while small minorities indicated some association with the physical and temporal aspects of hospitality.

This quantitative weight of evidence suggests then that when people think freely about what hospitality means to them, the first, and most important, feature for them is the behaviour of the people providing the hospitality. Similarly, when two sets of hotel guests were asked to indicate the words they would use to describe the physical aspects of hospitality in the respective

**Table 10.1** *Words associated with hospitality*

| Behavioural | [Physical] | [Temporal] |
|---|---|---|
| **Welcoming (34)** | Comfort (7) | Leisure (5) |
| Warmth of | | |
| Service | | |
| Friendly | | |
| Accommodating | | |
| Feeling welcome | | |
| **Service (32)** | | |
| Customer | | |
| Good | | |
| Polite | | |
| Welcoming | | |
| Excellent | | |
| **Friendliness (32)** | | |
| **Warmth (13)** | | |
| Of welcome | | |
| Of service | | |
| **Looked after (12)** | | |
| Being well | | |
| **Pleasantness/Politeness/Manners (9)** | | |
| **Attention (3)** | | |

*Source:* Brotherton, 2005: 144, http://www.tandf.co.uk/ journals. Reproduced with permission of Taylor and Francis Ltd.

hotels, the enumeration of their responses clearly indicated that they could be categorised as words expressing either an impression of or passing a judgement on these physical aspects (see Table 10.2).

The production of quantitative frequencies from the original qualitative data can be achieved very simply by using SPSS. The qualitative data are entered into SPSS as string variables – that is, the words themselves are typed in rather than numbers – and then the software is simply asked to produce the output frequencies for the relevant variables in the same way that it would be for numeric data, as described in Chapter 9. In cases where qualitative response options are predetermined rather than open-ended as here, then it is a straightforward matter to code them to facilitate enumeration. For example, in the project referred to above, the respondents were also asked to choose the season – spring, summer, autumn or winter – that they most associated with their experience of the service they had received in the hotel. In SPSS, all that is required to process the repondents' answers to this question is that the variable 'season' has its values defined in the variable view window for the data sheet as spring=1, summer=2, autumn=3 and winter=4. In this and other such cases, therefore, the data can be entered in numeric form from the outset.

Where the response option is not predetermined, but the actual responses exhibit clear sets of commonalities, then it may be possible to code the data

**Table 10.2**   Words used to describe the physical aspects of hospitality in the hotels

| Impression | [Performance] |
|---|---|
| Modern (14) | Very nice/Good/Excellent (16) |
| Clean (8) | |
| Comfortable (8) | Adequate/Mediocre/Quite basic (3) |
| Bright (3) | |
| Old-fashioned (12) but, nice/quite nice, | Very nice/Good Excellent (8) |
| classical/ornate, traditional, historical, | OK/Adequate/Average (4) |
| colonial, classy, charming, clean. | |
| On the other hand, drab and faded glory. | |
| Comfortable (5) | |
| Pleasant/relaxing (8) | |

*Note*: The data in this table represent the words used by the respondents in the two hotels, with those in Roman text being from hotel 1 and those in italic text from hotel 2.

*Source:*  Brotherton, 2005: 144. Reproduced with permission of Taylor and Francis Ltd.

before entry or recode the string data into numeric form after entry. For example, if when initially examining interview or questionnaire data it is clear that the same words or phrases occur frequently, it may be sensible to consider coding these numerically to make data entry and analysis simpler. Even when this is not undertaken before data entry, but it becomes evident once the basic frequencies have been produced, it can still be achieved by recoding the string variable into numeric form using the procedure for recoding numeric variables described in Chapter 9.

# 10.3 Basic Principles and Stages in Qualitative Data Analysis

It should be evident from the previous section that, regardless of the type of qualitative data you have, the basic principles and process of analysing this type of data are generic, whether you are testing or building a theory. Given that, whatever the form, the volume of qualitative data you have collected is likely to be considerable, the first problem is to address how these raw data can be organised to reduce their scale and complexity.

Unitising and coding the data are the first stages in this process. Unitising the data simply means choosing the unit, or focus, for the analysis. This might be individual words, ideas, phrases, events, images or even the questions used in an interview or on a questionnaire. The latter may be particularly appropriate where different people have been asked the same question and you wish to compare their answers. Table 10.3 contains an example of the value of this approach for revealing very different views from the staff in one hotel that, in

**Table 10.3**   Who is the yield manager in the hotel?

| Respondent | Reponse |
|---|---|
| DGM | The Rooms Division Manager. |
| Res. M | We don't have one as such, although the Rooms Division Manager assumes that role with my assistance. |
| RDM | The Reservations Manager and I do a bit of work between us, and the Reception Manager is beginning to get involved now as well. |
| HR | The Rooms Division Manager, well she maintains the system. |
| RM | We haven't got one, but the Rooms Division Manager, the Reservations Manager and myself are involved in it. |
| RC | I assume it's the Rooms Division Manager and the Reservations Manager. The Rooms Division Manager is actually managing it and the Reservations Manager helps with it . |
| R | The Reservations Manager. |

*Key*: DGM = Deputy General Manager; Res. M = Reservations Manager; RDM = Rooms Division Manager; HR = Head Receptionist; RM = Reception Manager; RC = Reservations Coordinator; R = Receptionist.

*Source:* Brotherton and Turner, 2001: 36

turn, surfaced a key issue – why is there not unanimous agreement over the simple issue of who the yield manager is?

Coding in general is a matter of attaching operational and/or conceptual identities to the data in order for these to be organised and categorised, then to be broken down and reassembled in a more meaningful form. In short, it is a process of ordering, reducing and summarising the data, whether this is purely an administrative task in the initial stages of the analysis or one more concerned with identifying themes and relationships later in the process. Once the data have been converted into a more manageable form by means of the coding process, the next step is to either examine this to identify any emergent structure or categories, if the data have been collected inductively, or to examine how the data relates to the conceptual framework used as the basis for the deductive research design and data collection. Once this structure has been established, either prior to data collection or as a consequence of its analysis, the data can be examined further to identify possible patterns, themes and relationships between the categories to either build or test theoretical propositions.

## 10.4 Qualitative Data Analysis Techniques

The techniques used to analyse qualitative data may be subdivided into those applicable to data obtained inductively or deductively. However, while it is true to say that there are techniques that are appropriate for one of these approaches and not the other, some can be used for each category or have their equivalents in the other category. Though it is possible that you have adopted an inductive approach to your research project, it is far more likely that you will have chosen a deductive route because of time and other constraints. Consequently, inductive techniques such as grounded theory, analytic induction, narrative, conversation and discourse analysis will not be discussed here, but details of these can be obtained from the books listed in the Further Reading section at the end of this chapter if required.

Content analysis and semiotics are perhaps the techniques most commonly applied to qualitative data obtained deductively, though they may be used to analyse such data obtained inductively. They are similar, but not synonymous, techniques in that they seek to derive meaning and make inferences from textual or visual data.

Content analysis is often viewed as a quantitative approach to analysing qualitative data as it tends to emphasise the counting, or enumeration, of key words, phrases, images and so on to produce frequencies, which can then be objectively compared. However, this use of content analysis is limited to identifying the denotative, or surface, meaning and can result in these meanings being decontextualised. That said, it is possible to counteract this by considering the underlying, latent or connotative meaning of the data by ensuring that the context or contexts are taken into account when inferences are made.

Semiotics sees this issue of context as a more fundamental consideration, that meaning can only be established by taking the context into account. It is concerned with the analysis of signs and what they are signs of. Semiotics, then, focuses on audible or visible cues and their underlying meanings. Given that the significance of a particular sign is contextually dependent, it follows that the same sign may have a different significance or meaning when it appears in different contexts. Thus, semiotics cannot be conducted in an acontextual manner. Furthermore, in addition to the signs and their significance varying according to their incidence in differing contexts, there is another element – the 'interpreter', who perceives, interprets and gives meaning to them. This contributes another dimension in that different interpreters may interpret the significance of a given sign in the same context differently.

Though much, if not most, qualitative data analysis and interpretation is likely to be conducted via written means, it is possible to utilise computing power to assist this process. As we noted earlier SPSS, for example, can be used to quantify qualitative data, but more specialised qualitative data analysis software packages do exist to support many of the inductive and deductive techniques referred to earlier. For example, there are NVIVO7, XSIGHT, ATLAS.ti and The Ethnograph packages, which tend to be the ones most commonly referred to in the literature. The extent to which you will have access to any of these, however, will depend on whether or not your institution has any of them available for you to use. Even if it does not, it is often possible to obtain trial or demo versions of them and these may be sufficient for your needs, so it is worth checking out the following web addresses:

◆ NVIVO 7 and XSIGHT: www.qsrinternational.com/products_free-trial-software.
  aspx
◆ ATLAS.ti: www.atlasti.com/demo.html
◆ The Ethnograph: www.qualisresearch.com

# 10.5 Justifying Qualitative Data Analysis Choices

Just as there is the need to explain and justify the selection and use of techniques and procedures when analysing quantitative data, these same issues have to be addressed with qualitative data analysis. In the case of quantitative data analysis, this is relatively straightforward because statistical techniques tend to be regarded as fairly objective and proven. As the analysis and interpretation of qualitative data are much more subjective and interpretative, however, it is not possible, in the main, to cite a particular statistic to claim validity or reliability. Similarly, the feasibility of any attempt to generalise from sample results to a wider population, if desired, is also problematic because it is unlikely that the sample used will have been determined statistically to facilitate the making of such inferences valid and reliable. These features can be serious threats to any qualitative data analysis and interpretation because they are likely to compromise the objectiveness, internal and external validity and reliability of the results.

How objective an interpretation is relates to whether or not it is possible for someone else to apply the same techniques and procedure and confirm that they produce the same results. How internally valid the results are raises the issues of authenticity and credibility – that is, how true they are and whether or not they can be believed. How externally valid qualitative data analysis results are depends on how transferable they are to other contextual conditions. How reliable such results are depends on their dependability over time or space.

Given that it may not be desirable, or indeed feasible, to claim that a set of qualitative results is externally valid or totally objective, the key issues are usually those of internal validity and reliability. By resisting the desire to claim that the results are generally applicable and accepting that subjective elements will have played a role in the interpretation of the data – explicitly documenting this by including a reflexive account of your views and beliefs and the potential impact of these on the analysis – you will make your claims more credible.

If you are to convince anyone that your results should be accepted as reliable, you need to ask the question, 'If someone else had conducted this research, would they have arrived at the same conclusions?' The issue here is that a minimisation of subjective bias is achieved in both the instruments and procedures of data collection and analysis. This can be demonstrated by ensuring that there is an audit trail for the whole process. This is akin to writing up the method used for an experiment that, if it is followed by another, should produce reliable results.

Another approach to dealing with validity and reliability issues is triangulation. Essentially, triangulation is a technique used to increase confidence in the accuracy and dependability of the results by utilising more than one data analyst or interpreter, source of data or data collection method. The idea of this is that, if the interpretations of more than one person analysing the same data independently or the same data are produced in different locations by different people or at different times, or else different types of data relating to the same issue or question 'questionnaire and interview data' all arrive at or point to the same conclusions, then this type of confirmatory process increases confidence in the process and results. In short, the results are validated from a number of different directions.

## SUMMARY

> » Qualitative data collected as part of a deductive study will generally be easier to analyse than quantitative data because a conceptual framework already exists to structure and compare these.
> » Some forms of qualitative data can be quantified to assist analysis, but care needs to be taken when doing this as it can lead to the context(s) being ignored.
> » Computer software can assist analysis of either enumerated or non-enumerated qualitative data, but once again, these aids tend to decontextualise the analysis.
> » Data structuring, summarising and reduction are key tasks within the process of analysing qualitative data as they all assist the identification of categories, patterns, themes and relationships in the data.
> » Techniques such as content analysis and semiotics are useful for analysing textual and/or pictorial data, particularly in deductively designed studies.
> » A major issue in qualitative data analysis is the ability of the researcher to instil confidence in the reader on the credibility of the methods and processes used to produce the final interpretation of the data.

## Further Reading

Blaxter, L., Hughes, C. and Tight, M. (1996) *How to Research*. Buckingham: Open University Press. Chapter 7.

Clark, M., Riley, M., Wilkie, E. and Wood, R.C. (1998) *Researching and Writing Dissertations in Hospitality and Tourism*. London: International Thomson Business Press. Chapter 10.

Denscombe, M. (1998) *The Good Research Guide for Small-scale Social Research Projects*. Buckingham: Open University Press. Chapter 11.

Finn, M., Elliot-White, M. and Walton, M. (2000) *Tourism and Leisure Research Methods: Data collection, analysis and interpretation*. Harlow: Pearson Education. Chapter 8.

Flick, U. (2002) *An Introduction to Qualitative Research*, 2nd edition. Thousand Oaks, CA: Sage. Chapters 14–18 and 20.

Hampton, A. (1999) 'Qualitative data analysis and interpretation', in B. Brotherton (ed.), *The Handbook of Contemporary Hospitality Management Research*. Chichester: John Wiley. pp. 287–303.

Hussey, J. and Hussey, R. (1997) *Business Research: A practical guide for undergraduate and postgraduate students*. Basingstoke: Macmillan. Chapter 8.

Jauncey, S. (1999) 'Observational research', in B. Brotherton (ed.), *The Handbook of Contemporary Hospitality Management Research*. Chichester: John Wiley. pp. 115–42.

Johns, N. and Lee-Ross, D. (1998) *Research Methods in Service Industry Management*. London: Cassell. Chapter 6.

Saunders, M., Lewis, P. and Thornhill, A. (2003) *Research Methods for Business Students*, 3rd edition. Harlow: Pearson Education. Chapter 12.

Sharp, J.A. and Howard, K. (1996) *The Management of a Student Research Project*, 2nd edition. Aldershot: Gower. Chapter 5.

Veal, A.J. (1997) *Research Methods for Leisure and Tourism: A practical guide*, 2nd edition. Harlow: Pearson Education. Chapter 8.

# Chapter 11

## Writing Up the Research Project

> ### KEY CONCEPTS AND ISSUES
>
> » *Who is going to be the reader and what will be important to him or her?*
> » *What questions will he or she have in mind when reading the work?*
> » *What do I have to do to convince him or her that my work is credible?*
> » *How do I write in an academic style?*
> » *What has to be included in the final, written version?*
> » *Why do I need to include references in my work?*
> » *How do I make sure I reference correctly?*

## 11.1 Introduction

In this final chapter we consider some key aspects of writing up the research study. Rather than trying to provide a model for writing the research report or dissertation, which in fact is a rather pointless exercise because different institutions will have different preferences and requirements, the approach taken here is concerned with encouraging you to make sure that some of the technical aspects of writing up, such as the references, are done correctly and to consider how issues of style and presentation should be approached, taking into account who the reader of this work will be and what is likely to be important to him or her. The purpose of this is not to provide you with a prescriptive blueprint to follow when writing up the work, but to supply a series of key thoughts to bear in mind when you are planning how to structure and present your arguments and evidence.

# 11.2 Style, Presentation and the Reader

One of the first questions you should consider when beginning to write up your research project or dissertation is, 'Who is going to read this and what are their expectations?'

Normally, your audience is going to be one or more of the academic tutors who will be marking the work. You may have previously been given information from the tutors concerning the purpose of the research work, in educational terms, and possibly an indication of the criteria they intend to use to mark or grade it. You may also have other information concerning what their expectations are in relation to the required content and preferred style of different aspects or parts of the work and the final report or dissertation. This type of guidance is invaluable as it tells you what is expected, what will gain credit, what you will be penalised for and so on. You ignore these things at your peril!

Given that you should have this type of specific guidance, which, as mentioned, does vary from institution to institution, there are no examples of this type of information here. It is more useful to consider the nature of the academics who will read your work and what is likely to be important to them. Of course, this still has to be something of a generalisation because individual academics have their own unique educational and experiential backgrounds, beliefs and priorities. Nevertheless, academics in general are sceptical people because scepticism lies at the heart of an academic's being. It will have been instilled in them during their training as academics, be expected in how they conduct themselves in academia and used in their academic work.

All of this means that they are not predisposed to take anything that they are told at face value – they need to be convinced by force of argument and supporting evidence. Thus, the academic who reads your work will not just accept or believe what you have written simply because you've written it. Therefore, one question you should bear in mind when writing up your report or dissertation is, 'Will the content and style of what I am writing enable the reader to accept what I say as convincing and therefore accept my results, conclusions and the method used to obtain these?' In other words, will it be credible enough to withstand the critical scrutiny of the reader?

So, what makes something credible in the eyes of the reader? There are a number of things to consider from the reader's point of view. Is this a worthwhile topic, and does it have the potential to add something new to what is known already? Does it have an appropriate focus or is it far too general? Is there a convincing rationale provided for undertaking the research? Does it have a clear and feasible research question to answer or an aim and objectives to achieve? The answer given to all of these should be 'yes' because these are all issues that should have been resolved before the work began.

Second, the academic may ask the following. Does this student demonstrate a sound and critical knowledge of antecedent (previous) work conducted in relation to this question or issue in the same field? In other words, is the student sufficiently aware of what came before, has this been evaluated in a critical manner, have obvious gaps or omissions in this been recognised and does the literature review contain a logical argument and substantive evidence to support a 'yes' answer to these questions? Does the review form a sound basis for the decisions that have been made regarding the conceptual framework used to inform the design of the empirical aspect of the research?

To put this in simpler terms, is the foundation for the work sufficiently strong for me to be confident that what is derived from or built on this basis is likely to be consistent and strong? If the foundations are seen to be weak, then this is likely to lead to the perception that whatever is built on these is weak also. In turn, this increases the academic's scepticism quotient and is likely to make him or her view the remainder of the work more critically.

Third, if, as the reader, I'm happy with the foundations for the empirical work, the next question is, has this work been suitably informed by the conceptual thinking lying behind it and have appropriate data collection and analysis methods and procedures been adopted that will enable the researcher to answer the research question or achieve the aim or objectives? That is, is there a logical link between the conceptual view of the issue and how this is to be investigated in the real world or are these two elements unconnected and living in separate worlds? The element that should connect the conceptual and empirical aspects of your work is the 'conceptual framework' and associated methodology. As we saw in Chapter 5, this is derived from or built on the review of the literature and is then used as the basis for designing the empirical investigation. Therefore, whoever is reading, and marking, your work will want to see that this framework is a logical synthesis of the existing state of knowledge on the issues being researched and the methods used to investigate them have been clearly explained and justified.

To give the reader confidence in your empirical research design, you not only need to explain fully what methods and procedures you have chosen to use and how these have been used, but you should also provide evidence to convince him or her that these decisions have a logical basis, are consistent and that there is evidence to support their validity. This is why the methodology section or chapter in a research report or dissertation is so important. It is another aspect of the process of convincing the sceptical reader that the results you have obtained should be regarded as valid and reliable because the methods and processes used to obtain them are sound.

Fourth, the results and their significance are a key part of the whole investigation and the reader will be very interested in what results have been obtained and what you believe they show or mean. The reader is likely to be asking questions such as, 'What are the results, are they presented clearly, can I understand them, has the author explained what types of data analysis have been used to obtain them and produced interpretations of what they mean, is there an indication of their significance, do they support any claims made about their significance?' Again, the reader will be trying to see if the results are believable in terms of the method(s) and process(s) used to obtain them and what you claim they show or prove. To be successful in these respects, they have to be clear and used in a sensible and credible manner.

What is vitally important in this respect is the need to be truthful about what your results show. It is tempting to think that your work will be regarded as failing if the results do not support your prior assumptions or hypotheses and try to ignore what they do show in order to claim that your work does support what you hoped to prove. This is always a mistake, which will be recognised by the reader and probably will be heavily punished in terms of marks.

You should not feel that if your results do not allow you to prove what you set out to prove, this is an automatic admission of failure and that it will lead to a loss of marks. Indeed, the reverse is more likely to be true. Honesty is always the best policy here because the reader will be looking to see if you are aware of the implications of your results whether these favourable or not – and your credibility will be enhanced if you evaluate them honestly.

Finally, in the conclusions section of your work, the reader will be looking to see if you can 'close the circle'. By this I mean bring together the conceptual and empirical parts of the investigation, identify and reflect on any errors that became evident after the event and highlight any remaining and/or new questions, inconsistencies, problems and so on that only became evident once the research had been completed. So, the reader will have questions such as, 'Are the conclusions justified, is there sufficient evidence to support them, are they sensible, have any omissions or errors been recognised and commented on appropriately and are there sensible suggestions for future work that needs to be done as a consequence of the findings from this work?'

In general, what the reader is looking for here is a clear indication that you have developed a suitable insight into not only the results and what they show but also into what you have learned from the process of actually conducting the research. Given that it is rare for a research project to go totally to plan, and that decisions made in designing and conducting it are not always the correct ones with hindsight, you should not be afraid to admit to any problems you encountered or mistakes made because how you dealt with them and/or recognised the implications of them will indicate that you have reflective insight.

On the question of the style of writing to use and the technicalities of formatting and presenting the document, once again you will undoubtedly have received some type of document from your institution outlining the style and format it requires you to use. Because such requirements do vary from place to place, again it does not seem sensible to make prescriptive comments on such issues here. However, one aspect is worthy of further comment because it is generally applicable and you may have some doubts about it. It is the require-ment that the document is written in an 'academic style'. What does this mean in practice?

Writing in an academic style is not an intuitive thing for many people as it is not how we would normally speak or write – it is quite formal and dispassion-ate. In technical terms, the academic style of writing involves using the third person rather than the first as it tries to convey an objective approach to the issues in question. In other words, it is a narrative based on evidence rather than subjective opinion or speculation. This means that you have to write as though you are an independent, uninvolved observer.

Your personal, subjective opinion is not required – only your objective and logical use and analysis of the evidence, whether you personally agree with it or not. So, using 'I' or 'we' is not permissible. Instead of 'I think' or 'I believe', use phrases such as, 'the evidence shows' or 'in the light of the available evidence it is clear that'. Similarly, phrases such as 'my results' or 'my conclusions are' should be avoided. Use 'the results' and 'the conclusions' instead.

A dispassionate, objective approach to writing up a research report involves stating the purpose(s) of it and providing a rationale to justify undertaking the research (see Chapters 1 and 3), comparing, contrasting and commenting on the evidence that already exists in the literature (see Chapter 4), explaining and justifying your conceptual conclusions and the methodological decisions underlying your empirical research design and procedures (see Chapters 2, 5, 6, 7 and 8), stating the results and the analytical techniques and procedures used to obtain these (see Chapters 9 and 10) and the conclusions derived from this process.

## 11.3 The Contents

As most institutions will have their own guidelines concerning the structure and sequence of a research report or dissertation, there is, once again, little point in trying to prescribe a particular format here. That said, the content of these types of documents is fairly, though not totally, universal in terms of the type of sections or chapters that must be included. What does, of course, vary is the particular order that these should be presented in and whether or not cer-tain aspects should be separated or can be dealt with in one subdivision of the work. For an extended version of what follows, including useful examples, see Baum (1999).

### 11.3.1 The introduction

This should be the first chapter or section of the document. Its purpose is to paint in the general background for the study – that is, locate the specific issue(s) being investigated within their wider context. Here you are trying to explain where you are coming from in terms of arriving at the specific focus of the research from the more general context it is derived from. This is sometimes thought of as the rationale for undertaking the study – why it is important, what benefits it will bring, who will be interested in the findings, what it will add to what is already known.

Within the introduction it is also usual to include the study's focus – the research question(s) to be answered or the aim/objectives to be achieved – to give the reader a clear indication of what it is designed to achieve.

Finally, it is often regarded as helpful to conclude the introduction with a short summary of the chapters or sections included in the document to give the reader an indication of what is to come.

## 11.3.2 *The literature review*

The literature review invariably follows the introduction, though some commentators suggest that the methodology section or chapter should precede it. However, my personal view is that the methodology section should follow the literature review as the question of what methodological approach should be adopted and the methods employed can really only be answered once the existing state of knowledge has been considered and reviewed. Whichever order is preferred or indeed demanded, the review of the literature, as discussed in Chapter 4, is your opportunity to demonstrate that you are aware of and have critically considered the current state of knowledge relating to your research topic or question.

This, of course, can be subdivided into sections, but they should be few in number and limited to major subdivisions because the review should be a discursive treatment of the material. Breaking the review into too many sections disrupts the flow of your argument and helps to create the impression that you may be merely describing, rather than critically evaluating, the material.

At the end of the review, there needs to be a summary or a concluding section that synthesises the discussion and highlights the key issues and questions that your empirical investigation is to focus on. This also serves as a useful link or bridge for the next chapter on methodology.

## 11.3.3 *The methodology chapter*

This is the chapter where you begin to make the transition from what is known already to your intentions regarding what you intend to do to add to this. Working from the review of the literature, you have both substantive and methodological inputs to help you formulate a conceptual framework and hypotheses that can be explained and justified by reference to the literature. You must also explain the methods and processes used to action the empirical data collection and analysis phases of your research and justify those choices.

This is your opportunity to convince the reader that your results and findings should be taken seriously because you have obtained them in a systematic and credible way.

### 11.3.4 *The results or findings chapter*

This chapter comes next and is also likely to include a section on the analysis, interpretation and implications of the findings. So, the results themselves need to be presented clearly in the first instance and then it is possible to focus on what the data are indicating. You will often see this type of format in papers in academic journals, where there is a results section followed by one often headed 'Discussion'. What you are trying to do here is tell the reader what has been discovered as a result of your research and then what this means or what implications it has.

### 11.3.5 *The conclusions chapter*

Finally, this chapter – which may also include an opportunity to make recommendations or suggestions for future research – is where you bring your work to a close and state if the original question has been answered or whether the aim/objectives have been achieved totally, partially or not at all. In other words, you can now comment on the relative success or failure of the project and reflect on what were good and bad decisions, which problems you encountered and any ongoing uncertainties.

## 11.4 References in the Text and Bibliography

Referencing the sources of information used and cited in the text of your work, and producing the corresponding full version in the bibliography, is something that seems to confuse many students in terms of understanding what to do (how to reference in a technically correct manner) and why it is necessary in the first place (its purpose). Hopefully, both of these issues will become clearer once you have read this section.

Taking the rationale for referencing first, one reason for it is that is demonstrates what is known as appropriate attribution. This means that if you are using another person's work, you make sure that the source of the work is properly recorded – you acknowledge that it belongs to that person. He or she is the original author and the intellectual effort that this individual has put into producing the work should be explicitly recognised by citing the appropriate details.

Technically, whether you overtly intend to or not, if you do not do this then you are likely to be accused of an unacceptable practice that may attract a penalty from your institution. This may be referred to as poor attribution practice, cheating or plagiarism, depending on how serious and endemic it is in your work.

I shall not discuss these issues further here as your institution will undoubtedly have informed you of how such practices are defined, how to avoid committing these sins and the penalties attached to them if you do and are caught.

A second reason for referencing is to produce evidence that you are aware of, and knowledgeable about, other work that has been produced relating to the topic or research question(s) you are dealing with. A good analogy here is that of a court trial. If a lawyer, representing either party, can refer to previous cases that are relevant to the one in question, supporting the point he or she is trying to make, then this strengthens his or her argument.

Moving on to the issue of how to reference correctly, there are many referencing styles or systems that have their own conventions regarding what should be included in the text and the references section for written or other types of sources. Indeed, you may have encountered these in the different books, journals and periodicals you have read as part of your research because different publishers have different 'house styles' for the referencing format they prefer to use in their publications. Whatever the particular style and format adopted, it is generally the case that the information required to produce a reference using one system will be sufficient to produce a similar reference using another system, even though how this is organised and presented will differ. Therefore, you should not feel that if your sources have used different referencing systems and formats this will stop you converting them into the system you are using.

Perhaps the most widely used referencing system is the Harvard system and this may well be the one your institution recommends or even insists that you use. If it is not, then I am sure you will have been provided with the details of an alternative system that the institution prefers and how to produce references using that system. Rather than waste time and space here discussing the alternative referencing systems, I intend to concentrate on the Harvard system as a vehicle to illustrate how textual and bibliographic references should be produced.

Taking text citations first, there are two main types of reference. These are commonly known as indirect, passing references or direct quotations. The difference between the two is that an indirect reference is used when you are writing the text using your own words but these have been derived from or influenced by another source. For example, you may be summarising findings from previous studies in your own words, but need to record the source of these studies to indicate where these conclusions can be found. Alternatively, you may want to note the source of the evidence you have used to produce your summary. In the case of a direct quotation, you are using someone else's words and not your own – you are quoting directly what someone else has previously said or written.

In the Harvard system, there is little difference between these two forms of text citation. Both require the author(s) surname(s) and the year of publication of the source cited. For a direct quotation, the page number(s) where the original text is located in the source are also included. Where the actual citation, whether indirect or direct, should appear in your text and the format it should take can vary slightly depending on how it fits into the flow of the narrative and whether it is a citation for a table or figure. Exhibit 11.1 contains some examples of these variations.

---

## Exhibit 11.1  Direct and Indirect Text Citations using the Harvard System

The information that should be included in a standard, indirect text citation is the author(s) surname(s) and the year of publication. All of this information or only the date may be contained within brackets, such as '(Brotherton, 2004)' or 'Brotherton (2004)', or with multiple authors, '(Brotherton and Wood, 2004)' or 'Brotherton and Wood (2004)'. Often, the fully bracketed form is used where the citation appears at the end of a sentence and the other where it appears within the sentence because this tends to fit in well with the flow of the text. However, it is possible to use the bracketed form within a sentence where this is more appropriate. For example, 'some authors argue that hospitality is a multifaceted concept (Brotherton and Wood, 2004) but other authors disagree (Smith and Jones, 2003)'. If the sentence had been worded differently, then the non-bracketed form might have been more appropriate. For example, 'While Brotherton and Wood (2004) argue that hospitality is a multifaceted concept, Smith and Jones (2003) disagree'.

The same principles apply to direct quotations, but then the start and finish of the quotation must be indicated and the page number(s) where this appeared in the original source must be included. It is also sometimes regarded as good practice to italicise the text of a quotation to make it even clearer where it begins and ends and to show that it is something other than your own words. For example, 'according to Brotherton and Wood (2004: 45) *the research evidence clearly indicates that hospitality is a multifaceted concept that requires more sophisticated investigation than has hitherto been undertaken*'. If the quotation is a long one – two to three sentences or a paragraph – then it is also often regarded as good practice to separate it from the main text by presenting it as a separate paragraph and possibly indenting it on the left and right sides. Where you are producing a citation for a table, diagram or figure taken from an original source, the normal conventions and format for a direct quotation apply, but with one small difference. It is regarded as good practice to locate the citation under the table, diagram or figure and to include the word 'source'. For example, 'Source: Brotherton and Wood (2004: 52)'.

So, as we have seen above, normally the difference between a direct quotation and an indirect reference is quite obvious in terms of whose words are being used – yours or someone else's – but there can be something of a grey area between these two, where most of the words used are your own but you want to quote one, two or a few words directly from the original source. In these circumstances, it is normal practice to use the standard, indirect form of citation – that is without including the page number(s). You simply indicate which of the words are not your own by using single quotation marks around them. For example, 'Brotherton and Wood (2004) take a different view of hospitality from many other authors and suggest that it is "a multifaceted concept"'.

You may also encounter some types of source that differ from the standard ones referred to above. Some examples of these are provided in Exhibit 11.2. These may include sources with no named author, government publications, secondary and electronic sources or other types of media, such as film, television or radio, and other variations on the standard formats. Exhibits 11.2 and 11.3 contain examples of how these can be cited in the text and bibliography using the Harvard system.

---

### Exhibit 11.2    Solving Possible Citation Problems in the Harvard System

**More than one publication by the same author(s) published in the same year**

This is a problem because both the text and bibliographic citation use the year of publication as a differentiating indicator. However, this problem is easy to solve. All you need to do is place a suffix after the year to differentiate one publication from another. For example, 'Brotherton and Wood (2004a)' and 'Brotherton and Wood (2004b)' indicate that there are two separate publications produced by these authors in the same year and that there are two separate entries in the bibliography or references section for these two different publications.

**When can you use 'et al.'?**

Et al. simply means – 'and others'. It is a form of shorthand to avoid having to cite all the authors' surnames in the text. It cannot be used where there are fewer than three authors or in the corresponding entry in the bibliography or references section.

It is normal practice to cite all the authors the first time the citation appears in the text and thereafter to shorten this to the surname of the first author, followed by 'et al'. For example, 'Brotherton, Wood, Smith and Jones (2004)' can become 'Brotherton et al. (2004)'.

**Dealing with quotations that flow over two pages or are discontinuous**

In some circumstances, you may wish to cite a quotation that begins on one page and ends on the next or you may wish to pick out and combine two or more pieces from different pages in the original text. The conventions for dealing with these are as follows. First, with a continuous quotation flowing over two pages, you cite the reference in the same way as you would for a normal quotation, but indicate the starting and finishing pages for the quote, inserting a dash between the two, such as 'Brotherton (2004, 19–20)'. Second, when the quotation is discontinuous, the page

*(Cont'd)*

numbers the separate pieces of text appear on in the original are separated by commas, so for example it could read 'Brotherton (2004, 21, 25, 32)'. In the quotation itself, the pieces are separated by a series of dots, such as, 'hospitality as a concept … is multifaceted … and one lacking sufficient explanation'.

### Citing multiple works by one author or different authors in the text

Where you wish to summarise evidence and/or ideas from more than one source, then it is normal practice to string these citations together. For example, in the case of multiple works by one author, you might say, 'All the work on this issue by Green (1998; 2000; 2004) has arrived at the same conclusion' or 'Green's work (1998; 2000; 2004) has arrived at the same conclusion' or 'Green has arrived at the same conclusion in all of his work (1998; 2000; 2004)'.

In the case of multiple authors, you may say, 'All the work on this issue has come to the same conclusion (Blue, 1994; Brown, 1996; Green, 2000; Yellow, 2004)' or 'all the work conducted on this issue (Blue, 1994; Brown, 1996; Green, 2000; Yellow, 2004) has come to the same conclusion'.

### What do I do when the source I've read cited another author but did not give the reference for this?

This is known as secondary referencing and should be used sparingly as it may reduce the credibility of your writing or argument. However, in cases where you have no other option, the following formats should be used. For example, in the text, this may appear as, 'Wood (cited by Brotherton, 2003) contends that …' or, in the case of a quotation, '"hospitality is a defunct concept" (Wood, cited by Brotherton, 2003: 45)'. In the bibliography, use the same format as for a chapter from an edited book.

The text citations you include in your write-up are essentially condensed, or shortened, versions of the full citation included in the bibliography or references section. However, there is a crucial relationship between these two beyond the difference in their length. It is, first, that the two must exist and, second, that the bibliographic details must be identifiable from the version in the text. As we have seen already, the reference in the text follows the format of author(s) surname(s) and year of publication, so logically the full bibliographic details in the references section should initially follow the same format because we only have these two pieces of information in the reference in the text from which we need to to be able to find the full reference. Exhibit 11.3 has examples of how different types of source should be cited in the bibliography.

## Exhibit 11.3    Bibliographic Citations using the Harvard System

The first principle to apply when creating a bibliography using the Harvard system is to organise the entries in alphabetical order by the author(s) surname(s) and initial(s). This is the first detail given in references in the text so it is logical that this is the first piece of information given in the full bibliographic entry. Similarly, as the corresponding references in the text only have one more piece of information – the year of publication – it is also logical that this comes next. Hence, the text reference 'Brotherton and Wood (2004)' becomes 'Brotherton, B. and Wood, R.C. (2004)' in the bibliography.

What are now required are the remaining details about the publication to enable those viewing the citation to obtain the source if they so desire. The ways in which these details are recorded differ slightly according to the type of source – that is, whether it is a book, paper in a journal, article in a magazine or newspaper, a dissertation or thesis, a sound or video recording, a website – but all follow the same basic principle of containing sufficient information to enable the source to be identified and obtained. Hypothetical examples of each of these and a way of setting each one out are shown below.

### For books

Author(s) surname(s), initials (year of publication) title, name of publisher, place of publication. For example, 'Brotherton, B. and Wood, R.C. (2004) *Hospitality: A radical view*. Sage, London'.

### For papers in journals

Author(s) surname(s), initials (year of publication) title of the paper, name of the journal, volume number, issue number, pages the paper appears on. For example, 'Brotherton, B. and Wood, R.C. (2004)' Hospitality – a radical view', *International Journal of Hospitality Management*, 22 (4), pp. 234–50'.

### For a chapter from an edited book

Chapter author(s) surname(s), initials (year of publication) title of the chapter, editor(s), initials and surname(s), title of the book, name of publisher, place of publication, pages the chapter appears on. For example, 'Brotherton, B. and Wood, R.C. (2004)' Hospitality – a radical view', in, G. Hathaway (ed.), *Hospitality in the Twenty-first Century*, Sage, London, pp. 45–60'.

*(Cont'd)*

### For an article from a magazine or newspaper

This format described here applies to these types of publication, which do not have volume and issue numbers. Where magazines have such pieces of information, the format given above for papers in journals can be used. Author(s) surname(s), initials (year of publication), title of the article, name of the magazine or newspaper, date of publication, page(s) the article appears on. An example from a newspaper would be 'Brotherton, B. and Wood, R.C. (2004) 'Hospitality – a radical view', *The Times*, 22 January, p. 6'. For an article from a magazine, an example would be, 'Brotherton, B. and Wood, R.C. (2004) 'Hospitality – a radical view', *Contemporary Hospitality*, January, pp. 6–8'.

### For work by an unidentifiable author

In such cases, either the normal format for the type of publication is used and the word 'Anon.' or the title of the publication can be used in place of the author's name. For example, 'Tourism Today (2001) 'Who believes traditional destinations are dead?', *Tourism Today*, 4 (1), pp. 1–2'.

### For government publications

Use the format given for books and, if there is no identifiable author, put the name of the organisation that commissioned the report. For example, 'Department of Culture (2002) *Reorganising the UK's Tourism Organisations*, HMSO, London'.

### For theses or dissertations

Follow the same basic procedure that you would for books, but here, of course there will be no publisher or location information as these are unpublished works. However, the equivalent information exists in the form of the name of the institution that conferred the award and its location. For example, 'Jones, B. (1999) 'Service Quality in UK Restaurants', PhD thesis, Deptartment of Hospitality Management, John Wrasse University, Boston, UK'.

### For electronic sources

There are many different types of electronic sources for documents, but the general principles for citing them are the same as those for more conventional publications. What is required is for sufficient details to be provided to allow them to be identified and accessed.

The general format for this type of source is author(s) surname(s), initial(s) (where there is no identifiable author, 'Anon.' or the website name can be used) (year of publication) title, location (that is, name of website), place (if applicable). URL (that is, website address), date accessed. For example, 'Hogg, T. (2001)

'Ruritania's tourism future', University of Ruritania, Real City. Available at: http/ur.ac.ru/ruritania tourism research institute/research papers/july-2001/html [accessed 30 September 2004]'.

The statement that both forms of the citation should exist may sound rather obvious, but experience suggests that this does not always happen. It is easy, when writing the text and citing sources as you go, to forget to also enter the full reference in the bibliography. Similarly, it is tempting to pad out a bibliography with more citations than have been recorded in the text to make it look as though you have read more widely than you actually have. Both of these things should be avoided, for fairly obvious reasons, but there is another reason, one that is rooted in the use of the Harvard system. It is a basic tenet of this system that all the bibliographic citations have corresponding citations in the text and vice versa. If there is a mismatch between them, then the reader may become suspicious and, more importantly, you may lose marks!

Note also that there are some differences of opinion regarding the nature of the bibliography in this system. Some regard it as a complete record of all the sources consulted, regardless of whether they have been cited in the text or not. Thus what I have referred to earlier as the bibliography they would call a list of references, as it only contains sources cited in the text. Where this is the desired practice, you would have a references section and a bibliography may contain those sources listed in the reference section plus others consulted but not cited in the text. Personally I find this rather confusing and illogical and would suggest that you regard the bibliography as the definitive list of references cited in the text. If you wish, it is possible to have another list entitled 'Other sources consulted' that would give details of sources not cited in the text.

If you need further guidance on how to reference other types of sources, there are many websites that have guidance documents. By entering 'Harvard referencing system' as the search term into Google, you can access these easily.

## SUMMARY

»  Before you start writing, consider the nature of who is going to read your work and what is likely to be important to him or her.
»  Remember, you have to convince the reader that your study is worthwhile and has been designed and conducted in a credible manner.
»  Make sure that you adopt the right style of writing and presentation for the nature of the work and its audience.
»  Structure and sequence the document in a logical manner.
»  Ensure that you have referenced all your sources correctly, both in the text and in your reference section or bibliography.

# Further Reading

Blaxter, L., Hughes, C. and Tight, M. (1996) *How to Research*. Buckingham: Open University Press. Chapter 8.

Clark, M., Riley, M., Wilkie, E. and Wood, R.C. (1998) *Researching and Writing Dissertations in Hospitality and Tourism*. London: International Thomson Business Press. Chapter 19.

Denscombe, M. (1998) *The Good Research Guide for Small-scale Research Projects*. Buckingham: Open University Press. Chapter 12.

Finn, M., Elliot-White, M. and Walton, M. (2000) *Tourism and Leisure Research Methods: Data collection, analysis and interpretation*. Harlow: Pearson Education. Chapter 12.

Flick, U. (2002) *An Introduction to Qualitative Research*, 2nd edition. Thousand Oaks, CA: Sage. Chapter 19.

Hussey, J. and Hussey, R. (1997) *Business Research: A practical guide for undergraduate and postgraduate students*. Basingstoke: Macmillan. Chapter 9.

Johns, N. and Lee-Ross, D. (1998) *Research Methods in Service Industry Management*. London: Cassell. Chapter 8.

Preece, R. (1994) *Starting research: An introduction to academic research and dissertation writing*. London: Pinter. Chapter 9.

Saunders, M., Lewis, P. and Thornhill, A. (2003) *Research Methods for Business Students*, 3rd edition. Harlow: Pearson Education. Chapter 13.

Sekaran, U. (2000) *Research Methods for Business: A skill-building approach*, 3rd edition. New York: John Wiley. Chapter 13.

Sharp, J.A. and Howard, K. (1996) *The Management of a Student Research Project*, 2nd edition. Aldershot: Gower. Chapter 8.

Veal, A.J. (1997) *Research Methods for Leisure and Tourism: A practical guide*. Harlow: Pearson Education. Chapter 15.

Wolcott, H.F. (2001) *Writing Up Qualitative Research*, 2nd edition. Thousand Oaks, CA: Sage.

# References

## Chapter 1

Gill, J. and Johnson, P. (1991) *Research Methods for Managers*. London: Paul Chapman.

Neuman, W.L. (1984) *Social Research Methods: Quantitative and qualitative approaches*. Needham Heights, MA: Allyn & Bacon.

Robson, C. (1993) *Real World Research*. Oxford: Blackwell.

Sekaran, U. (2000) *Research Methods for Business: A skill-building approach*, 3rd edition. New York: John Wiley.

Shoemaker, S. (1994) 'Understanding the market research process: a guide to using an outside research supplier', *International Journal of Hospitality Management*, 13 (1): 39–56.

Wilson, D. (1997) 'The insidious erosion of ethics', *The Times Higher Education Supplement*, 16 May, p. vi.

## Chapter 2

Easterby-Smith, M., Thorpe, R. and Lowe, A. (1993) *Management Research: An introduction*. London: Sage.

Hussey, J. and Hussey, R. (1997) *Business Research: A practical guide for undergraduate and postgraduate students*. Basingstoke: Macmillan.

Mitroff, I. and Kilman, R. (1981) 'Methodological approaches to social science', in P. Reason and J. Rowan (eds), *Human Enquiry*. Chichester: John Wiley. pp. 43–51.

Taylor, S. and Edgar, D. (1999) 'Lacuna or last cause? Some reflections on hospitality management research', in B. Brotherton (ed.), *The Handbook of Contemporary Hospitality Management Research*. Chichester: John Wiley. pp. 19–38.

## Chapter 3

Brotherton, B. (2004) 'Critical success factors in UK budget hotel operations', *International Journal of Operations and Production Management*, 24 (9): 944–69.

Brotherton, B. and Watson, S. (2000) 'Shared priorities and the management development process: a case study of Bass taverns', *Tourism and Hospitality Research (The Surrey Quarterly Review)*, 2 (2): 103–17.

ESRC (2005) *Research Ethics Framework*. Swindon: ESRC.

King, G., Keohane, R.O. and Verba, S. (1994) *Designing Social Enquiry: Scientific inference in qualitative research*. New Jersey: Princeton University Press.

Sekaran, U. (2000) *Research Methods for Business: A skill-building approach*, 3rd edition. New York: John Wiley.

Weiers, R. (1988) *Marketing Research*, 2nd edition. London: Prentice-Hall.

# Chapter 4

Bell, J. (1993) *Doing Your Research Project*, 2nd edition. Buckingham: Open University Press.

Brotherton, B. and Booth, W. (1997). 'An application of SERVQUAL to a hotel leisure club environment', *The Proceedings of the EuroCHRIE/IAHMS Autumn Conference*, Sheffield Hallam University, pp. 117–21.

Brotherton, B. and Burgess, J. (1997) 'A comparative study of academic research interests in US and UK hotel and restaurant companies'. *The Proceedings of the Sixth Annual CHME Hospitality Research Conference*, Oxford Brookes University, pp. 317–48.

Brotherton, B., Heinhuis, E., Miller, K. and Modema, M. (2002) 'Critical success factors in UK and Dutch hotels: a comparative study', *Journal of Services Research*, 2 (2): 47–78.

Cresswell, J. (1994) *Research Design: Qualitative and quantitative approaches*. London: Sage.

Fink, A. (1999) *Conducting Literature Reviews: From paper to Internet*. Thousand Oaks, CA: Sage.

Frochot, I. and Hughes, H. (2000) 'HISTOQUAL: the development of an historic houses assessment scale', *Tourism Management*, 21 (2): 157–67.

Glaser, B. and Strauss, A. (1967) *The Discovery of Grounded Theory*. Chicago, IL: Aldine.

Knutson, B., Stevens, P., Wullaert, C. and Yokoyoma, F. (1990) 'LODGSERV: a service quality index for the lodging industry', *Hospitality Research Journal*, 14 (2): 227–84.

Lee, Y.L. and Hing, N. (1995) 'Measuring quality in restaurant operations: an application of the SERVQUAL instrument', *International Journal of Hospitality Management*, 14 (3/4): 293–310.

Saleh, F. and Ryan, C. (1991) 'Utilising the SERVQUAL model: an analysis of service quality', *The Service Industries Journal*, 11 (3): 324–45.

Stevens, P., Knutson, B. and Patton, M. (1995) 'DINESERV: a tool for measuring service quality in restaurants', *The Cornell Hotel and Restaurant Administration Quarterly*, 36 (2): 56–60.

# Chapter 5

Brotherton, B. (2004a) 'Critical success factors in UK corporate hotels', *The Services Industry Journal*, 24 (3): 19–42.

Brotherton, B. (2004b) 'Critical success factors in UK budget hotel operations', *International Journal of Operations and Production Management*, 24 (9): 944–69.

Brotherton, B. and Watson, S. (2000) 'Shared priorities and the management development process: a case study of Bass Taverns', *Tourism and Hospitality Research (The Surrey Quarterly Review)*, 2 (2): 103–17.

Clark, M., Riley, M., Wilkie, E. and Wood, R.C. (1998) *Researching and Writing Dissertations in Hospitality and Tourism*. London: International Thomson Business Press.

Cooper, D.R. and Schindler, P.S. (1998) *Business Research Methods*, 6th edition. Singapore: Irwin/McGraw-Hill.

# Chapter 6

Brotherton, B. (1999a) 'Case study research', in B. Brotherton (ed.), *The Handbook of Contemporary Hospitality Management Research*. Chichester: John Wiley. pp. 115–42.

Brotherton, B. (1999b) 'Comparative research', in B. Brotherton (ed.), *The Handbook of Contemporary Hospitality Management Research*. Chichester: John Wiley. pp. 143–72.

Brotherton, B. (2000) 'The comparative approach', in B. Brotherton (ed.), *An Introduction to the UK Hospitality Industry: A comparative approach*. Oxford: Butterworth-Heinemann. pp. 1–22.

Brotherton, B. (2003) 'Is your mirror the same as mine? Methodological issues in undertaking and interpreting cross-cultural studies', *Tourism Today*, 3 (Autumn), pp. 26–37.

Jauncy, S. (1999) 'Observational research', in B. Brotherton (ed.), *The Handbook of Contemporary Hospitality Management Research*. Chichester: John Wiley. pp. 191–206.

Jones, P. (1999) 'Experimental research', in B. Brotherton (ed.), *The Handbook of Contemporary Hospitality Management Research*. Chichester: John Wiley. pp. 97–114.

Lashley, C. (1999) 'Action research', in B. Brotherton (ed.), *The Handbook of Contemporary Hospitality Management Research*. Chichester: John Wiley. pp. 173–90.

Lucas, R. (1999) 'Survey research', in B. Brotherton (ed.), *The Handbook of Contemporary Hospitality Management Research*. Chichester: John Wiley. pp. 77–96.

Sekaran, U. (2000) *Research Methods for Business: A skill-building approach*, 3rd edition. New York: John Wiley. Chapter 7.

Yin, R.K. (1994) *Case Study Research: Design and methods*, 2nd edition. Thousand Oaks, CA: Sage.

# Chapter 7

Brotherton, B. (2004a) 'Critical success factors in UK corporate hotels', *The Services Industry Journal*, 24 (3): 19–42.

Brotherton, B. (2004b) 'Critical success factors in UK budget hotel operations', *International Journal of Operations and Production Management*, 24 (9): 944–69.

Brotherton, B. (2005) 'The nature of hospitality: customer perceptions and implications', *Tourism and Hospitality Planning & Development*, 2 (3): 139–53.

Jauncey, S. (1999) 'Observational research', in B. Brotherton (ed.), *The Handbook of Contemporary Hospitality Management Research*. Chichester: John Wiley. pp. 115–42.

Leidner, R. (1993) *Fast Food – Fast Talk: Service work and the routinization of everyday life*. Berkeley and Los Angeles, CA: University of California Press.

Neuman, W.L. (1994) *Social Research Methods: Quantitative and qualitative approaches*, 2nd edition. Needham Heights, MA: Allyn & Bacon.

Watson, J.L. (ed.) (1997) *Golden Arches East : McDonald's in East Asia*. Stanford, CA: Stanford University Press.

## Chapter 8

Hemmington, N. (1999) 'Sampling', in B. Brotherton (ed.), *The Handbook of Contemporary Hospitality Management Research*. Chichester: John Wiley. pp. 245–62.
The Economist (1997) *The Economist Numbers Guide: The essentials of business numeracy*, 3rd edition. London: Profile Books.

## Chapter 9

Brotherton, B. (2004) 'Critical success factors in UK budget hotel operations', *International Journal of Operations and Production Management*, 24 (9): 944–69.
Finn, M., Elliot-White, M. and Walton, M. (2000) *Tourism and Leisure Research Methods: Data collection, analysis and interpretation*. Harlow: Pearson Education.
Kinnear, P.R. and Gray, C.D. (2000) *SPSS for Windows Made Simple: Release 10*. Hove: Psychology Press.
Pallant, J. (2001) *SPSS Survival Manual: A step-by-step guide to data analysis using SPSS for Windows (Version 10)*. Buckingham: Open University Press.
Ryan, C. (1995) *Researching Tourist Satisfaction: Issues, concepts, problems*. London: Routledge.

## Chapter 10

Brotherton, B. (2005) 'The nature of hospitality: customer perceptions and implications', *Tourism and Hospitality Planning & Development*, 2 (3): 139–53.
Brotherton, B. and Turner, R. (2001) 'Introducing yield management in hotels: getting the technical–human balance right', *Journal of Services Research*, 1 (2): 25–47.

## Chapter 11

Baum, T. (1999) 'Presentation of research findings', in B. Brotherton (ed.), *The Handbook of Contemporary Hospitality Management Research*. Chichester: John Wiley. pp. 305–30.

# Index

academic writing style 220
access 154–5
action research 127–9
aims 7, 51–4
alternate hypotheses 92
analytic induction 212
analytical survey 114–15
applied research 14
argot 156
association, measures of
    Cramer's V coefficient 190
    crosstabulation 188–90
    Pearson's r 191, 197
    phi coefficient 190
    Spearman's $r^2$ 191, 197
average *see* mean

balanced scales 146–7
bartlett's test of sphericity 202–3
between-group variation 170
bias
    questionnaire design and 116–17
    respondent 118
    sampling 117–18, 164–74
bibliographic referencing 226–9
bi-polar scale 144, 147
bivariate
    data analysis 188–95
Boolean logic 68

cases
    atypical 123, 172
    critical 125
    extreme 125
    ideal 125
    revelatory 125
    unique 123, 125
case studies
    holistic 124–6
    embedded 124–6
    multiple 124–5
    single 124–5
case study
    design 122–6
    research 45, 122–6
categorical variables 86, 97, 192
causal relationships 33, 78, 86, 89, 91–2, 106, 114
causality, conditions for 91–2
central tendency 182–6

characteristics of scientific research 7–12
    confidence 9–10
    generalisable 10–11
    objective 10
    parsimonious 11–12
    precision 9
    purposeful 7
    replicable 8–9
    rigorous 7
    testable 7–8
chi-square test
    for independence 192–3
    for goodness of fit 200–1
citations
    Harvard system 223–9
classification questions 141, 143–4
closed questions 132–4, 137, 143
cluster
    analysis 202
    sampling 170–1
coding 140, 176, 209–10
collective exhaustion 96–7
comparative research 119–22
    case-oriented approaches 122
    negative approach 120
    positive approach 120
    variable-oriented approaches 120, 122
comparisons
    inter-case 121, 126
    intra-case 121, 124, 126
concepts 80–2, 91, 93
conceptual framework 78–87, 91–2, 218
conclusion section, research report and 219
concurrent validity 101
confidence 9–10, 195
confidence intervals 168, 195, 197
constructs 80–2
content analysis 212
construct validity 101
content validity 101
control
    experimental design and 109
    groups 109
convenience sampling 171–2
convergent validity 101
correlation 78, 103, 187, 190–1
correlation coefficients 187, 190–3
Cramer's V coefficient 190
criterion related validity 101

cross-national studies 121
Cronbach's alpha coefficient 103, 187–8
cross-tabulation 188–90
cross-sectional studies 115

data
  collection 131–62
  empirical 79
  interval 184
  nominal 184, 188
  observational 154–6
  ordinal 184
  qualitative 38, 208–10
  quantitative 38, 175–206
  primary 64
  ratio 184
  raw 176–7
  secondary 64
data analysis methods
  qualitative 207–14
  quantitative 175–206
data reduction 88, 202–5
deduction 18–19
deductive
  approaches 18–19, 34–5, 79, 109
  research 18–19, 80
dependent variable 82, 84–9, 91–2, 120, 145
descriptive
  research 12–14
  statistics 182–88
  surveys 114–15
determining
  validity 100–2, 106, 144, 154, 213
  reliability 102–3, 106, 134, 154, 187, 213
developing aims and objectives 51–4
differences, measuring
  chi-square test 192–3, 200–1
  student t-test 198–200
dimensions 94
directional hypotheses 91–2, 196
discriminant validity 101
dispersion, measurement of
  inter-quartile range 184
  standard deviation 167, 184
distributing questionnaires 115–16, 118, 134
double-barrelled questions, and questionnaire
  design 147, 150

ecological validity 154
eigenvalues 202–3
empirical
  evidence 35
  research 14–16
epistemology 27–30
equivalence
  conceptual 120–1
  measurement 120–1

error
  administrative 118–19
  non-response 116–17
  sampling 116
  response 118
  systematic 116
ethical considerations 55–7
ethnography 127
experimental research 33, 108–11
experiments
  field 37
  laboratory 33, 108–11
explanatory research 12–14
exploratory research 12
external validity 102, 213
extreme cases, sampling and 125

face-to-face questionnaires 115, 136
face validity 101
factor analysis 88, 202–5
field interviews 154, 157
field studies, research process and 37
focus groups 153
framework, conceptual 78–87, 91–2, 218
frequency distributions 182

generalisability 10–11
generalisation 119, 121–2, 164–5, 168, 171

Harvard system of referencing 223–9
hypothesis
  development 91–2
  null and alternate 92
  one and two-tailed 196
  testing 195–201
hypotheses 80, 90–2
  causal 91–2
  correlational 91–2
  directional 91–2, 196
  non-directional 91–2, 196

ideographic methodology 16
independent samples t-test 197–8
independent variable 82, 84–6, 88–92, 120, 145
induction 16–18, 79
inductive research 16–18, 79
inferential statistics 195–201
information
  primary 64
  secondary 64
  tertiary 64–5
information gathering *see* data collection
itemised rating scale 146–7
internal consistency 187–8
internal validity 109, 213
interpretivist paradigm 16
inter-quartile range 184

interval
  data 98–9, 184
  scale 98–9, 144, 176
intervening variable 82, 84–5, 87–8
interviewing 151–3
interviews
  face-to-face 136, 151–2
  field 154, 157
  group 153
  individual 151
  semi-structured 151
  structured 151–2
  telephone 151–2
  unstructured 151

judgement sampling 172

Kaiser-Meyer-Olkin test of sampling
    adequacy 202–3
knowledge and reality 25–30
kurtosis 186

laboratory experiments 33, 106, 109
layout, questionnaire 132–50
leading questions, questionnaire
    design and 148, 150
level of confidence 168, 195, 197
Levene's test for equality of variances 198
Likert scale 98, 144–5, 147, 179
literature
  accessing and obtaining 67–70
  evaluating 70–2
  reviewing 70–2
  searching 67–9
  sourcing 67
  what is it? 63–5
literature review
  role and placement in inductive
      and deductive studies 63, 72–3
  what is it? 65–7
  why is it necessary? 60–3
  writing it up 72–5, 221
loaded questions, questionnaire
    design 148, 150
location, measuring
  mean 184
  median 184
  mode 184
longitudinal study 115

mailed questionnaires 115–16, 134
mean 168, 184–5
measurement
  of variables 82–92
  reliability 95, 100–3
  scales 95–100
  validity 95, 101–2

measuring association
  Cramer's V coefficient 190
  crosstabulation 188–90
  Pearson's r 191, 197
  phi coefficient 190
  Spearman's $r^2$ 191, 197
measuring differences
  chi-square test 200–1
  student t-tests 198–200
measuring dispersion
  inter-quartile range 184
  standard deviation 184–5
measuring location
  mean 184
  median 184
  mode 184
median 184
metaphors 159
method section, of research report
    218, 221–2
methodological
  assumptions 27–30
methodologies
  phenomenological 36–8, 39
  positivistic 32–6
mode 184
models 90
moderating variable 82, 84–8
multi-stage cluster sampling 171
mutual exclusivity 96–7, 176

naturalistic enquiry 37, 127, 154
nature of literature 63–5
nature of research 2–6
nominal
  data 97, 184, 188
  scales 97, 143
non-parametric tests 200–1
non-participant observation 37, 127, 154
non-probability based sampling 171–3
non-response error 116–17
normal distribution 185
note-taking 156–7

objectives 7, 51–4
objectivity, scientific research and 6, 10
observation
  participant 37, 127, 154
  non-participant 37, 127, 154
observational research 126–7, 154–7
one sample t-test 198–200
one-tailed hypotheses 196
ontology 27–30
open-ended questions, questionnaire
    design and 132–3, 137, 143
operational definition 93, 101
operationalisation 34, 92–5

ordinal
  data 97–8, 184
  scales 97–8, 144, 177
outliers 193–4

paired samples t-test 197–8
paradigms
  interpretivist 36–8
  phenomenological 36–8
  positivistic 30–6
paradigms and methodology 16–19, 30, 39
parametric tests 196–200
parsimony, scientific research and 11–12
participant observation 37, 127, 154
Pearson's product moment correlation
      coefficient (r) 191, 197
periodicity 170
phenomenology 16, 36–9
phi coefficient 190
philosophies
  phenomenology 36–9
  positivism 32–6
piloting questions 150–1
plagiarism 61, 222
population
  defining 165–6
  elements 165–6, 168
  heterogeneity 165
  homogeneity 165
  parameters 165–8
  variability 165–6
positivism 18, 30–6, 39, 109
postal questionnaires 115–16
precision 9, 99–100, 146
predictive validity 102
primary
  data 64
  research 14–16
probability-based sampling 168–71
principal components analysis 202–5
projective technique procedures 150, 157–61
  association 159
  choice ordering 161
  completion 159–60
  construction 160
  expression 160–1
pure research 14
purposive sampling 172
*p* values 192, 195, 198, 200

qualitative
  data analysis 207–14
  sampling 171–3
qualitative data analysis
  basic principles and stages 210–11
  justifying choices 213–14
qualitative data, what kind? 208–10

quantitative
  data analysis 175–206
  sampling 168–71
questionnaire
  design 132–51
  piloting 116, 150–1
questionnaire surveys 107, 111–19
  direct implementation 115–16, 118, 134
  distributed implementation 115–16, 134
questionnaires
  semi-structured 135
  structured 133–4
  unstructured 113–14, 143
questions
  attitudinal 143–4
  behavioural 143–4
  categorical/classificatory 141, 143–4
  closed 132–4, 137, 143
  coding 140
  double-barrelled 147, 150
  leading 148, 150
  loaded 148, 150
  non-standard forms 149–50, 157–61
  open 132–3, 137, 143
  perceptual 143
  problems to avoid 147–9
  recall-dependent 148
  standard forms 149–50
quota sampling 173

randomisation 168
random numbers 168–9
random sampling 168
range 184
ratio
  data 99, 184
  scales 99, 143, 177
raw data
  cleaning up 176
  re-coding 177
recall-dependent questions, questionnaire
      design and 148
re-coding data 177
recommendation section of
      research report 219
reductionism 36
referencing 222–9
  text 223–6
  bibliographic 226–9
regression 193–5
reliability 102–3, 106, 134, 154, 187, 213
  inter-rater 102
  split-half 103, 187–8
  test-re-test method 102
replication 8–9, 61–2, 114, 126
  literal 126
  theoretical 126

replicative studies 11
representativeness, sampling
    and 112, 117–18, 186
research
    aims 7, 51–4
    ethics 55–7
    issues 19–22
    nature of 2–6
    paradigms 16–18
    problems 19–22
    proposals 54
    purposes 7
    questions 19–22, 50–1
    topics 43–50
    types 12–16
research designs
    action 127–9
    case study 45, 122–6
    comparative 119–22
    experimental 108–11
    observational 126–7
    survey 112–19
research report
    conclusions 219, 222
    introduction 217, 220–1
    literature review 218, 221
    methodology 219, 221–2
    style, presentation and the reader 217–20
    recommendations 219
    results 218–19, 222
respondents 113, 136–40
response
    bias 118
    rates 116, 137–40, 164
results section of research report 218–19
rigour, the scientific method and 7

sample 164–74
    bias 165, 167
    composition 165
    frame 166
    inferences 164–5
    initial 167
    precision 166–7
    realised 167
    representativeness 112, 117–18, 165, 186
    respondents 166
    selection 117, 164–73
    size 166–9
    statistics 166, 168, 195
    subjects 166, 171
sampling 163–74
    area 170–1
    cluster 170–1
    convenience 171–2
    error 116, 167
    frame 169–70

sampling cont.
    judgement 172
    multi-stage 171
    non-probability based 171–3
    population and 164–8
    probability based 168–71
    purposive 172
    quota 173
    simple random 169
    snowball 172
    strategies 164–73
    stratified random 170
    systematic random 170
    techniques 163–74
scales
    balanced 146–7
    interval 98–9, 146, 176
    itemised rating 146–7
    Likert 98, 144–5, 147, 179
    nominal 97, 143
    ordinal 97–8, 177
    ratio 99, 143, 177
    selecting 99–100
    semantic differential 147
    unbalanced 146–7
scientific research 6–12
schools of thought 29–30, 38–40
secondary
    data 64
    research 14–16
semantic differential scale questions 147
semiotics 212
semi-structured questionnaires 135
sequencing, questionnaire design
    and 132–51
skewed data 183–5
Spearman's rank correlation
    coefficient $(r^2)$ 191
split-half reliability 103, 187–8
spread see dispersion
SPSS
    association, measuring 188–95
    Bartlett's test of sphericity 202–3
    bivariate data analysis 188–95
    central tendency, dispersion and
        skewness 182–3
    charts and graphs 183
    chi-square test for goodness of fit 200–1
    chi-square test for independence 192–3
    cluster analysis 202
    correlation coefficient analysis 190–3
    Cramer's V coefficient 190
    cross-tabulation 188–90
    data range 184–5
    data recoding 177
    data reduction 202–5
    data sheet 178–9, 182

SPSS *cont.*
   data view 177–8, 180–2
   defining variables 78–80
   descriptive statistics 182–8
   eigenvalues 202–3
   entering data 178–80
   factor analysis 202–5
   formatting data 178–80
   frequency distributions and tables 182–3
   hypothesis testing 195–201
   inferential statistics 195–201
   inter-quartile range 184
   Kaiser-Meyer-Olkin test of sampling
      adequacy 202–3
   kurtosis 186
   Lenene's test for equality of variances 198
   missing responses 176, 179
   non-parametric tests 200–1
   output window 183, 185, 187, 189–90,
      193, 201, 203
   parametric tests 196–200
   phi coefficient 190
   principal components analysis 202–5
   *p* values 192, 195, 198, 200
   regression analysis 193–5
   residual outliers 193–4
   select cases option 181–2
   scatter graphs 190
   skewness 185–6
   split file option 181–2
   split-half reliability 103, 187–8
   standard deviation 167, 184
   string variables 209
   student t-tests 196–200
   t-test values 198–200
   univariate data analysis 182–8
   variable view 178–80
standard deviation 167, 184
statistical significance 192, 198–200
statistics
   descriptive 182–8
   data reduction 202–5
   inferential 195–201
structured interview 151–2
structured questionnaires 133–4
student t-tests 196–200
survey
   design 112–19
   implementation 115–16
   questions 132–61
   research 112–19
   response rate 116–17
surveys
   advantages and disadvantages 113
   analytical 114–15
   descriptive 114–15

telephone interviews 151–2
telephone questionnaires 115, 151–2
test-retest reliability 102
text referencing 223–6
theoretical
   framework 78–81
   models 90
   research 14–16
theories and theory 89–90
topics
   finding and refining 43–50
triangulation
   data 214
   methods 214
t-tests 196–200
two-tailed
   hypotheses 196
   tests 196–200

unbalanced scales 146–7
unit of analysis 124–6
univariate
   data 186
   data analysis 182–8
unstructured
   interviews 151
   questionnaires 133–4, 143

validity
   concurrent 101
   construct 101
   content 101
   convergent 101
   criterion-related 101
   discriminant 101
   ecological 154
   external 109, 213
   face 101
   internal 109, 213
   predictive 102
variability
   between clusters 170
   population 164–73
variables
   exploring relationships between 86–90
   categorical 86, 97, 192
   dependent 82, 84–9, 91–2, 120, 145
   independent 82, 84–6, 88–9, 91–2, 120, 145
   intervening 82, 84–5, 87–8
   moderating 82, 84–8
   re-coding 177

wording principles, questionnaire
   design and 147–9
writing the literature review 72–5, 221
writing the research report 216–30